EXPLORING LEARNING

Tina Bruce was formerly Director of the Centre for Early Childhood Studies at the Froebel Institute and is presently working as a freelance early-childhood consultant. She has, with the British Council, advised at the Cairo Kindergarten Training College, and received the award, 'International Outstanding Woman Scholar in Education in 1989', at the Virginia Commonwealth University, USA. She is the author of *Early Childhood Education* (Hodder & Stoughton, 1987) and *Time to Play in Early Childhood Education* (Hodder & Stoughton, 1991).

Pat Gura was research assistant to the Froebel Blockplay Project. She holds advanced diplomas in both Early Childhood Education and Educational Research.

EXPLORING LEARNING: YOUNG CHILDREN AND BLOCKPLAY

Edited by Pat Gura
with the Froebel Blockplay Research Group
directed by Tina Bruce

P·C·P
Paul Chapman
Publishing Ltd

Paul Chapman Publishing Ltd
144 Liverpool Road
London
N1 1LA

British Library Cataloguing in Publication Data

Exploring learning: young children and
blockplay.
I Gura, Pat   II Bruce, Tina
372.1102

ISBN 1 85396 171 X

Typeset by Best-set Typesetter Ltd, Hong Kong.
Printed and bound by Athenaeum Press Ltd, Newcastle upon Tyne.

B C D E F G 8 7 6 5 4 3

CONTENTS

INTRODUCTION
Tina Bruce

DOING EDUCATIONAL RESEARCH: A RESEARCH DIRECTOR'S PERSPECTIVE

This book aims to share with busy adults working directly with young children, the way those participating in the Froebel Blockplay Project went about exploring blockplay as an integral part of the whole curriculum. Perhaps it will encourage other groups to develop their own collaborative projects. We have learnt that collaborative research can have a very powerful influence on curriculum development.

ARE WE RESEARCHERS, PRACTITIONERS OR EDUCATORS?

The answer to the above question lies in the relationship between theory and practice. In effect, the Froebel Blockplay Project expresses in modern terms the Froebelian principle that theory and practice should be interwoven, and not two separate strands.

At times there can be an uneasy relationship between researchers and practitioners. Margaret Clark (1989, p. vii) expresses this clearly:

> It seemed important to 'demystify' research so that practitioners and students in training appreciate that research may have something to say which is relevant to education; it can be couched in terms which they understand and yet can still be rigorous; not least, they can be helped to adopt a research approach to the evaluation of their own practice.

COMBINING THE ROLES OF RESEARCHERS AND PRACTITIONERS

The language we use reflects the way we view life. For example, the word 'researcher' usually carries more status than 'practitioner'. On the other hand, 'educator' carries a different meaning. The pioneers of early childhood education are often described as educators. Froebel, Montessori, Steiner, the McMillan sisters and Susan Isaacs all started their own schools and worked together with colleagues to try out ideas, to do research and to develop their practice in the everyday setting of the school community. They were all skilled at sharing their knowledge and sharing in a group – and beyond to the wider community. An educator is a researcher and practitioner combined.

SEPARATING THE ROLES OF RESEARCHER AND PRACTITIONER

These pioneer educators interwove theory with practice. However, during the twentieth century, there emerged a gradual separation of the two. Educators began to see themselves mainly as practitioners, and researchers did not necessarily have much experience of the classroom.

Jonathan Silin (1987, p. 17) suggests that the growth in understanding of psychology and sociology has tended to push into the background the philosophical and principled base leading to the articulation of educational principles, which enabled the pioneer early childhood educators to tussle with the practical problems of translating these principles into practice.

Once educators were not (first and foremost) concerned to work from first principles and to think for themselves, they were increasingly at the mercy of those with the power to influence through research findings and theory. These would often be totally unconnected to educational philosophy and principles.

Consequently, instead of being in a position to further good classroom practice, they tended to be used by it, and remain 'vulnerable to any claims made which are said to come from "research evidence" provided these appear sufficiently impressive' (Clark, 1989, p. vii).

A situation arose whereby assertions made about children's learning, or teaching methods, had to be made increasingly within the terms set by the research methodology of these disciplines. In other words, researchers were setting the agenda for early childhood education by the 1960s and 1970s, and educators receded into the role of practitioners, on the whole accepting the given agenda. There is a vicious circle here. If teachers see themselves as practitioners rather than as educators, their self-esteem is affected. This in turn has an impact on the way teachers are regarded by others. Colin Fletcher (1988, p. 1) makes the point that 'It is accepted by academics that mature professionals have an "understanding". It is not so often the case that their understanding is held to be equivalent to that of the academics'. He wants to see practitioner perspectives given the same status as academic perspectives. However, he still does not suggest a shifting of the agenda back to the days when educators combined the two roles.

Recently, there has been an implicit embracing of the educator approach. The Thomas Report on primary education (1985) emphasizes the need for a whole-school policy and for all the staff to develop shared meanings and a coherent approach. In effect, the emphasis is on the teacher as active learner and reflective practitioner, working from first principles as part of a team. This is taking us back again to combining the roles of researchers and practitioners.

BECOMING EDUCATORS AGAIN

The Froebel Blockplay Project has emphasized the need for those taking part in it to see themselves as educators. This approach stems from a long research tradition (Appendix I looks at this aspect in further detail). The project has encouraged participants actively to explore theory with practice in their own school and with colleagues in other schools and early-years settings, building on the traditions inherited through the Froebel Institute.

The Froebel Blockplay Project has in effect been about shifting the agenda back to the spirit of the pioneers of early childhood education, interweaving theory with practice while working with children and their families, and so rediscovering what it is to be an educator.

EDUCATORS NEED A STRONG SELF-IMAGE

Jennifer Nias (1987, p. 184) says 'Who and what people perceive themselves to be matters as much as what they do'. The blockplay project has been about empowering all involved: children, parents, and staff in school and college. There have been subtle changes in the way they see themselves since the beginning of the project. This may be in lasting ways. The feeling of empowerment makes it possible for theory to begin to inform practice, for research evidence to be evaluated and for further areas to be studied.

PIONEER SPIRIT

During the eighteenth century, Froebel developed one of the first sets of blocks for use in the early childhood curriculum, known as the Gifts. As his work developed with children and parents, he moved steadily towards structuring his work with children on the basis of a strong framework of general principles (Bruce, 1991). The participants in this collaborative project have continued in this tradition (using educational principles and current research literature and theory) in the practical setting of blockplay in the classroom.

It is hoped that this book will encourage those who work directly with young children to see the importance of taking up the educator role. Otherwise, it is only possible to receive what others consider to be good practice. Educators create good practice, and because they have a sense of ownership of it, they can begin to articulate what is important in their work with children and their families, and to share it. They can use research as a rich resource, rather than being used by it.

This book has been written by a group of educators. It places 'the focus of early childhood education where it belongs, on the study of children in school, and the development of theoretical constructs for explaining the influence of their school experience' (Zimiles, 1977, p. 70).

Perhaps it will encourage others to become educators, to join together and to make the early childhood curriculum move forward, and so benefit the children and families they meet. Perhaps that is what is meant when we say we need pioneer spirit.

THE SHAPE OF THE BOOK

Details of the Froebel Blockplay Project's starting-point, and the way we began to work together, can be found in Appendices I and II. Some readers will want to know more about these aspects of the project early on in the book, some later and some, perhaps, not at all.

In the first chapter, Jane Read introduces the history of blockplay in the Western world. Chapter 2, by Tina Bruce, looks at the way children and adults interact while using blocks together. In Chapter 3 the Froebel Blockplay Research Group examines aspects of blockplay involving representation and communication. The importance of awareness, making links between the presentation and provision of blockplay and the child's development is estab-lished in Chapter 4 and Appendix III by Pat Gura. Chapters 5, 6 and 7 look at the mathematical, scientific and problem-solving opportunities in blockplay. The Froebel Blockplay Study Group writes about these areas in terms of being mathematical, speaking mathematics, being scientific and solving problems. In Chapter 8, the group turns its attention to ways of keeping records of blockplay in the busy classroom setting. The next two chapters (9 and 10) tackle the very practical issues of creating a favourable environment, and using educational principles, theory and research as powerful classroom tools to aid the development of good practice. Appendix IV, compiled by the Danebury Nursery Class, gives more detailed practical help in relation to the last two chapters. The reflections were written by Tina Bruce in consultation with the group.

ACKNOWLEDGEMENTS

Warmest thanks are extended to *community playthings*, of Robertsbridge, with whom we discovered a common bond in the work and writings of Frederick Froebel and who responded with such generosity to our appeal for gifts or loans of blocks to enable the research to develop beyond the basics. Unit blocks and hollow blocks were given and loaned unconditionally. Most of the blocks in the illustrations are those made by *community playthings*. Our thanks are also due to James Galt, of Altrincham, who generously donated a quantity of smaller-scale blocks that we were able to use to complement and contrast with the larger-scale blocks.

We would also like to thank Sue Gifford and Richard Harrison, of the Mathematics Department, the Froebel Institute College, for sharing our excitement and helping us to reflect on aspects of blockplay.

Our special thanks go to Sydney Lodge, BEM, in reprographics, Froebel Institute College, for his generosity of spirit, especially towards dawn raiders, and to Sarah Gerrard, Head of Library and Media Services, Roehampton Institute, and the Froebel Institute College Library staff for expediting our extensive literature searches and Pauline Vincent (Art).

We cannot thank the children because they did not do it for us but with us. Instead, we salute them. We also salute the parents who, under the guidance of Carol Price (reception-class teacher at the time), contributed their recorded observations of the blockplay of 6-year-olds, at Our Lady of Victories Primary School, Putney.

Our final thanks are to Jill Redford, the Principal, Froebel Institute College, for her personal interest in the project, to the Governing Body, chaired by Rory Hands, of the Froebel Institute College, Roehampton Institute, who funded the research and to Marten Shipman, then Dean of the School of Education at Roehampton Institute, who (together with Greg Condry in the Centre For Early Childhood Studies) encouraged the idea and helped it to take shape.

CONTRIBUTORS

This book is the culmination of a collaborative action-research project into children's blockplay (1987–90) based at the Froebel Institute College, Roehampton Institute. Children, nursery nurses, teachers and college staff participated on equal terms, each making a unique contribution to the whole. The children named in the text represent the dozens of others whose blockplay was observed and recorded. Adult participants were as follows: Ann Bridges, Debbie Albon, Tracie Taylor, Dorothy Wickson, supported by headteacher Rob Ratcliffe (Danebury Primary School, Nursery Class, Roehampton); Lizzie Linklater, Liz Gibbons, with headteacher Jill Vereycken, and the nursery staff (Eastwood Nursery School, Roehampton); Rakshah Shah, Brenda Duckett, Lynne Bartholemew, Sharon Galvin, Tracey Bond, supported by headteacher Dionne Ziranek (Grove House Nursery School, Southall); Peter Missiuro, supported by Fay Mirkovich, Head of Partial Hearing Unit (Holman Hunt Primary School, Fulham, Partial Hearing Unit, Nursery Class); Krystina Dabrowka, Gayna Cooper, supported by headteacher Frances Mulligan (Our Lady of Victories Primary School, Putney, Early Reception Class), and Jane Read, Archivist, Froebel Early Childhood Collection.

The project was led by Tina Bruce with Pat Gura as research assistant, both from the Froebel Institute College. Data from the records of all the participating groups are the source of the practical experiences of blockplay that illuminate the issues discussed in the following pages. All participants advised on the book as a whole, with Chapters 3, 5, 6, 7, 8, 9 and 10 being worked on initially by subgroups who determined the weighting to be given to the different aspects of blockplay contained in them and helped to write the earlier drafts. It is doubtful if any one of us could have written down and contributed as much if we had not been part of this group.

NOTE ON ILLUSTRATIONS

The majority of the drawings of children's block constructions are based on photographs. Using photographic negatives and an enlarger the images were projected onto a board and details of the construction outlined.

Although the figures differ in scale, the actual scale of most of the blocks used is that given in Figure 4.1. Those figures in which children appear offer the best guide to scale.

1
A SHORT HISTORY OF CHILDREN'S BUILDING BLOCKS
Jane Read

Blocks are far more elusive to trace historically than other toys. There are little limestone animals from Persia that date back to 1100 BC, the fragment of a doll from ancient Babylon, rattles, balls and yoyos from Greece and Rome, but nothing resembling building blocks. When one considers the seemingly natural and inherent desire children display for building, blocks would appear to be the archetypal toy. It is possible that, because wood decays, other toys took precedence in lists and illustrations, and this is the reason for the lack of definitive proof of their historical origins. Most toys surviving from the earliest times are of clay and occasionally lead or bronze; we can probably assume they represent the wooden toys that existed but that have not survived. Perhaps clay blocks were not recognized as such among the general rubble of an archaeological site.

The earliest hint that blocks may have existed as far back as the fourth century BC comes from a reference in Plato's *Laws*, paragraph 643, where education is being discussed as a training for later life. Plato uses building as an example: 'the future builder must play at building . . . and those who have the care of their education should provide them when young with mimic tools' (1953, p. 24). We can only speculate as to what Plato meant by this.

Few examples of toys survive from the Dark and Middle Ages. Woodcut illustrations and illuminated manuscripts have given no visual evidence of blockplay. In Bruegel's painting. 'Children's Games' (1560), we have our first evidence that playing with bricks was an activity children engaged in. In one corner of the picture, house-building bricks are lying around and a simple construction has been partly made.

Ben Jonson's play *Bartholomew Fair* (1614) lists cheap English toys, but building blocks are not mentioned. The seventeenth-century Moravian educationalist, John Amos Comenius, in *The School of Infancy* (1633), suggests that children under 5 should be allowed to play freely: 'They are delighted to construct little houses, and to erect walls of clay, chips, wood, or stone, thus displaying an architectural genius' (1896, p. 45). However, the examples of children's occupations shown in his book, *Pictus Orbis* (1657), do not include block building. Towards the end of the seventeenth century, John Locke put forward his ideas on education. Although he does not mention building blocks as such, he writes in *Some Thoughts Concerning Education* (1692)

> I know of a person of great quality...who by pasting on 6 vowels (for in our language Y is one) on the 6 sides of a die and the remaining 18 consonants on the sides of the 3 other dice, has made this a play for his children that he shall win who at one cast throws most words on these 4 dice.
>
> (Locke, 1884, p. 131)

As a device for teaching spelling, these reflect a growing desire to make learning more enjoyable, and we can imagine that a child might also use these for simple construction. It is perhaps also significant that the letters were pasted on dice. One wonders if this was from choice, or simply that cube-shaped building blocks did not exist as an alternative. An anonymous book, *Arche Noah* (1693), was published by Dillinger on the Danube, and this describes toys and activities. These included playing with dolls, riding on sticks (hobby horses) and building houses (Fritzsch and Bachmann, 1966).

During the seventeenth century, relative stability in Europe made conditions favourable for the growth of the German toy industry, based on the wood-carving skills of the German peasantry. Nuremberg had already established itself as an important centre for trade, and German toys thus began to spread to many other countries, including England.

Growth of the toy industry was matched by a gradual change in attitude towards children and their education, heralded by such writers as Comenius and Locke. The idea that children were miniature grown-ups who were expected to occupy themselves with learning and hard work began to give way to a more liberal outlook in which childhood was recognized as a state valuable in its own right and that acknowledged the child's need to play. Rousseau was particularly influential in the spread of ideas, through works such as *Emile*. This led to a demand for toys, among the upper classes at least. The kind of toys bought and enjoyed can be found from various sources – diaries, household accounts and portraits both of family groupings and specifically of children – but building blocks do not feature.

Towards the end of the eighteenth century, alphabet blocks and picture cubes, often representing scenes from religious and general history, became and continue to be very popular. These products of the growing toy industry were originally hand coloured and, like most educational toys, were very expensive. In 1798 Maria Edgeworth and Richard Lovell Edgeworth published *Essays on Practical Education*, a work that was to be very influential. This is interesting on two counts. In the chapters 'On Arithmetik' and 'Geometry', they discuss the use of half-inch cubes for teaching arithmetic and wooden models for teaching geometry. These match the alphabet and picture blocks as a means of making learning more enjoyable, and represent a move away from learning purely from books and by rote. The chapter on 'Toys' gives us evidence of their use: 'The first toys for infants should be merely such things as may be grasped without danger and which might, by the difference of their sizes, invite comparison . . . square and circular bits of wood, balls, cubes, triangles' (Edgeworth and Edgeworth, 1798, p. 5). For slightly older children they suggest 'they should be provided with the means of amusing themselves, not with painted or gilt toys, but with pieces of wood of various shapes and sizes, which they may build up and pull down, and put in a variety of different forms and positions' (*ibid.* p. 11). In the 1801 edition, the following advice is added: 'We have found that 2 or 300 bricks formed of plaster of Paris, on a scale of a quarter of an inch to an inch, with a few lintels, etc. in proportion, have been a lasting and useful fund of amusement' (p. 36). These toys fulfil the requirements for toys 'which continually exercise their senses or their imagination, their imitative, and inventive powers' (1798, p. 2). The Edgeworths recognized that what seems to many adults sheer destructiveness is often a spirit of inquiry: 'either he wishes to see what his playthings are made of, and how they are made, or whether he can put them together again if the parts be once separated' (*ibid.* p. 2).

David Stow, a merchant who established an infant school in Glasgow in the 1820s, encouraged the use of blocks in school playgrounds. He noticed that children took up different aspects of the task in hand, some fetching and carrying, others building and some adopting the role of architect (Jones, 1980).

Stow's ideas are echoed by those of Samuel Wilderspin, with whom he had been in contact and who had established an infants school in Spitalfields. In *The Infant System* (1834), Wilderspin describes the use of wooden blocks as a playground activity, resorted to when the toys he initially provided were lost and broken. He gives (*ibid.* p. 85) the dimensions of the blocks as

> about 4 inches long, an inch and a half thick and two inches and a half wide, and of these a thousand were obtained. With these children are exceedingly amused from the variety of forms in which they may be placed, and of buildings which may be erected with them.

Later, in *A System for the Education of the Young* (1840, p. xi), Wilderspin describes an infant playground in which some children engage in erecting their various buildings: 'some are building solid oblong pillars, others are busy erecting squares, other pentagons, other hexagons and so on as they feel inclined'. Wilderspin includes in his description a little cart

> to enable the children to take the wood bricks away and place them in their proper places as on no account are they to be left out when the children are done with them. . . . The pupils being supplied with the necessary articles for amusement, the teacher must not fail to remember that the choice is always left to the children. If they play at what they choose they are free beings and manifest their characters; but

if they are forced to play at what they do not wish, they do not manifest characters but are cramped and are slaves and hence their faculties are not developed.

(Ibid.)

This attitude to a child's right to spontaneous and free play and its beneficial effect on character development was formed before Froebel's ideas had spread to England. Wilderspin was also an advocate of the use of blocks for teaching arithmetic, and had a hundred inch cubes for this purpose (1823, p. 31).

At this time we begin to find visual evidence that building with blocks (especially in the form of bought sets) was an activity carried out within the home. In John Abbott's book, *The Mother at Home*, published in New York by the American Tract Society in 1833, there is an illustration of a mother watching her children, a boy and two girls, building a house with some plain wooden blocks. In England, a painting entitled 'Children with Bricks' was painted by Charles Robert Leslie in the late 1820s. Toys were still very expensive but improved manufacturing processes, for example, the introduction of chromolithography in the mid-nineteenth century, brought down the price of such toys as alphabet and picture blocks – one cannot imagine that Wilderspin would have been able to afford a large sum for his thousand playground blocks.

More expensive and more sophisticated sets of building blocks were on sale from the end of the eighteenth century, and we find these advertised in the catalogues of German toy manufacturers, such as Bestelmeier and Biberach. Bestelmeier was the largest producer. Their catalogue of 1803 has about 1,200 entries; the illustrations show model houses, farms, barns, ruined buildings and towns. The boxes contained detailed plans and required considerable construction skills, making them more suitable for older children and adults. The specific nature of the parts restricted the builder to making the houses, etc., as illustrated.

A wish for greater variety, which would allow free rein to a child's imagination, led to the production of construction sets that supplied the basic materials of building – blocks of various sizes and shapes, columns, arches, etc. In some sets, features such as windows and doors were engraved, stained or stamped onto the blocks. This might be termed the 'architectural' tradition in building blocks, and it continued throughout the century and can still be seen today.

FRIEDRICH FROEBEL

In the specifically educational field, the person who took building blocks and formulated a detailed theory of play involving them and other occupations was Friedrich Froebel. Regarded by some as the apostle of free play and criticized by others for the rigidity of his ideas in practice, Froebel had a varied career before becoming a teacher. He studied widely in the natural sciences, gaining a perception of the importance of geometric forms as the basis of all natural material, and in mathematics, building and architecture, each of which stresses precise and unchanging relationships. It was in Frankfurt (where he had gone to work and to continue his studies as an architect) that, in 1805, he met Herr Gruner, the Director of the Frankfurt Model School, and became drawn into teaching. Froebel's complex philosophy grew out of his own childhood experiences and the prevailing romanticism of his day. His stress on the importance of each child as a person with the right, indeed the necessity, to establish and fulfil his or her own personality and form of development, led to the educational approach we value today. Although Wilderspin spoke of the importance of allowing a child free play in the playground, he favoured the rigid gallery form of classroom, which was a feature of nineteenth-century schools, and the system of learning by rote. Froebel believed that through play and self-chosen activity children came to spontaneous freedom of action. It was the highest form of child, indeed human, development. It was not trivial. He believed in the interconnection of all living things, a connection that encompassed the infinite. Through finding one's own true self one can intuit a sense of the infinite.

The Gifts and Occupations Froebel devised over a period of years reflect his concern to provide children with materials that will help them to become aware of the interconnection between objects – an awareness children will then apply to the world around them and thence to the universe. They were all suitable for table-top use: Gifts 3–6, those specifically designed for building, are sets of blocks, each cut from an eight-inch cube. The manner in which each set is partitioned progresses logically from simple to complex in terms of number, shape and size of the component blocks.

We can see how they fulfil Froebel's intention of giving a child playthings that 'will, in a miniature way, show parts and wholes and also the relation between them ... that the whole is not complete without each of its parts and that each part is dependent upon the whole for any real significance or value' (Harrison and Woodson, 1903, p. 74).

This led Froebel to insist on a procedure for using the Gifts – the child first had to learn to take each Gift out of its box, rather than simply tipping it out. Every block in a particular Gift had to be used and any new construction made by transforming the existing one, rather than knocking it down and starting again. A table was provided for using the Gifts, divided into one-inch squares to encourage the orderly placing of bricks in precise relation and symmetry. Froebel saw the Gifts as being capable of representing three forms:

1. Forms of life, by which a child creates objects seen in the world around him or her.
2. Forms of beauty, which are those where pattern and symmetry predominate.
3. Forms of knowledge, by which abstract mathematical statements are given physical form.

Froebel saw certain Gifts as being more suited to exemplifying some forms rather than others.

After using the blocks, the child had to reconstruct the Gift and replace it in its box. Having mastered one Gift the child could then proceed to the next in sequence. While a child was using the Gifts an adult would be present to supervise and provide guidance when necessary. Froebel's method led to a gradual build-up of competence, manual dexterity and an eye for form – a progression that, in his view, led to the freedom of ordered activity.

Froebel was aware in his own lifetime of objections to his system – for example, that continuous adult supervision would rob play of its naturalness, and he insisted that he valued opportunity and attentiveness rather than a rigid direction of activities. However, one can see how teachers might adopt Froebel's Gifts but then go on to direct a child's activities, thus robbing them of their life and imposing an unintended formality and complexity. One cannot ignore the didactic intention underlying the Gifts, which was not only the display of mathematical relationships between the whole and its parts but also the desire to awaken in the child an intuition of his or her place in the universal scheme, as perceived by Froebel. It is clear from this that large boxes of blocks would not fulfil Froebel's intention – small boxes give children the consciousness that they can reunite them into a whole, a consciousness lost when they can choose as many or as few as they wish.

This represents Froebel's mature thinking, as expressed in his later writings. In *The Education of Man*, originally published in 1826, Froebel discusses using blocks very similar to those used by Wilderspin, from one to twelve inches in length, and he mentions a set 'in which the greatest number of blocks – at least 500 – are of the described brick shape and size' (1887, p. 284).

Commentaries were written on the use of the Gifts – for example, *The Gifts of the Kindergarten* (by Goldammer), first published in England in 1882, with its extensive illustrations of constructions possible with each Gift. The Gifts came to be used not only in kindergartens established in Britain, America and Europe as a whole but also in some of the more enlightened board schools – although not always as Froebel intended.

MARIA MONTESSORI

In the early twentieth century, when Froebel's Gifts were under attack for exhibiting a restricting didacticism, Maria Montessori produced her concept of building toys, which also carried an explicit didactic function. There was to be no free and spontaneous play with her apparatus – a child must put the blocks in the correct order to create a tower and a stair (Montessori, 1912). Montessori's blocks were a part of her material for educating the senses.

Froebel's ideas were a force to be reckoned with in any educational debate, and this can be seen in the arguments between supporters who wanted to retain his system intact and a more progressive school that recognized Froebel's value but saw a need to use his methods to make them more relevant to late nineteenth- and early twentieth-century realities.

Another American, Patty Smith Hill, also made practical changes to educational, school-based blocks. Her enlightened education in America in the 1870s included not only playing with blocks, barrels and boards but also constructing objects in a carpenter's shop. In her own professional education she became interested in Froebel's valuation of play as an important method of learning, but drew on the ideas of Dewey and Stanley Hall on child growth and development, and Earl Barnes and Luther Gulick on the psychology of play. She went on to design the Patty Hill blocks – the forerunners of the large hollow blocks we see today.

As these were up to three feet high, they enabled children to construct houses, shops and other buildings large and sturdy enough for them to enter and act out dramatic situations. The Hill floor blocks were stabilized by the addition of grooved corner-pillar blocks into which the other blocks would fit and the use of pegs and holes, copper-wire rods and girders. In 1905 Patty Hill went to lecture at Teachers' College, Columbia University, which was to become the outstanding centre for advanced professional teacher training.

Caroline Pratt, a contemporary of Patty Hill, also found herself at odds with the kindergarten training of the day and she turned to handwork for a more meaningful form of education, studying at the Sloyd School in Sweden. However, she found that this too did not provide the kind of occupation she felt children would find stimulating. At the turn of the century she arrived in New York and came into contact with Hill's work at the Horace Mann Kindergarten attached to the Teachers' College, where the Hill blocks were in use.

Although she found much to admire in the Hill blocks, she had her own ideas about how she wanted to use blocks and had the necessary skills to create what were to become known as the 'unit system' blocks. These form the basis of many sets found in nursery schools today (and seen in many illustrations throughout this book). They were in the proportion of 1 to 2 to 4; that is, half as high as they were wide, twice as long as they were wide (Provenzo, 1983).

The practical use to which these were put in the City and Country school, where Pratt worked with Harriet Johnson and Lucy Sprague Mitchell, is described in *Experimental Practice in the City and Country School* (1924, p. 8):

> We pin a large amount of faith to block building for younger children. The reason for this is that blocks are the most adaptable materials for their use that we can find. . . . The ordinary visitor takes the products of the children on their face value – looking for an approach to the adult's conception of the things produced. We on the contrary should be alarmed if we saw such an approach.

She goes on to describe the construction of a play city in the River Yard of the school in permanent materials – board and metal – in which the children 'reorganized their experiences and information and extended both . . . the children as a group had the information and experience for building a city; the teacher helped them organize and extend it' (*ibid*. p. 21).

Harriet Johnson writes about the City and Country School in her book. *Children in the Nursery School* (1928, p. 183):

> power to deal effectively with his environment accrues to a child through the use of constructive material. The Hill blocks or those used in the City and Country School or other sets planned to meet the same requirements make it possible for a child to plan and execute constructions as large and as elaborate as he can devise. They are in an entirely different category from the smaller sets of blocks restricted in actual number and having no stable unit form with which Parents have had until recent years to be content. These small collections of vari-sized and shaped blocks force the child continually to adapt his plans and his purpose to their limitations.

The block systems designed by Pratt and Hill are based on multiples of two – unlike those constructed according to the Golden Ratio, which conform to relationships found within the natural world. The mathematical basis for Golden Ratio blocks is that formulated by the Renaissance mathematician, Leonardo Fibonacci, each block deriving from a golden rectangle measuring $2 \times 3\frac{3}{16}$ inches (Provenzo, 1983).

Although England lacked educational theorists on blockplay at this time, photographs in the Greater London Record Office Photograph Library show that some schools, as well as kindergartens, were allowing their pupils more imaginative use of building blocks. In addition, the Board of Education *Report of the Consultative Committee upon the School Attendance of Children below the Age of Five* (1908) includes a chapter on 'The Ideal Institution for Such Younger Infants', in which 'Bricks of various sizes' are recommended as suitable apparatus (p. 22).

A few years later, two well-known English writers produced books on the construction of imaginary environments within two years of each other. In 1911 H. G. Wells published *Floor Games*. As the title indicates, Wells regarded floors as the ideal surface on which to construct: 'The jolliest indoor games for boys and girls demand a floor and the home that has no floor upon which games may be played falls so far short of happiness' (*ibid*. p. 9).

Wells also thought little of the blocks sold in toyshops:

> How utterly we despise these silly little bricks of the toyshops! They are too small to make a decent home for even the poorest lead soldiers . . . and there are never enough, never nearly enough. We see rich people going into toyshops and buying these skimpy, sickly, ridiculous pseudo-boxes of bricklets because they do not know what to ask for. . . . Their unfortunate under-parented offspring mess about with these gifts, and don't make very much of them and put them away.
>
> (*Ibid*. p. 18)

Wells was lucky enough to have a box of blocks given to him by two older friends who had a 'Good Uncle'. He had engaged a

> deserving unemployed carpenter through an entire winter making big boxes of bricks . . . there are whole bricks 4½ × 2¼ × 1 and an eighth inches, there are half-bricks 2¼ × 2¼ × 1 and an eighth inches and there are quarters . . . and of each

size – we have never counted them but we must have hundreds. We can pave a dozen square yards of floor with them . . . we can scheme and build, all 3 of us, for the best part of an hour and still have more bricks in the box.

(*Ibid*. p. 16)

Wells then details the games they played: '"The Wonderful Islands" and the "Building of Cities": We always build twin cities because 2 of us always want to be lord mayors and municipal councils' (*ibid*. p. 41). Wells also wrote a book specifically about war games called *Little Wars* (1931), in which the bricks are utilized in the constructions for 'The Battle of Hook's Farm'.

In John and Elizabeth Newson's book, *Toys and Playthings in Development and Remediation* (1979), the proportions of Wells's blocks are praised for the flexible and versatile structures that can be made, and they approve the modular principle as one that has both clarity and simplicity – an important educational factor.

The second writer on blockplay is Edith Nesbit, who published *Wings and the Child* in 1913. She, too, criticized the boxes of blocks available in toyshops:

They are lacking both in quality and in quantity. No box of bricks that can at present be bought for money will build anything that can satisfy an imaginative child. In the bricks themselves there is not enough variety. The stone bricks, it is true, have broken out into a variety of ugly shapes and a blue colour.

(Nesbit, 1913, p. 55)

Nesbit, whose own childhood was in the late 1860s, asks the reader what he or she remember from their his or her childhood:

You loved your bricks, I think, especially if you lived in the days when they were of well-seasoned oak, heavy, firm, exactly proportioned, before the boxes of inexact light deal bricks, with the one painted glass window, began to be made in Germany. How finely those great bricks stood for Stonehenge and how submissively Anna, the Dutch doll, whose arms and legs were gone, played the sacrifice.

(*Ibid*. p. 22)

In Part 11 (p. 105 *et seq*.) she goes on to describe the building of 'magic cities', constructed on a large table rather than on the floor, where they would be prone to damage, both deliberate and accidental, and which incorporate all sorts of materials as well as building blocks – boxes, cotton reels, pieces of tile and pipe, broom handles, dominoes, books, cigars and cigarettes, chess pieces and natural materials, such as shells, fir cones, acorns and sedge.

Nesbit constructed a magic city for the Children's Welfare Exhibition at Olympia in 1912; *Wings and the Child* was written in response to requests for suggestions and advice received there. She stresses the good training for hand and eye as well as the stimulus to the imagination and the learning of habits such as precision and neatness, patience, good temper: 'for no one can build anything in a rage' (*ibid*. p. 155), and perseverance: 'All these grow strong while you build your cities and try to make visible your dream' (*ibid*.).

During the nineteenth century sets of wooden blocks with titles like 'Principal Edifices of Europe' and 'Country Seats' had appeared on the market.

With these a child was not merely playing with blocks but was, to quote the description on the lid of 'Country Seats', 'A Little Connoisseur of Wood'.

These were joined in the 1870s by sets of stone blocks, with door and window details stamped on or specially shaped. The Richter sets, first patented in 1880, known as 'Anchor Blocks', were cast from cement and could be bought in very large sets weighing over half a hundredweight and including 328 different shapes and sizes of stones. The sets contained detailed construction plans and grids but could obviously be used to make abstract as well as representational constructions.

Jones (1980, p. 30) quotes Mr W. Foster, headmaster of the board school at Mendham in Suffolk, who wrote in 1890 'We have used your Anchor Blocks in our infant school for some time and I can therefore testify to their suitability for infant education. These stones have an influence of the highest order for educational purposes'.

In England the firm of Lotts was the chief rival to Richter, although initially it simply packed blocks sawn by another local firm. However, it bought the English plant producing the Richter blocks and called in an architect, Arnold Mitchell, to advise on cutting the blocks into shapes suitable for such constructions as cathedrals. Later, smaller sets for domestic buildings were produced with embossed blocks, mullioned windows, etc. Lotts blocks achieved recognition when Queen Mary bought the first set at the British Industries Fair in 1918, and a set sent to H. G. Wells in 1920 met with his approval.

FRANK LLOYD WRIGHT

It is interesting to note that, despite the long and widespread availability of these specifically architectural sets of blocks, it was the Froebel building Gifts that attracted the attention of Frank Lloyd Wright's mother at the Philadelphia Centennial Exhibition in 1876. She had decided before her son's birth that he would be an architect; Wright acknowledges in his book, *An Autobiography*, that the Froebel Gifts she provided for his play had proved an important formative influence on him: 'The smooth shapely maple blocks with which to build, the sense of which never afterwards leaves the fingers: so *form* became *feeling*. . . . Here was something for invention to seize and use to create' (1932, p. 11, original emphasis).

The ground plans of two of Wright's famous early buildings, the Imperial Palace Hotel, Tokyo, and Midway Gardens, Chicago, have been reconstructed using Froebel's blocks – offering visual evidence of their practical effect on his work (Provenzo, 1983, pp. 4–5).

ALBERT EINSTEIN

It would be of great interest to know exactly what kind of blocks Albert Einstein played with as a child in the 1880s. In his book, *Thematic Origins of*

Scientific Thought (1973), Gerald Holton stresses the importance of visualization in Einstein's approach to problem-solving. He describes Einstein as 'quietly sitting by himself at an early age, playing by putting together shapes cut out with a jigsaw, erecting complicated constructions by means of a chest of toy building parts' (*ibid*. p. 367).

The language Einstein used in describing the genesis of his theory of relativity reflects the importance of this aspect of his childhood play experiences: 'the arguments and building blocks were being prepared over a period of years, although without bringing about the fundamental decision' (*ibid*. p. 197).

Holton also draws our attention to Einstein's comment 'that he was brought to the formulation of relativity theory in good part because he kept asking himself questions concerning space and time that only children wonder about' (*ibid*. p. 356). The value of blockplay in helping children understand and experience the practical realities of spatial concepts emerges during the course of this book.

CHARLES CRANDALL

During the nineteenth century, attempts were made to design a system for building blocks that would make them more stable but not too intricate for children to assemble, and that would take apart easily when required. In 1867 Charles Crandall patented a tongue-and-slot system in America, which looks like a precursor of Sticklebricks. Because these interlink, they are not, strictly speaking, blocks, as they are not freestanding and stackable.

Crandall's firm produced a wide variety of building blocks including nesting alphabet blocks and stacking sets – an obelisk constructed from these was set up in Central Park in 1880 and a set based on it patented in 1882. A huge construction using Crandall's tongue-and-slot blocks was displayed at the Philadelphia Centennial Exhibition in 1876 – the same year in which Wright's mother discovered the Froebel building Gifts.

LEGO AND OTHER CONSTRUCTION KITS

In 1869 a spring-clip system was patented and developed into the Klipit sets manufactured by J. H. Skinner of Norfolk from 1910. A system resembling Lego was patented in 1889 in which blocks had a row of single buttons that fitted into recesses in the base of other blocks. Lego appeared in the 1930s, having been invented by a Dane, Papa Christiansen. Other systems include threading wooden blocks onto wire rods, and sliding blocks between rods. In the 1890s, sets of building blocks using cement and window putty were produced by the firm of Jarrett in Gillingham, thus adding practical building skills to those of architectural design.

Other sets that appeared in the early twentieth century include the British Wenebrik, marketed in 1915, which reflects the particular interest in smaller-scale domestic architecture. In contrast to this was the American Bilt-E-Z set, made in Chicago in 1924. The child built with stamped metal panels, which were capable of creating that new phenomenon, the skyscraper.

SUMMARY

New materials, such as metal and plastic, came to be used in construction toys, and various ingenious methods for stabilizing structures were employed. However, the basic freestanding, stackable wooden block – in various shapes and sizes, in coloured wood and plain, with and without details stamped on them, simply stacked in a tower or carefully arranged into a complex building or city – remains a universally popular toy both at home and in schools. Such blocks have been favourably compared with other toys by the writer and structuralist philosopher, Roland Barthes. In *Mythologies* (1973; first published 1957) Barthes argues (p. 53) 'A few sets of blocks, which appeal to the spirit of do-it-yourself are the only ones which offer dynamic forms'.

Unlike other toys they allow a child to discover for him- or herself:

> The merest set of blocks, provided it is not too refined, implies a very different learning of the world: then the child does not in any way create meaningful objects, it matters little to him whether they have an adult name; the actions he performs are not those of a user but those of a demiurge. He creates forms which walk, which roll, he creates life not property. Objects now act by themselves, they are no longer an inert material in the palm of his hand. But such toys are rather rare.
>
> (*Ibid*. p. 54)

Finally, a poem from Robert Louis Stevenson's anthology, *A Child's Garden of Verses* (1985, pp. 81–2) entitled 'Block City'. It speaks for itself:

> What are you able to build with your blocks?
> Castles and palaces, temples and docks.
> Rain may keep raining, and others go roam.
> But I can be happy and building at home.
>
> Let the sofa be mountains, the carpet the sea,
> There I'll establish a city for me:
> A kirk and a mill and a palace beside,
> And a harbour as well where my vessels may ride.
>
> Great is the palace with pillar and wall,
> A sort of a tower on top of it all,
> And steps coming down in an orderly way
> To where my toy vessels lie safe in the bay.
>
> This one is sailing and that one is moored:
> Hark to the song of the sailors on board!
> And see on the steps of my palace, the kings
> Coming and going with presents and things!

Now I have done with it, down let it go!
All in a moment the town is laid low.
Block upon block lying scattered and free,
What is there left of my town by the sea?

Yet as I saw it, I see it again,
The kirk and the palace, the ships and the men.
And as long as I live and where'er I may be,
I'll always remember my town by the sea.

2
CHILDREN, ADULTS AND BLOCKPLAY
Tina Bruce

INTRODUCTION

Western societies tend to value that which is measurable and part of the tangible experiences of life. It might be of crucial importance for the development of humanity if more emphasis were to be placed on what could be, ought to be, and on alternative, imagined worlds (Meek, 1985). The way adults and children use blocks together will either help or hold back this process.

THE THREE APPROACHES OF THE RESEARCH PROPOSAL AND THE BASELINE SURVEY

The research proposal aimed to look at approaches to the curriculum that might be *laissez-faire*, didactic or interactionist (see Appendix I). Initially, a baseline survey was carried out by each school in order to establish how blocks were being used.

LAISSEZ-FAIRE

The baseline survey revealed that current practice and organization of blockplay tended to be unintentionally *laissez-faire*. That is to say, it was not the policy of any of the schools. In practice, the block area was set up but not necessarily all the time, and children were often left to use blocks without adults.

Presentation

The presentation of blocks may have had an impact in that children seemed to be held at an early level of blockplay. During sessions, the block area became increasingly uninviting, as blocks became scattered. The baseline survey revealed that schools did not possess complete sets of unit blocks, or that children removed blocks from the set and transported them elsewhere. Typically the schools offered children blocks mixed with other media. These included play people, train sets, cars, etc.

This led to discussion about what constitutes order or mess in a classroom. The unintended *laissez-faire* approach seemed to lead to children abandoning the blockplay area once it became too untidy. Consequently, blockplay was often effectively over by 10 a.m.

Timetabling

Timetabling was important. If the school offered initially only indoor play, with the option from 10 a.m. of playing outside, there seemed to be a mass abandonment of other activity. The blocks particularly often suffered from such an arrangement, as children would be expected to tidy up before leaving the block area. In contrast to putting away pencils, clearing up might appear to the child as a penalty to be paid for playing with the blocks. In fact, one child was overheard telling her friend not to use too many blocks 'because you have to put them away afterwards'.

Process and Product in Blockplay

The group also began to realize from the collection of baseline data that there was virtually no regard for product in the blockplay. Bruner (1976) argues that both process and product are important. Some children tended to knock down any end-products, causing their creators to leave the area in a state of resignation, or upset and frustrated. In reality, only the children who dominated the blockplay were in a position to build constructions that stood any chance of remaining for any length of time, without threat of demolition. Demolition is one of the joys of blockplay, and one way or another will be part of it. However, an unintended *laissez-faire* approach encourages demolition in particular ways, which may not be the most educationally desirable.

As the group reflected on this, it became clear that this situation was not what participants saw as ideal. Participants had joined the project in order to explore such issues together. There was great interest in the picture that began to emerge, and commitment to developing practice from this point.

From unintended *laissez-faire* beginnings, the group moved towards the exploration of interactionist strategies. The act of observing and recording blockplay, which had become a regular adult activity, served as a bridge between non-involvement and positive interaction. The energy of the participants went into consideration of the role of the adult in blockplay, which also had an impact on the curriculum in general. Participants shared an implicit respect for the *laissez-faire* approach in its reticence to invade and dominate children's play.

DIDACTIC

As the discussion developed, anxiety was expressed that almost before they knew it, adults would find themselves dominating. Such studies as that of Wells (1987) indicate that adults do indeed tend to take over, and become didactic when they join children's play. This is also noted by Hutt *et al.* (1988, p. 227): 'More often than not adults, in interacting with either a single child or a small group of children, tend to dominate the interaction.'

The didactic approach emphasizes tasks set by adults. Adult-directed tasks encourage dependency, narrowness, a desire to please those in authority, conformity and a lack of creativity, imagination or the ability to create and solve problems. It leads to the need to feel secure through sticking to what is known and understood, rather than risk-taking and exploration (Dweck and Legett, 1988).

The didactic approach was never explored as the result of my decision as director of the project. The didactic approach brought us all great unease, and did not sit easily beside the initial training of either teachers or nursery nurses. It did not fit with the current research and theory the group was exploring, either on general inservice courses or in the blockplay project. Transmitting knowledge about how to build a tower, etc., through demonstration, or stipulating what children are to construct (e.g. a house) or setting specific construction tasks, would have undervalued research that pointed to the need for children to initiate, to be active in their learning, to make decisions and choices, to negotiate, to set their own problems and to problem-solve with help where needed.

The group's discussions moved from unintended *laissez-faire* to interactionist strategies.

INTERACTIONIST

The participants in the blockplay project worked in a determined way to develop strategies that would help children's blockplay to develop with quality. This meant that adults needed to find more helpful ways than didactic approaches offer in giving children information, or making suggestions about what they might do: 'A little technical help given when the children have shown that they cannot solve the problem themselves may be necessary, particularly in some bridging constructions or when making a roof for an enclosure' (Parry, 1978, p. 10).

Children sometimes meet difficulties they cannot resolve alone. There are times when they need information and help in finding strategies that enable them to carry out an idea. At other times they are able to solve their problems without adult help. This would include collaborative learning through and with friends, using books, paying focused attention to the medium, manipulating and exploring it, remembering what the material will do from previous occasions or learning through watching. The children have appreciated the appropriate and sensitive strategies adults in the project worked hard to achieve. It makes children want adults with them, and there has been great development in the richness of the blockplay. One participant commented in her notes towards the end of the project 'At every stage we've really had to go back to basics and sort out our own thinking before we move forward'.

STRATEGIES DEVELOPED USING THE INTERACTIONIST APPROACH

The Role of Adults

Children find it easier to play if they are helped and encouraged to do so by adults: 'If there is one single message which comes through . . . it is the importance of the caring adult both in directing the child's play in an appropriate way at the appropriate moment, and in gauging the child's mood state and deciding in which circumstances it is inappropriate to intervene' (Hutt *et al.*, 1988, p. 194).

Children need to play alone, and they need to play in groups, and one of the most powerful ways to become involved in rich play is through partnerships (Sylva *et al.*, 1980). Children develop these with other children; hence the crucial importance for young children of who is and who is not their best friend.

An adult joined two girls at the point where a block construction had been completed. She wondered how it was done, tried and failed to make a similar construction. The girls explained 'You need a friend'. They gave a demonstration. One held the block while her friend arranged the other blocks against it so that they would balance as a whole (Figure 4.14).

Children also develop play partnerships with adults if given the opportunity. The Froebel Blockplay Project gave great emphasis to adult–child play partnering.

A Team Approach to Blockplay

Initially, adults tried a very gentle approach. Attention was given to classroom organization and presentation. This involved adults planning together who would be in the block area and when. It meant looking at where the block area should be, and having a distinct block area. It meant considering the space available for blockplay, offering it indoors and outdoors where possible, and considering how to make it available and when. Ideally, it was felt that blockplay should be available all the time.

Gender Issues

A marked gender influence was at work to begin with, with boys tending to form groups and take over the blockplay area. This meant that many children were prevented from moving beyond their starting strategies – watching, on the edge, or repeating what they did last time. The dominating group had the effect of pushing them to the periphery with few blocks for their use. This lack of space and lack of materials constrained development of blockplay for children not in the dominant group.

A girl and boy collaborated in the making of a house for Cinderella and Prince Charming to live in after they married. There is space to sunbathe on the roof. It is important to note that the story, which became an 'alternative' to Cinderella (a tale of dreams turned sour) was improvised as the building progressed. A dynamic relationship developed between the kind of construction that emerged and the plot of the story. The adults' role was to be interested and to act as a sensitive audience to the unfolding story. The boy and the girl worked co-operatively, neither dominating, and each contributing.

Encouraging Children to Use the Block Area

Some children were never in the block area to be observed. In her notes, the research assistant describes how she initiated blockplay through the strategy of storying, so that children began to watch the blockplay, join in with it or take it over. Some children were not finding out what blocks were like because they never used them.

Play partnering can be initiated and led by adults, as in this case, or by children. Sometimes the adult leads, and sometimes the child leads (Bruce, 1987). Two girls were partners in their blockplay:

A says 'Let's build'. B says 'Yes'. They build a pile. Pat, the adult, says 'I've got a family. Here's me.' (One cylinder.) 'Here's my husband.' (Another cylinder.) 'And here's my children, Lucy and Mark.' (Another two cylinders.) 'And here's my cat.' (An eighth unit.) 'We need a house.' A says 'We'll build you a house'. During the tidying of the blocks, she heard B saying 'Be careful of Patti's cat'. In her hand she had an eighth unit and was stroking it, and said 'We'll wait until all the blocks are away and then we'll put it in (with the others). We don't want it to get hurt, do we?'

In this example, the children took over the story the adult used as a strategy to get things off the ground when help was first needed.

Encouraging Adults to Be in the Block Area

There are many ways for adults to join the block area without dominating. Some adults tried a side-by-side strategy, as in the Cinderella example. That is to say, adults joined children in the block area but were aware of the tendency to dominate and so did not initiate a conversation. They watched children.

They listened to what children said. They were participant observers, simply showing interest (Corsaro, 1979).

Children Need Help

Observations highlighted that children might first be attracted to the area because of its presentation but then be at a loss to know how to use it, not yet knowing the possibilities of blockplay. Children cannot easily plan how to use an area they do not yet know much about. They tend to build the same things each time, perhaps in order to feel secure, or perhaps to get to know the material. They might stay on the edge of the area, watching and performing very simple actions, apparently uninvolved. It may be that these are simply sensible starting strategies for children to adopt. What emerges from the blockplay project is just how sensible children are.

Acting on Observations

Adults either waited for children to say something or made a remark or movement with the blocks attempting to connect with what they had seen the child do or say. There are links here with Goetz's (1981) research, who emphasizes the importance of praising children when they make a new form out of blocks and actually pointing out to them that they have made something different and new. The manner in which this is done forms part of the ethos of the setting: being warm, attentive, enthusiastic and sensitive is of fundamental importance. In this way, the adult's first move into conscious play partnering was to join in with what they thought children were doing. Bruner *et al.* (1976) says we need to observe in order to diagnose the 'incipient intention' of the child.

Adults began to report girls joining the block area, and boys being more willing to share. Children were developing effective strategies for working together, as in the Cinderella construction, and side by side. Children were gaining mastery of blocks and using them in increasingly complex symbolic play. Again, in the Cinderella construction, the children wanted to build a staircase on the side of the building. This was difficult, and so they talked about having a chute that could be a fire escape, which was simpler to make.

This linked with the work of Wolf and Gardner (1978, p. 118), who define symbolic play as 'the ability to represent actual or imagined experiences through the combined use of small objects, motions and language'. Blockplay lends itself to this.

Respecting and Enabling Children's Ideas

Wynne Harlen and Paul Black (1989), investigating the effective teaching of primary science in the National Curriculum, note:

systematic observation of children's ideas has shown that if these are ignored and children are expected to accept the 'right' answer, then only confusion results. Children retain their initial ideas because it is these which they will have worked out for themselves, and which, for the moment, make sense to them in terms of their experience and their logic. These are the ideas which children use in trying to understand new phenomena as their experience expands.

There are parallels between this approach and that of the Froebel Blockplay Project. Harlen and Black emphasize that it is time to have the courage of our convictions. They point out that in reality, few opportunities are given for children to express their ideas. Pat Gura (personal communication) points out that after Guanella and Johnson's studies in the 1930s there is a gap of some thirty years before studies of spontaneous blockplay reappear.

The blockplay project, looking at the 3–7-year-old level, takes up Froebel's statement that we need to 'begin where the learner is'.

The *laissez-faire* approach tends to leave children where they are. The didactic approach gives children only the 'right' ideas. The interactionist approach begins where children are, helping them to use what they know, and to move with them into new knowledge and understanding. In order to do this in an interactionist way, adults need to know as much as possible about the development of young children, and the context of learning. They also need to be clear about what they are helping children to know and understand, as with two boys who were constructing separately but near to one another. They used all the basic block forms as they played and seemed to be going over everything they knew about their mastery of blocks. It seemed to be a celebration of their knowledge and mastery of blocks. The contribution of the sensitive, interested and skilled adult is indirect on the whole, but at times adults also need to take a direct role, otherwise (as the blockplay project found) the children's play is less rich.

THE IMPORTANCE OF ACTION

So far we have looked at interactionist strategies that encourage both children and adults to use the block area to good effect. We have seen that this enables the development of materials mastery, which enables rich play to develop. Hutt *et al.* (1989, p. 231) distinguish between open-ended, transparent structuring and closed, opaque structuring, which constrains the child's activity, often in counterproductive ways. What becomes clear is that children need many opportunities to master, control and become competent in their blockplay. They need to explore the potential of blocks and what can be done with them, alongside developing ideas through them. In this way, they reach the point where they not only have ideas about the possibilities of blocks and can represent events and experiences with them but they can also carry out these ideas effectively and to their own satisfaction.

A girl (4 y.) is making a freestanding enclosure. She is using her knowledge of how to make right angles with blocks (Figure 5.4).

Materials mastery has a central place in blockplay. Materials mastery involves aspects of knowledge and understanding that form the bedrock on which the possibility of advance planning, acting on a plan or reflecting on it rest. After all, a good worker knows the tools and, through this active knowledge, learns about their potential. Children need to know about blocks, and so come to envisage what blocks will do. Forman (1982) sees the early manipulation of blocks as the basis of metacognition and reflection. Hutt *et al.* (1988) value manipulation and exploration if these lead to the novel use of materials and problem-solving. Because they search consistently for concrete evidence that children are learning, they do not give a high value to what they call fantasy or ludic play, on the grounds that children do not evidence direct learning from it. In reality, it may well be that fantasy play and true planning can only develop once manipulation and exploration have become sufficiently established, since this involves symbolic behaviour, which is removed from action.

The Basic Forms of Blockplay, and how Children Use Them

The basic forms of blockplay are described in Chapter 4 and Appendix III. Different researchers have described the different patterns children use, make and develop when playing with blocks or in more general situations. Children need opportunities to repeat, vary, mix and match. Participants found that it was very helpful when observing the children's blockplay to know about basic forms, and to have some understanding of aspects humans share as part of their common development, and to see how each child uses them uniquely.

The studies that helped most were those of Johnson (1933), Guanella (1934), Piaget (1962) and Athey (1981, 1990), whose work on schemas links with Bruner's (1973) notion of modularization. These studies are all concerned with the emergence of behaviours that are generalized, repeated, mixed and matched and varied, and that become increasingly complex.

Stunt-Building

As blockplay becomes more daring, stunt-building, as Harriet Johnson calls it, begins to emerge. This kind of risk-taking develops from manipulating, exploring, using what you know and experimenting with it and pushing ideas to the limit. Gradually, experienced blockplayers can make what they want to make because they not only have ideas but are also competent in using the grammar of blocks. When they have experienced high-level blockplay through manipulating, exploring, watching, listening to others talk about them and so come to appreciate blocks, they are in a position to perform at a complex level in their blockplay.

PROVISION

Complete Sets of Blocks

It seemed important for children to experience complete sets of blocks that were carefully and thoughtfully presented, with supporting interest tables and outings (this is discussed in more detail in Chapters 9 and 10). It became obvious to children that blockplay was a priority for adults, and valued in the curriculum. The children found their blockplay initiatives were being encouraged, noted and celebrated. In other words, the blockplay project had created the setting in which progress could be made.

Use of Accessories

At the beginning of the project, the children tended to use blocks as an accessory to play with cars, farms, play people, etc. As adults began to emphasize the blocks themselves, the situation changed. Accessories were added after constructions were made. Children still 'storied' using play people and so on, but now, because the constructions were more complex, the stories had gained.

A group of children made a construction they then imagined to be a building. They then used play people and ladders on it. The building helped the story, and vice versa. The play was richer in terms of both the construction and the use of accessories. Hutt *et al.* (1988, p. 98) suggest that mixing materials from different areas, such as sand and water, is beneficial. The blockplay project found that this was only the case if both micro-environments were given appropriate attention in their own right. Otherwise, if blocks were used with accessories, the block constructions were less sophisticated.

Blockplay Celebrates what Humans Have in Common, and the Uniqueness of Each Person

Although there seem to be particular forms common to all children in the way they draw (Kellogg, 1979), and use blocks (Johnson, 1933), it is also evident that children use these entirely uniquely (Athey, 1990), and show individual preferences and style, both in the way they use the basic forms and in the themes they choose to explore through them (Wolf and Gardner, 1978). Wolf and Gardner found that some children show tendencies to be 'patterners' and some to be 'dramatists', although children need to be both. A patterner involved in blockplay would make configurations and patterns. A dramatist would use the blocks as artefacts in a story, e.g. pretending the blocks were chairs, making a table and using other blocks for the people sitting down for a meal.

It seemed in the project that children need opportunities for pure blockplay as this enables the patterner in the child to develop. It also leads to more complex constructions, which serve as artefacts the dramatist in the child can then use in conjunction with other accessories to make stories. H. G. Wells, E. E. Nesbit and Frank Lloyd Wright all had rich childhood experiences of blockplay, which encouraged both the patterner and the dramatist within them to develop and feed off each other inextricably. For the first two, the dramatist is dominant, but having a concrete 'stage set' helped the story to develop. For the architect, the patterner is to the fore, but the developing constructions could be rearranged time and again until they satisfied.

THE IMPORTANCE OF LANGUAGE

Problems Arise when Children are Asked to Verbalize in Advance of Action

Rather than pushing children to verbalize what their actions will be in advance, as in the plan–do–review cycle of the American High Scope programme, adults in the blockplay project gave children opportunities to manipulate and explore the blocks while giving a verbal accompaniment to the child's actions. The adult spoke in the light of what they observed the child to do or say, as in genuine conversation. In this way the child is not under pressure to speak his or her plans, although the atmosphere is encouraging of dialogue. It seems that once pressure to speak on the adult's terms is removed from children and adults, provided adults are aware of the importance in human development of anticipating through language, the children begin to engage in blockplay with enthusiasm.

Lack of Pressure to Speak is Important

Stephen Krashen (1981) stresses the importance of lack of pressure to speak in language development. He suggests that this may be why babies are such successful learners of language compared with adults. They are given what he calls 'comprehensible input'. For example, the adult points to the empty plate, then to the bowl of food, and says 'Would you like some more?' Babies need only vocalize or speak if they want to do so. He contrasts this with the pressure on pupils to speak in many language teaching programmes.

Language without Action Decontextualizes Situations

Decontextualized situations cause difficulties for children, as Martin Hughes (1986) suggests. If children are helped to create rich blockplay situations, and this means helping them to develop materials mastery in situations that are verbalized for them by the adult, they quickly show evidence of natural advance planning. They may not be able to articulate their advance plans verbally, but it may not be appropriate that they should have to. As Lilian

Figure 2.1

Katz (1990) argues, because children are capable of reading at 4 years does not mean they should read at such an age. It may be more appropriate that they do other things that broaden rather than narrow down their lives. Asking children to advance plan in a formal way may, in the long term, constrain the imagination and discourage flexible thinking, which is the stuff of good scientific research and the expressive arts. Katz also points out that the way we educate young children has a cumulative effect on their later performance.

A 4-year-old selects an arch, and makes a repeating pattern on the floor. The blocks are placed with increasing precision. Advance plans, prior knowledge and competence fuse (Figure 5.3).

Strategies that are less direct may help children to considerations of what they might do in advance, which are of deeper quality in the end.

A girl (3 y.) was interested in a caterpillar she found in the nursery garden. Next day, she arrived in school with a soft toy caterpillar, saying she was going to build one like it with blocks. She did so, and sketched it. Checking her sketch, she found she had given the caterpillar an extra leg on one side. Next day, she used her sketch to guide a reconstruction, remembering to deduct a leg (Figure 2.1).

We have seen that getting to know the material through physical manipulation and exploration is of central importance, and a vital part of the backcloth to blockplay. So is the sensitive adult who verbalizes the experience for the child, without pressure to speak, and encourages true conversations to take place through having a shared experience and a shared focus. These strategies help children to think ahead, ponder and meander in deep and worthwhile ways.

Valuing Unspoken Behaviour and Spoken Language

Gesture, facial expression and body language are as important as spoken language. Halpern, Corrigan and Alvierez (1983) suggest that children understand things at an action level by doing before they talk about them. The relationship between language and thought fascinated such researchers as Fraser, Bellugi and Brown in the 1970s, and this fascination engendered further consideration of the wider aspects of communication in the 1980s. Communication is not only verbal: it is nonverbal too, and this is particularly so in young children.

We have seen that Stephen Krashen's work emphasizes the importance of comprehensible input. It is no good using verbal language unless the person spoken to understands what is said. People need clues to help them, particularly if the words are new to them. Krashen gives the example of talking about his eyes, nose, ears or mouth to someone who does not know the language. They are none the wiser. If, as he speaks, he touches his eyes, nose, ears and mouth, it is easy to understand what he is saying. We need action in order to bring about understanding.

In Welsh and French-Canadian immersion schools, children are spoken to in a context that involves just such first-hand experience and action, with meaningful, comprehensible language input. This approach was used in the blockplay project. It leads to real conversations and not, as so often happens, to adult monologues and closed question-and-answer sessions. We need to value nonverbal behaviour as much as verbal behaviour, especially with very young children or anyone learning a new language.

A child gathers all the blocks that look the same (four planks). He holds them in celebration. There is no intention to construct with them. His action suggests to the adult that he is matching the blocks mathematically.

Watching

Watching is also important. We have many instances of children watching other children construct, and then using ideas gained in this way in their own blockplay, sometimes several days later. It could be argued that these children are aimless, purposeless or 'off task'. In fact, the children do have their own task and purposes, rather than the task the adult had in mind. Those participating in the blockplay project would argue that such children were more likely to be gathering together ideas and formulating thoughts ready for future use.

The Daci International Conference in London in July 1988 ('Dance and the Child') emphasized the need for children to make, appreciate and perform dance. It may well be that in the blockplay study, children watching other children construct were appreciating block constructions and how to make them. They also learnt to appreciate them by seeing buildings on outings, looking at interest tables using blocks and books of architecture and sculpture.

All this helps children to wallow in and experience ideas, which make for rich blockplay.

SUMMARY AND CONCLUSIONS

Indirect strategies, which are interactionist in character, make blockplay rich. These include the crucial partnership role of the adult, other children, the mastery and control of materials, the importance of action with language and a deep valuing of the unspoken. It means careful presentation of blocks, interest tables and outings as shared experiences. It involves the importance of participant observation, and a commitment to help children appreciate, make and perform in their blockplay, through understanding the way children develop basic forms and explore content. It means celebrating the progress children make, and valuing their learning with them.

Through these strategies, children begin to construct and represent things they know and think about in their blockplay. They play in a sustained way, showing deep commitment, concentration and involvement. They come to value their own and the efforts of others. They admire, celebrate and come together around an experience they can begin to share with the community in which they operate. Vygotsky (1978) believed that play shows children operating at the highest level of which they are capable. Froebel, watching the way children used his Gifts, often with parents in his community school, believed such play to be the most spiritual and highest level of the child's functioning. There have been times during the blockplay project when we have felt very close to the thinking of both Froebel and Vygotsky in ways that put us in touch with what it is that young children need in their development. Parents who became involved also seemed to sense this.

Rich blockplay does not just occur. It develops when the adult acts as a powerful catalyst working hard to enable it. This needs to develop in a sustained way; that is, as part of a framework embedded in a set of general and broad principles.

3
REPRESENTATION AND COMMUNICATION
Froebel Blockplay Research Group

Blockplay, like spoken and written language, drawing and painting, mathematics, dance and mime, is a symbol system that can be used to say things. In this chapter we begin by considering some of the characteristics shared by verbal language and blockplay and indeed all true languages. Striking similarities can be found in the way in which complexity develops and in the fact that all languages have a grammatical structure or *syntax*. We next look at the uniqueness of blockplay as a nonverbal language that can be used to say certain kinds of things more powerfully than words or words alone can say[1] and, finally, at the ways in which spoken language, drawing, gesture and other media can support and complement each other.

BLOCKPLAY AS A NONVERBAL LANGUAGE

When we look at the development of speech and communication in babies, we can see how vocal sounds are explored, played with, strung together and invested with meanings either by the child or caregivers. Eventually, grammatical combinations emerge that make it possible for the child to make statements and to interact verbally with others (Whitehead, 1990, pp. 55–60).

Just as children explore and play with vocal sounds in their early speech, they explore and play with spatial relationships in early blockplay. Blocks are arranged on top of, underneath, in front of, behind, to the left, to the right of each other. When making a series of two-block stacks, Akash (3 y. 3 m.) is heard using the term 'on top of'. Another 3-year-old, working from left to right, places several assorted blocks at spaced intervals along the top of a longer, single-length block.

Using the Special Features of Blocks

The properties of blocks are discussed in detail in Chapter 4. Here we will focus on one of the properties, that of *length*, and try to show how the availability of different-length blocks increases the range of ideas that can be explored and represented with blocks.

Length

An important characteristic of unit blocks is that they offer the possibility of using different numbers of blocks to make lines that are the same length. This means that a horizontal or vertical line can be expressed *either* by using a single-unit block in either position *or* by placing smaller blocks end to end, horizontally, or one on top of the other, vertically. These very different processes result in the same overall form.

Which of these processes is chosen depends on knowledge and experience with blocks, present concerns and the blocks available at the time. Shorter-length blocks would be used if the child was exploring repetition, rhythm, part–whole relationships, one more, number, spatial relationships such as on top of, next to, underneath, beginning and ending, and many more ideas. Longer-length blocks can be used to span wide gaps between blocks and are used in experiments with balance.

If the interest is simply in *enclosure*, or *squareness*, four-unit blocks can be arranged accordingly. On the other hand, if the enclosure is also to express *circularity*, many of the shorter blocks will be needed (Figure 3.1).

The Child Develops Rules for Using Blocks

From these examples, we can see that the exact division, proportioning and shaping of unit blocks support children's simultaneous thinking *about*, as well as *with*, the material. This combination of features allows children to keep a check on the effect of their actions in the light of this, and to reconsider and rearrange their blocks (Forman, 1982, p. 98). As children explore, we can observe the emergence of a repertoire of basic block forms: lines, surfaces, masses and enclosures. These can be varied and combined into more complex, original wholes (Johnson, 1933; Guanella, 1934).

Eisner (1982, p. 53) defines the arrangement of parts within the whole as the *syntax*. This term is more familiarly associated with spoken and written language, where it means the modification of word forms as in making plurals and past tenses as well as 'the organization of words into meaningful ordered combinations' (Whitehead, 1990, pp. 11–12). The everyday term for this is *grammar*.

In relating this to the visual arts and architecture, Eisner (1982, p. 63) writes that 'painters determine the composition of visual elements . . . architects arrange spaces'. Eisner's description of architects and architecture can be

Figure 3.1

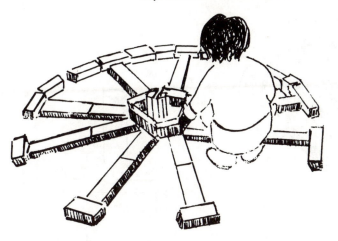

translated into blockplay terms: a three-dimensional block construction with integral windows and doors illustrates fluency in arranging spaces into meaningful, ordered combinations.

Fluency in the use of blocks offers children the means of controlling space to represent ideas. These may be about the continuing present, the past or the future, about the real or imagined worlds. They may be about abstract shape and form.

SAME IDEA, DIFFERENT SYMBOL SYSTEMS

In the last section, blockplay was presented as a symbol system, sharing the general syntactical characteristics of other symbol systems, such as drawing, movement and spoken language. Similar ideas may be expressed in all these systems and, indeed, it has been found that some generalized conceptual concerns are persistently explored and represented across different media and contexts.[2] These include spatial relationships, projective relationships, movement, shape, form etc.

Research into early representation[3] indicates that the form and the act of forming are often, in the words of Kepes (1965, p. ii), 'co-existent and interchangeable'. Thus, in blockplay, the idea of an *enlargement* and the act of *enlarging* (Figure 3.2) and a *reduction* and *reducing* (Figure 3.3) are fused. Many more instances of this fusing of form and action were seen in blockplay: a *connection* and *connecting*; a *mass* and *amassing*; an *enclosure* and *enclosing*; an *alignment* and *aligning*; an *intersection* and *intersecting*.

Figure 3.4 shows a child exploring one such general idea across different media. Nazir's (3 y. 10 m.) series of grid-like arrangements is one of the ways in which she represented her interest in bisecting and intersecting lines or trajectories. She had earlier been observed drawing criss-cross patterns in the

Figure 3.2

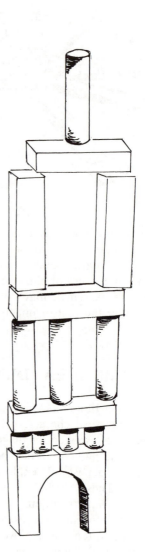

Figure 3.3

Figure 3.4

wet sand, while a favourite game currently is noughts and crosses. In time, the construction and reading of maps and graphs could be a developmental extension of these early representations of grids.

The action is *frozen* in the form, which in turn is a record of action. The form stays, allowing the individual to stand back and reflect on its form and content.[4]

A basic mental structure, or *schema*,[5] such as intersection and bisection, remains constant, regardless of whether it is represented two- or three-dimensionally, verbally or through movement, as in counter-marching, the interweaving of sound as in music, or the tactile, visual, kinaesthetic process of darning a sock or weaving cloth.

In recognizing the similarities in the representational potential of different media we need to be careful not to overlook the *unique* opportunities each one offers to represent and communicate *particular* kinds of experience. As Eisner puts it, 'Not everything can be said through anything' (1982, p. 49).

THE UNIQUENESS OF BLOCKS

Blocks are objects in their own right and can be explored as such. They can also be used to explore and represent ideas external to them. Borrowing from Papert (1980, p. 11), we consider in the next section the role of blocks as *objects to think with*. The ideas are discussed under six headings: (1) three-dimensional topological space; (2) physical balance; (3) structural integrity in three dimensions; (4) equivalence; (5) visual harmony; and (6) stage design.

Three-Dimensional Topological Space

Sauvy and Sauvy (1974, p. 17) suggest that traditional education is only marginally concerned with helping children 'construct their space'. Ideas essential to this process are concerned with connection, separation, proximity, enclosure, regions, boundaries, spatial-temporal sequence, continuity, discontinuity, lines and horizontal and vertical co-ordinates.[6]

A group of 5–6-year-olds were building in a room on the ground floor beneath the music room. This was a new blockplay venue for them. Building was proceeding at a steady pace when suddenly a thunderous noise erupted above our heads and the light fixture in the room started to rattle and sway most alarmingly. Without exception, the children froze. 'Don't worry,' said the adult, 'it's only people moving furniture about in the room above.' 'What, on the ceiling?' was one incredulous response. 'How comes they're making our light shake about?' (Meaning: How could they do that without our seeing them?)

It dawned on the adult that her explanation was about as comprehensible to the children as the frequently delivered parental instruction to the young not to splash bathwater onto the floor as it ruins the kitchen ceiling. (An alternative for the flat-dweller is the suggestion that water on the floor annoys the people underneath.) Until we have constructed mental maps of the spaces we inhabit, such comments have mind-boggling implications, as we can see from the children's reaction on this occasion.

They insisted on having a look in the room above. In terms of theory generation, there was only one contender: a ghost. 'Nuns used to live here in the olden days. My mum told me.' By the time they had exited their own room, turned left, right, mounted two right-turning flights of stairs, followed by a final left turn, they were lost in space, relative to their starting-point. It was almost an irrelevance that the room in question was found unoccupied. They checked the ceiling, naturally. Those who expected to find heavily booted nuns walking there hid their disappointment (or relief) well. The relationship of this room and its spatial features to the room where they had been building was as elusive as ever.

The beginnings of understanding began to emerge as the children accepted the suggestion that they construct a building with the blocks, with an upstairs and downstairs and made pretend people with cylinders. Blocks allow for the scaling down of space, so that spatial relationships can be studied.[7]

Children's study of topological space is not always tied to specific events as in this case, and will often be of a more general nature as children explore and reflect on spatial relationships in activities like blockplay.[8]

Physical Balance

This aspect of blockplay is more fully explored in Chapter 6. Meanwhile, a few examples will serve as an indication (Figures 3.5, 3.6 and 3.7).

Structural Integrity in Three Dimensions

This concerns relationship of parts to wholes and understanding – for example, that the roof of the house goes on last and is tied to the floor via the walls (Figure 3.8). A full discussion is offered in the next chapter.[9]

Equivalence

Blocks offer a unique opportunity for even the youngest children[10] to explore ideas to do with equivalence, expressed through spatial transformations: *translation* (Figures 3.5 and 3.9); *reflection* (Figures 3.7, 3.14, 3.15 and 3.16); *translation with reflection* (Figure 3.10); and *rotation* (Figures 3.11, 3.12 and 5.12).

Playing around with spatial transformation is much simpler with blocks in the early years than with materials that leave a permanent mark. First, there is nothing between hand and block to impede manipulation. Second, the position of a block can be changed repeatedly until the child is satisfied. Third, the physical forms of lines, angles and curves are 'given' in the blocks and do not have to be physically created. Last, since this is a three-dimensional medium,

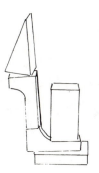

Figure 3.6

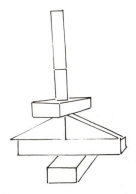

Figure 3.7

Figure 3.8

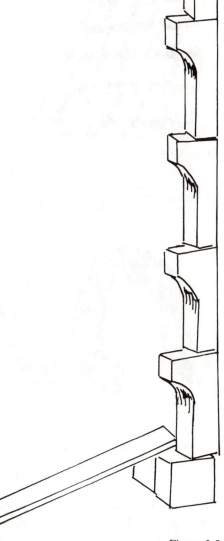

Figure 3.5

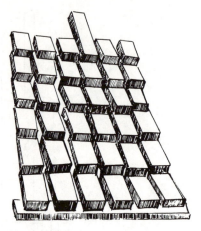

Figure 3.9

Figure 3.10

Figure 3.11

Figure 3.12

there are no problems in representing projective relations. Attention can be concentrated entirely on the arranging of blocks.

Visual Harmony

There are links between this aspect of blockplay and the search for equivalence. The design of the blocks invites the creation of spatial designs that emphasize visual harmony (Figures 3.2, 3.3, 3.9, 3.10, 3.14, 3.15 and 3.16). Further discussion is offered later in this chapter and in Chapter 6.[11]

Stage Design

This refers to the use children make of blocks in the creation of settings for their narrative and dramatic play.[12] Cuffaro (1984) characterizes dramatic play with blocks as requiring the child to (1) create the context of play rather than finding it; (2) deal with reality and scale in translating ideas to the medium; and (3) step outside of self gradually to a symbolized self in play (*ibid*. p. 125).

A few examples from our records will help to illustrate points (1) and (3). Point (2) is dealt with in Chapter 4, where the creation of symbols with blocks is discussed.

Venus and Thomas (4 y. 6 m.) have made a post office using the hollow blocks. Venus is the customer and Thomas the shopkeeper. Venus enters the shop and speaks in gobbledegook. Thomas looks blank and says he doesn't understand. Venus says it's all right, she'll go and write it down. She goes away and comes back with a note she has written:

> Venus: *Cos you don't understand me, I've wrote it down for you.*
> Thomas: *That's a good idea. Shall I read it?*
> Venus: *Yes. Tell me what it says.*
> Thomas: *It says you want some pens for your office.*
> Venus: (Looking pleased) *That's right. Have you got any?*

Venus seems to be exploring ideas about communication by playing at being someone whose speech is not understood. Thomas falls in with this and plays at being helpful. This form of play enables children to operate at higher levels of thinking and behaviour than is possible for them in their everyday roles. The self becomes subordinate to the game. What they do in their play represents children's emerging structures (Vygotsky, 1962; Bruce, 1987).

Andrew (3 y. 6 m.) made a very solid wall into which was inserted a door (Figure 3.13). A crowd of play people was assembled waiting to be allowed through. The movement of Andrew's lips suggested he was using private speech. One by one, he opened the door for each member of the waiting crowd, slid them through, closed the door, moved the queue to fill up the vacant space and repeated the performance until all were on the other side of the wall. Between each round there was a pause after the reshuffling of the crowd. Possibly someone was asking to be allowed through? Each time the door was opened, Andrew smiled to himself.

What ideas might have been absorbing him? Perhaps the repeat patterning of the sequence of moves? Or the very powerful themes of *being in charge* and *being at the mercy of*? This kind of play allows children to *decentre*, that is, to consider a situation or a problem from several points of view (Donaldson, 1978, pp. 17–32; Bruce, 1987, pp. 134–45).

INDIVIDUAL STYLE

In addition to the differences that blocks, as such, can make to what can be represented, there are differences between individuals in the general style of their representations. These differences are sometimes striking. Tina Bruce, in Chapter 2, refers to research[13] that found that some children tended towards dramatic and vocal forms of representation, and others towards pattern and

Figure 3.13

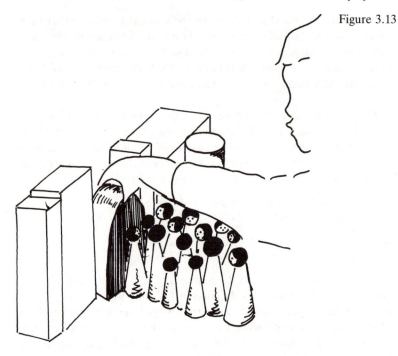

visual forms. Jane Read mentioned several famous blockplayers, including the physicist, Albert Einstein, who appears to have been a visualizer. Papert (1980, p. vi) recalls how he used images of gears 'to carry many otherwise abstract ideas into my head'.

In the present study, we came across examples of both visualizers (or patterners) and dramatists, and also a third group who appeared to be able to mix styles.

Arabella (4y.) was a dramatist whose constructions were minimal. They seemed to serve more as starting-points to narrative rather than having any pretensions to form in their own right. Her 'hotel' consisted of a two-dimensional, rectangular enclosure.

> Arabella: *This is a hotel.*
> Adult: *I can't see the way in.*
> Arabella: *It's a hotel only just for children. A private hotel for children so they can get some peace and quiet. They can climb over the wall to get in and out. They only live next door.* (At this point in the narrative, she makes a step next to one wall.)
> Adult: *You mean children can go there without any grown-ups when it gets noisy at home?*
> Arabella: *Yes. My sister sleeps in the same bedroom. She's only little. Sometimes she wants me to play with her when I want to go to sleep. She sings sometimes and keeps me awake* (pause) *but sometimes you might want a bit of company. I have a bunk-bed and when I want company, I reach down and hold my sister's hand.* (There is a pause while she places several blocks inside the hotel.) *The hotel has bunk-beds.*

Katy (4 y.) had a strong tendency towards visual, patterned forms of representation (Figure 3.14). It wasn't her practice to name her structures, although she listened with interest and often amusement to the efforts of her peers to make literal sense of the forms she created. Peter (5 y.) was a patterner, whose structures were usually labelled on completion. This labelling was not usually extended into narrative. His striving for visual harmony is evident in his rocket house (Figure 3.15). Peter's friend, Elliot (5 y.), could be described, on the basis of his blockplay, as having a feel for both pattern (Figure 3.16) and narrative. Influenced by Elliot, Peter was able to mix styles on the occasion described next.

Peter is arranging the blocks while Elliot watches. He completes his arrangement and announces to Elliot that it's a monster with two heads (Figure 3.17):

(Elliot ponders for a few moments before commenting): *Yeah! But what if he* (pointing to one end) *wants to go in for his tea, and he* (other end) *doesn't? And* (pause) *what if* (smiling broadly) *he wants to go to the toilet and he doesn't!*

(Peter now picks up the theme): *How about if he's sick and he's not and his mum won't let him go to school?*

(By this time they are both grimacing in horror at the many dilemmas facing Peter's monster. Elliot makes one final contribution): *What if he wants to go to his nan's and he doesn't?* (Both children fall into silent contemplation of the monster, which has by now acquired a busy life and a family.)

Adult Priorities and Expectations

It is probably fair to suggest that most of us feel more comfortable in responding to dramatists and verbalizers than to visualizers and patterners, because they so often make their meanings explicit. It is also a fact that in the recent past special emphasis has been placed on supporting and extending linguistic and literary competence in early childhood education and consequently we may be more inclined to home in on a narrative sequence.

Because of the emphasis in our culture on verbal forms of representation, adults often have difficulty in accepting and evaluating nonverbal forms without some verbal explanation, or elaboration from the child.

We certainly can't expect that children will be able to explain or describe to us in words something that may have no verbal equivalent. Sometimes a block arrangement is what remains as a by-product of a kinaesthetic experience. Ferguson (1977) suggests that many of the problems scientists and engineers confront cannot be described in verbal form and instead they use mental imagery, sketches and three-dimensional models.

Johnson (1933, p. 145) emphasizes the expressive qualities of children's block structures and their concern with form and balance, rather than utility: 'not the bald form of what they wish to represent – but with its essence'. She stresses the importance of adult respect for blockplay as a nonverbal means of expression, more like poetry than prose. Picasso (1952) also uses the analogy with poetry when writing about painting: 'Painting is poetry and is always written in verse with plastic rhymes, never in prose. . . . Plastic rhymes are

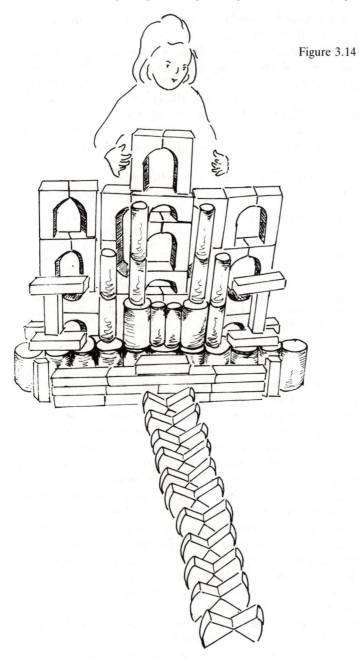

Figure 3.14

Figure 3.15

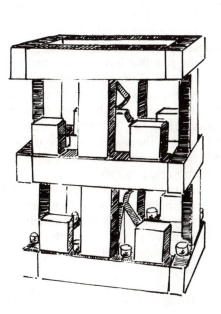

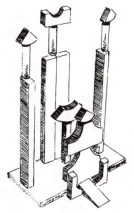

Figure 3.16   Figure 3.17

forms that rhyme with one another or supply assonances either with other forms or with the space that surrounds them' (cited in Arnheim, 1970, p. 56).

In discussing children's drawings, Kellogg (1979) is critical of adults who seem to believe, by the questions they ask children about their creations, that words and art forms are interchangeable. She suggests that words can never describe visual processes with accuracy. Children seem to have a better appreciation of this than adults, as demonstrated in the example Kellogg gives of one child who, in response to adult questions about her picture, said 'This is not a story, it's a picture to look at' (*ibid*. p. 9). Kellogg goes on to suggest that children have an innate capacity to enjoy the visual form relations they create.

Johnson (1933, p. 35) suggests in relation to very young children that their patterning with blocks is more closely tied to motor activity than to the repeated application of a rule that has been internalized. The builder is carried along by the rhythm and feel of the pattern (Figure 3.9).

It would be unreasonable to expect children who are experiencing blocks, *in muscle* (*ibid*.) to be able to discuss what they are doing, although some may volunteer a description. However, there is no reason why an interested adult cannot try to reflect back to them something of the spirit of their activity. At the same time, this may be pitched so as to offer some extension in the direction of a shift from muscle to mind.

Athey (1990) comments on the frequency with which the analogy is drawn between scribbling and babbling. She goes on to point out that where babbling is usually reciprocated by adults, this is not usually so with scribbling. Both Athey (1990) and Matthews (1987) stress the need for children from the earliest days to receive feedback about their early nonverbal representations in order for these to develop fully.

Pairing Art and Literacy Learning

Dyson (1988, p. 26) notes that drawing is often paired with dictation and writing. She looked at this in relation to a group of 6-year-olds and found that some children were helped by the verbalizing process to clarify the ideas they had been attempting to express in their drawings. She describes this as a 'process of negotiation' between talk and picture (*ibid*. p. 31). She also found that after completing their drawing some children simply dictated a record of the drawing process. Perhaps this indicates that they do not see the point of repeating themselves in terms of the *content* of their drawings, which is there for all to see. Alternatively, they may describe their work in this way because it is the formal attributes of objects and events they are interested in.

Dyson also cites one child who never drew anything other than monsters, even though he claimed to be able to make houses as well. When asked by the teacher why he didn't draw houses he replied 'I don't know. Because I don't know what to say about them' (*ibid*. p. 30). It is worrying to think that some practices may lead children into representing in drawing, blockplay, clay-modelling, etc., only that which they are also able to talk about. What might be the effect on the more expressive, abstract forms to which Johnson refers and which we have met frequently during the course of the present study? Equally important is the effect on cognition, discussed in the next section.

What and How?

Eisner (1982, p. 49) suggests that the forms of representation we become skilled in, such as words, drawing and movement, affect the way in which we experience events, and the way we experience events affects our representations. We have all experienced the effect of a new word on our consciousness. Once we know the word we start to hear it. Similarly an unfamiliar piece of music may simply wash over us until we stop to listen, and the more we listen the more likely we are to begin to hear and appreciate the interweaving of sound patterns. The artist, writer, architect and mathematician have heightened sensitivity to different aspects of the same situation. Their viewpoints are determined by the medium in which they work.

Members of the study group have experienced a change in the way they experience the built environment. Through observing blockplay, and looking at the layout of buildings inside and out, our sensitivity and insights about form relationships, part–whole relationships, physical structures, proportion, scale, pattern, decoration and composition have increased our critical awareness. We are able to feed this back into our interactions with the children and this helps to make them more aware.

We saw earlier in the chapter how a representation takes form in the external world and becomes something that can be reflected upon. Froebel expresses this in terms of the 'inner' becoming 'outer' and the 'outer' becoming 'inner'.[14] It allows for what Eisner (1982, p. 56) calls the 'editing' process, which involves revising 'the ideas expressed through the form chosen. In this way a representation serves not only as a means of communicating ideas, but also of modifying them'. According to an account by Wolf and Gardner (1980), the final version of Picasso's 'Guernica' is built on top of 200 preparatory sketches and, even after many revisions, Leonardo da Vinci never regarded the 'Mona Lisa' as completed (*ibid.* p. 50).

Earlier we saw Arabella, Katy, Peter and Elliot externalizing their representations and through them refining their ideas. As a study group, we represented our observations of blockplay to each other in words. Tina Bruce has described how this enabled us to engage in reflective discussion. The present book represents a study of blockplay and has undergone many revisions as we have struggled to find forms of words that correspond to what we mean.

The notion of reflecting on, editing and revising our representations ties in with Piagetian thinking. Piaget (1953) studied the way in which children use what they already know to develop further their ideas and understandings. There is continuous negotiation between 'inner' and 'outer'.

Eisner represents metaphorically the relationship between *how* and *what*: 'The kind of nets we know how to weave, determine the kind of nets we cast. These nets in turn, determine the kinds of fish we catch' (1982, p. 49).

The child in the Dyson study who always drew monsters because they were the only subject he felt confident of being able to draw and talk about, seems to be trapped in a closed loop that deprives him of the opportunity to .explore and become sensitive to other realms of experience and forms of representation. The effect could be long term. Harnet (1988) calls for a range of symbolic media, including blocks, to enable children to record their work in ways meaningful to themselves.

Good practice seeks to extend and not confine children in how they represent their experience. Verbal and nonverbal adult–child interaction, in which the initiative is shared, can enable children to develop their sensitivity to and understandings of the unique properties of different materials and the merits of different representational forms, so that they are able to decide what is best done with blocks, for example, and what might be better served in another medium – or even by mixing representational forms. In our interactions, our aim should surely be to enable children to weave many different nets?

One 4-year-old used blocks, speech and enactive gesture to represent a rainbow . . . with raindrops. The rainbow was formed by placing a quarter eliptical curve on top of an upright unit block. 'This is the rainbow, and this (hand and finger movements) is the raindrops.'

Our assessment of children's representations rests on our ability to appreciate the meanings they are trying to communicate and by what means.

COMMUNICATING ABOUT BLOCKPLAY

In drawing attention to the nonverbal aspects of blockplay, our intention has not been to suggest that block structures be greeted with silent rapture on the part of adults. The important thing is to be on the right wavelength. Children often ask us to come and look at their 'building'. In this situation it is useful to bear in mind the definition of *building* given in the dictionary: 'the art, business, or act of assembling materials into a structure' (Longman, 1988, p. 188). Only sometimes, when children arrange blocks, are they attempting to suggest a structure with walls and a roof.

A form of representation that is essentially nonverbal can acquire an explicit *communicative* function through the interaction of users of the particular symbol system (Franklin, 1973). Theatre-goers share with actors and dramatists understandings of theatrical convention. There are similar understandings between dancers and choreographers and their audiences. Meanings are passed on, picked up and negotiated between individuals or between members of a group and even between groups, who share understandings of the system and the kinds of things that can be said with it. This discussion is further developed in Chapter 4.

Gesture, Talk and Blockplay

The syntactical structure of blockplay enables children to control space to secure meanings. It is interesting to note that British and American sign languages, which also have a syntactical structure, make 'linguistic use of space' (Sacks, 1989, p. 87). There are other similarities. Both sign language and blockplay employ sequence and movement and are capable of producing poetic as well as prosaic statements. With so much in common between the two systems, perhaps we could make more and better use of gesture in our interactions with each other in the block area, in addition to speech? This idea is developed in Chapter 10.

Attention has been drawn to the rhythmic, physical quality of early pattern-making. A sympathetic adult response might be initially to reflect this in rhythmic sound and gesture. In such ways, we may enable children to reflect on their actions, so that they begin to move from involuntary to voluntary performance and eventually develop into the highly competent designers whose creations are illustrated throughout this book.

Talk between children and between adults and children thrives in the block area and contributes to the development of its conventions and communicative power within the group, as well as to the development of individual under-standings and competence (Franklin, 1973). The process of negotiating mean-ings is discussed in more detail in Chapters 4 and 6. All we need say here is that both children and adults need to develop communal understandings relevant to blockplay so that child–child/adult–child discussions can take place on the basis of shared experience and insights. In such a context visual and verbal aspects of the situation interact and mutually support each other.

This has important implications for the way in which we organize for blockplay, which includes not only allowing non-builders into the block area but also in other opportunities made for members of the group to consider each others' efforts and achievements. These issues are explored more fully in Chapters 8, 9 and 10.

The Elements of Art

From our observations we developed the general frames of reference discussed in Chapter 4 that we needed in order to identify both the commonalities and the differences in children's use of blocks. The terms we adopted to describe these reflected line, pattern, shape and form, mass, volume, positive and negative space, movement, direction, sequence and spatial relationships. Where we know that children have been attempting to create real-world likenesses to things remembered, then it seems legitimate to focus on this content.

Athey (1990) and Matthews (1987) suggest that we can, as appropriate, discuss children's representations in terms of either their form or content or both. Matthews points out that, in fact, by referring to one of these, we may at the same time be describing the other. This happens as we saw earlier in this chapter, when we discussed children's representations of general conceptual concerns, such as *intersection*. In referring to Nazir's vertical grid-like ar-rangements (Figure 3.4), the adult remarked with complementary gestures on the fact that she had stacked her blocks in a criss-cross pattern.

Looking at this from the point of view of the child as developing artist, Schirrmacher (1986, p. 6) also proposes that line, form and shape, i.e. the formal 'elements of art', should guide our comments on children's drawings and constructions. There are links between these elements and mathematics as can be seen in the vocabulary they share. These topics are discussed more fully in Chapters 5 and 6.

Schirrmacher suggests that we may need to become familiar with the formal elements of art through reading, courses in art appreciation and possibly engaging in art projects in our own right. It certainly helps to appreciate what these elements are in relation to blockplay, if adults can make time for personal hands-on experience in using blocks.

When referring specifically to the art of blockplay, we would also want to include in our verbal interactions comment about constructional aspects of the situation, physical balance, fit, part–whole integration and problem-solving.

A further suggestion made by Schirrmacher is that when invited to look at a creation, we hold back from commenting immediately to give ourselves time to look and consider what to say and, second, to give children the opportunity to lead the discussion. Our records confirm the wisdom of this. On so many occasions, given a few seconds' hesitation on our part, children will start the ball rolling, often by naming their structures.

REPRESENTATIONAL CONVENTIONS

When the adult sketches as the children build, this provides a wealth of opportunity for discovering how we each solve our graphic representational problems.

> (Saam (4 y.) was making a block structure. The nursery nurse was sketching it as he went along. He came to look over her shoulder.)
> Saam: *What are you doing?*
> Adult: *What d'you think?* (She offered him the opportunity to study her sketch. He glanced occasionally from sketch to block structure.)
> Saam: *I think you're drawing my building.* (He returned to his structure, added a few blocks, then came back to look again at the adult sketch, which by now included the additions he had just made.) *Yes, you are drawing mine.*

If the adult had simply told him what she was doing in response to his initial query, Saam would have had no incentive to find a means of checking, which, in the event, also helped him to discover something about the way in which the adult was attempting to achieve a paper-and-pencil equivalence to his structure. This serves as a reminder of the need to encourage and help children to become skilled not only as producers but also as critics who can consider the work of others in what Eisner calls a 'competent way' (1982, p. 65). Each time the children elect to sketch their block structures, they are faced with the problems of scale and projection. 'You have to do it more small than it is, when you do a drawing of your blocks', one 6-year-old pronounced excitedly after several attempts at sketching a structure that spread over several square yards. Through his sketching from life, he had just become consciously aware of something he had been doing intuitively in his paintings and drawings for some time. In this he is typical of all young children. Another child (5y. 5m.) insisted on explaining to the adult why certain features of the block structure were not represented in her drawing of it: 'Some blocks are behind other blocks in buildings but you can't see them in drawings.' The child was very concerned that the adult understood this. Barnes (1987, p. 11) suggests that 'Even if we discount for the moment any expressive artistic qualities drawings have, as a way of making children look closely they are unique'.

SPACE EXPLORATION

To help them enhance their critical awareness of art and architecture, we need to go with children to places where natural and sculpted forms can be experienced in the round. We also need to physically explore spaces together as part of our shared group history of 'space' exploration, using the vocabulary of space that will help to link these experiences to their own work. To back up this first-hand experience, books and pictures that celebrate architectural and natural forms from across cultures and geographical areas should also be available for sharing. These also offer opportunities for reflecting together on how others have solved their representational problems. In such ways we can help them become more competent viewers as well as doers.

SUMMARY AND CONCLUSIONS

In this chapter, blockplay has been considered as a symbol system, capable of representing experience through the arrangement of forms in space. What can best be said with blocks may not be directly translatable into other forms of representation. The chapter has been particularly critical of practices that pressure children to make translations from one representational form to another. The children in the blockplay study decided for themselves whether or not to make a sketch of their block structures just as they chose whether or not to describe them in words. The fact that they often chose to do both was because of the genuine shared interest that developed within groups between adults and children about blockplay. Sketching and verbal description became a mutually accepted means of reflecting together.

Where there is a felt need to translate from blocks to words, and/or blocks to sketch, or vice versa, we can help children negotiate the passage between these different forms of representation by interacting in ways in sympathy with their intentions.

Good practice seeks to extend and not confine children in how they represent their experience. While recognizing stylistic differences between children and the special abilities this sometimes indicates, it would seem to be in every child's interest to be competent in both verbal and spatial domains. The writings of Eisner have been particularly influential in enabling us to recognize that *how* we represent our experience plays an important part in determining *what* we come to know and understand. This has implications for the whole of our development.

We finish with a quotation from Barnes (1987, p. 16) who is writing here of the importance of art to young children. He refers to the rapid pace of change in modern society and suggests that 'the flexibility of thought that we associate with creativity is almost a prerequisite for keeping pace. . . . It may be that the truly creative thinkers as children become those adults who can see positive alternatives where others fail to envisage them'.

NOTES

1. Franklin (1973) considers the emergence of nonverbal representation including gesture, use of objects in play, painting, modelling and understandings of graphic forms. The implications for education are also discussed.

2. See note 5.

3. See note 5.

4. Forman (1982); Sigel (1986); Matthews (1984, 1987); and Athey (1980, 1981, 1990).

5. A Piagetian 'schema' is a pattern of behaviour that is generalizable. According to Athey (1990, p. 78), schema evolve from early action and perception. They enable individuals to explore their environment and relationships with others in an organized and selective way. Further discussion of schema can be found in Piaget (1962); Piaget (1969); Nicolls (1986); Sharp (1986); Bruce (1987); Matthews (1984, 1987); Nutbrown (1988); Athey (1980, 1981, 1990).

6. See also Matthews (1984, 1987) and Athey (1980, 1981, 1990).

7. Forman (1982, p. 98).

8. This aspect of blockplay is related to the field of study known as 'environmental cognition'. Hazen (1982) found that children who actively explored new environments as opposed to being led passively around them, had a greater knowledge of the environment. Evans (1980) offers a detailed review of the literature. This includes discussion of the writings of Piaget whom Evans regards as the virtual founder of environmental cognition studies. Map making and map reading, together known as 'mapping', are important aspects of environmental cognition. Hatcher (1983) and Billett and Matusiak (1988) suggest a developmental progression in mapping beginning with the making of models using lengths of track and blocks. Links from these studies can be made to other work on mapping in the early years, e.g. Spencer, Harrison and Darvizeh (1980) and Spencer and Darvizeh (1983).

9. Dillon-Goodson (1982) studied the development of part-to-part and part–whole relationships in block construction by setting up a situation involving a series of arch constructions children were asked to copy. The series began with a simple three-block arch and proceeded through arches of arches to arches of arches of arches. Dillon-Goodson draws an analogy between the development of skilled action, such as that demanded by the arch-building problem, and the hierarchical complexity the child has to come to terms with in the course of language development. Results indicated a relationship between perception, planning and skill in placing blocks.

10. Foreman (1982).

11. Gelfer and Perkins (1987, 1988) describe an experimental study aimed at raising the level of children's understanding and appreciation of the formal elements of art, using blocks as the representational medium. Once a week, for six weeks, consciousness-raising sessions were held when adults and children shared hands-on

experience of building and discussing models and looking at photographs and paintings. Children could play freely with blocks between structured sessions. Compared with no-treatment controls, the experimental group scored higher when their art concepts were subsequently tested and there was evidence of these understandings having an influence on their block constructions. Payne (1990) describes similar work relating to art appreciation with under-5s, although blocks were not the medium. Our experience in the Froebel Blockplay Project suggests that consciousness-raising sessions are unlikely to be needed if the general climate is geared towards both action and reflection and we ourselves have a genuine interest and some understanding of the formal aspects of the built environment.

12. Guanella (1934, p. 16) refers to this aspect of blockplay as 'histrionic art'.
13. Wolf and Gardner (1978).
14. Cited in Bruce (1987, p. 17).

4
DEVELOPMENTAL ASPECTS OF BLOCKPLAY
Pat Gura

James (4 y.) struggles to make a tall three-sided vertical enclosure with the unit blocks. At last he succeeds: 'I've done it!' he shouts delightedly. 'When I was a little baby, I couldn't do that.'

THE DEVELOPMENT OF BLOCKPLAY

This discussion of developmental aspects of blockplay starts with a group of 6-year-olds who have decided to build a car ferry. They discuss details and particular aspects they want to include. Some help from the teacher is needed in planning, dividing the work into subunits and negotiating who does what. Rachel and Harry opt to do the car deck, while Sinead takes on the stairs and upper deck.

Sinead struggles with her stairs and needs to talk this through with the others. The method she has adopted is known in architectural jargon as 'corbelling', i.e. a stepped line of blocks. To raise such a staircase of free-standing material in a confined space to a predetermined height involves complex practical mathematics. For example, how far away from where you want to finish do you start? Then there is the tendency for this type of stair to fall over backwards. A ramshackle but serviceable arrangement of supports eventually keeps the staircase in one piece.

Meanwhile, the approach road is found to end in a sheer drop onto the deck of the ferry. Harry thinks drivers could be asked to treat the problem as skiers approach a jump, i.e. 'very fast!' But on tracing a similar flight path with a block in his hand for a car, he concludes this would land them on the opposite side of the ferry in the sea. He surveys the block supply and eventually selects a narrow

*wedge: 'This slope will do the trick', he says and attaches it to the end of the
road. Rachel becomes absorbed with the problems of traffic flow and a one-way
system is devised. They have to work out how to do this away from the car deck,
so that they can see and feel their way through the problem. Harry cuts out some
circles, free hand, and apologizes because they are not quite round (an under-
statement). Each is inscribed with an arrow. These are placed on the ground
and it is discovered they can be rotated to point in any direction. The investigation involves much body movement and clockwise pacing and positioning of
arrows. The results then have to be transferred carefully to the car ferry. 'No
entry' signs are added as Rachel insists that some people might try to drive
between the end pillars. The information on road signs is found in a reference
book. Sinead makes a café and puts up a sign, before finishing the upper deck
with a safety barrier.*

Sinead, Harry and Rachel use blocks regularly. They often work together
and can take each other's basic block-building skills for granted. The hull
and upper deck, without the detail, were quickly put together, the children
moving in synchrony with each other, as if the sequence of moves had been
choreographed.

They obviously shared a well-differentiated idea of the distinguishing features of a car ferry (even if streamlining wasn't one of them), and understood
the relationships of the various parts to the whole, before they started.

They also demonstrated a sufficiently *differentiated* knowledge of blocks to
enable them to choose the most appropriate from those available, for the
various parts of their construction. Last, they understood, roughly, how to
combine the blocks into a *structurally integrated* whole to match their idea of a
car ferry. The problem of the staircase was solved by trying various known
strategies in turn and by improvisation. The logistics of the one-way system
were worked out first by disembedding the problem and studying it separately,
then transferring the knowledge back to the car deck. Real-world considerations were adapted to the material and the material to real-world considerations. Using the tools available they tried to think like car-ferry designers,
thinking about car-ferry users.

These children have acquired a good working knowledge of blocks, which
they are integrating with other knowledge and competencies and adapting to
suit their present representational needs.

Now let's have a look at 4-year-old Helen, who is placing one block on top
of another, in a stack.

*Each block is different in shape and size and she is taking great care to check
each one for balance before completely removing her hands. Half-way up she
very gingerly centres the cross block horizontally on top of the block below. This
is difficult as she has to judge a position she can't see. When the tower is finished
to her satisfaction, she walks away.*

*Manda approaches. She is just 3 and it's her first day at nursery school. She
runs her fingers over some blocks nearby, while studying Helen's arrangement
then, without warning, she takes hold of the cross block in the centre of the*

tower, as if to lift up the entire structure. Her dismay at the resulting rubble indicates she had no idea this would happen.

Manda's working knowledge of blocks has just begun.

The Material

The process of materials mastery, or 'knowing your blocks', is continuous and consists of two interacting elements:[1] *differentiation* – the process by which understanding becomes increasingly detailed and specific; and *integration* – the process of linking parts into wholes.

Differentiation

A child's understanding of blocks begins to emerge from the grasping, sucking, releasing, banging, hide-and-seek activities of the infant playing with a single block, sometimes alone and sometimes interacting with significant others.[2] Froebel understood the need for exploration to start with *wholes* in the design and order of presentation of his Gifts. Only after the child had experienced the whole were they offered the parts.[3] The single block eventually becomes part of a new whole, in this case, a *set* of blocks (Figure 4.1).

As a set, blocks may at first be regarded as relatively undifferentiated *stuff*, which is useful for carting around in trucks and prams and for filling and emptying from containers. Gradually children begin to separate out the differences between this and other kinds of stuff, including the fact that this particular kind is called 'blocks'. Having begun to establish some of the common physical characteristics of blocks, they go on to discover the character of each block and differences between one block and another.

Sadie (3 y.) was taking the blocks nearest to her, i.e. the arches, from the shelf. After arranging them in a row, curve downwards, she paused, rotated one, explored the resulting upward curve with a finger, then called out: 'I've changed it, I've changed it!'

Amy (4 y.) puzzles over why her companions keep rejecting the quarter circle she wants to place vertically on the tower they are building together. Every time she places it upright on the stack, someone says words to the effect: 'No, Amy, that one's no good, yet. It can go at the top, when we've finished.' After several rejections she inspects her block. She places it upright on the carpet and tries balancing another block on top of it. Observing that this slides off, she holds the quarter circle steady, still in the upright position, with one hand, and runs the index finger of the other along its curved edge. She then lays it flat and runs the tips of her fingers over its horizontal surface, before tentatively trying to balance a block on top of it. She succeeds and uses her new knowledge to construct a tower, with the quarter circle as a base.

Amy was not a beginner with blocks when this observation was recorded. However, the response of the other children to this particular block aroused her curiosity and caused her to stop to think about it.

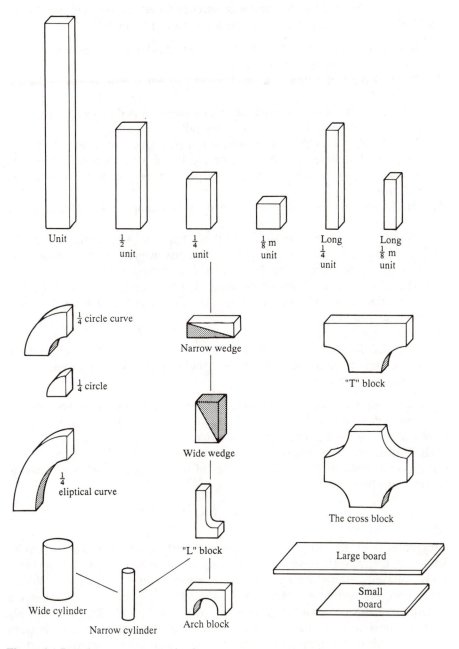

Unit
$\frac{1}{2}$ unit
$\frac{1}{4}$ unit
$\frac{1}{8}$ m unit
Long $\frac{1}{4}$ unit
Long $\frac{1}{8}$ m unit

$\frac{1}{4}$ circle curve

$\frac{1}{4}$ circle

$\frac{1}{4}$ eliptical curve

Wide cylinder

Narrow cylinder

Narrow wedge

Wide wedge

"L" block

Arch block

"T" block

The cross block

Large board

Small board

Figure 4.1 Based on *community playthings* design. Scale: $\frac{1}{4}$ unit $= 3.5 \times 7 \times 14$ cms

The kinds of knowledge the child will discover about the physical qualities of unit blocks and the relationships between them include the following:

1. Blocks are solid, wooden, free-standing, stackable, transportable and resistant to bending or squashing.
2. Blocks have feel, texture, a smell, especially when new, colour and grain pattern.[4]
3. They give off sounds of different quality when tapped or banged together or against other objects, or when they fall to the ground.
4. Each block has angles, edges and surfaces, shape, form, length, width, height and volume, and they can be combined with each other to create further angles, edges, surfaces, shapes, forms, lengths, widths and volumes.
5. Blocks occupy spaces that correspond to their shape, form, length, width and volume.
6. Blocks can be named according to their shape, length, width, volume.
7. A block can be used in different orientations, which greatly increases the number of different forms that can be made from a set.
8. There are length/volume equivalences between blocks, e.g. four quarter units placed end to end make up the same length and have the same volume as a unit.
9. Blocks can be arranged and rearranged.
10. They are discontinuous (or discrete), in contrast to clay or water, and can be scattered, gathered together in conglomerate piles or systematically connected to create continuity.

Edward forgot he was dealing with a discontinuous material one day when he asked two other children if they would mind just moving their extensive block representation of the school a little to one side as it was in his way.

The process of differentiation involves much active experimentation and investigation of both the physical properties of the blocks and the mathematical relationships between them.

Integration

Integration is to do with the *interconnection* and *interdependence* of parts to wholes. A house, with ground floor and upper storey, is a useful example of an interconnected, interdependent system of smaller units or modules: floors, walls, ceilings, openings, stairs, etc. For children to be able to construct something of this order of integration with free-standing blocks, they not only have to know how to make up each of the smaller units but also how to combine these in the right order into structural wholes. We discovered at an early stage in the study that young children, coming across a pile of blocks, do not necessarily connect this with the building of buildings. A brick in a wall is not necessarily understood as part of a whole by the young child. Walls and houses are seen as wholes and amongst the *givens* of the built environment we take for granted. Remarks made by the children brought this home to us vividly.

Seema (4 y. 4 m.) announced she was going to make a tall building. She mounted the recently introduced stepstool until she was standing on the platform at the top. Having got there, she hesitated, then turning to a nearby adult said: 'Can you start up here?' The adult handed her a block. 'You can't,' said Seema. 'You can't start up here.'

Knowledge of how structures hang together is developed out of children's experiments in combining blocks (see also Chapter 7).

Just as children learn to identify blocks in ever-increasing detail through exploratory action, they are similarly involved in discovering how to make simple block forms and to integrate these into increasingly complex structures.

BASIC BLOCK FORMS

The basics of blockplay[5] are summarized in Figure 4.2. The development of the ability to integrate blocks structurally begins with the *adding* of blocks to an indeterminate pile (Figure 4.3), in which there is no systematic attempt to create discrete connected or interconnected wholes. Children often return to this as a game involving the use of all the blocks. Although a pile may be indeterminate in form, placement is not random. Simple one-dimensional linear structures follow (Figures 4.4 and 4.5). A combination of vertical and horizontal linear forms can be seen in Figure 4.6. Linear forms are followed by two-dimensional 'areal' arrangements, i.e. plane surfaces (Figures 4.7 and 4.8) and enclosures (Figures 4.9 and 4.10). Established forms are progressively combined with those emerging (Figures 3.3 and 4.11), with the three-dimensional envelopment of space marking the climax (Figures 4.12 and 4.13). The car–ferry built by the 6-year-olds demonstrates a higher level of structural integration than the tower Helen built and Manda unintentionally dismantled. The difference is developmental, with both age and experience with blocks playing a part.[6] Most of our children were encountering blocks in a sustained way for the first time at the age of 3, and showed by their behaviour that they needed to start by getting to know the blocks in their own time and their own way, including discovering which blocks 'measure each other', as one 4-year-old expressed the idea of same-length blocks and that the same form (a line, a plane surface or an enclosure) can be made with different permutations on the shape and size of blocks used. In other words, as Piaget's concept of schema suggests, the overall basic form remains constant but the exact method of construction may vary, depending on the blocks available and the child's present purpose. General cognitive concerns[7] interact with the more specific exploration of how blocks work. Lines, areas and enclosures result from the co-ordination of general basic ideas, such as *next to*, *on top of*, *again*, *beginning*, *ending*, *joined*, etc.

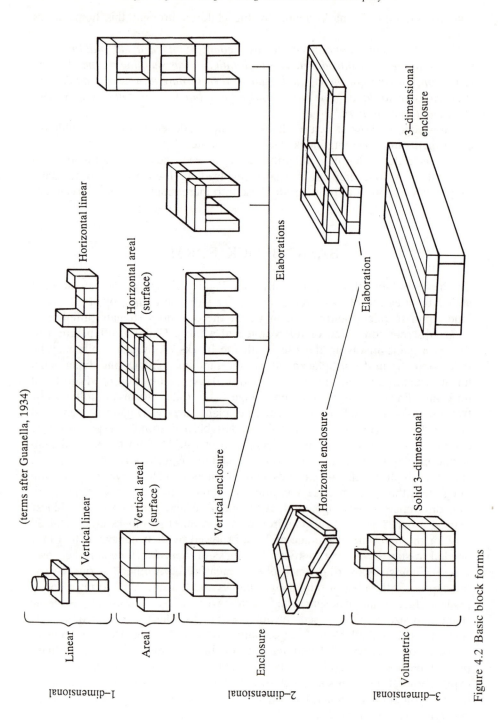

Figure 4.2 Basic block forms

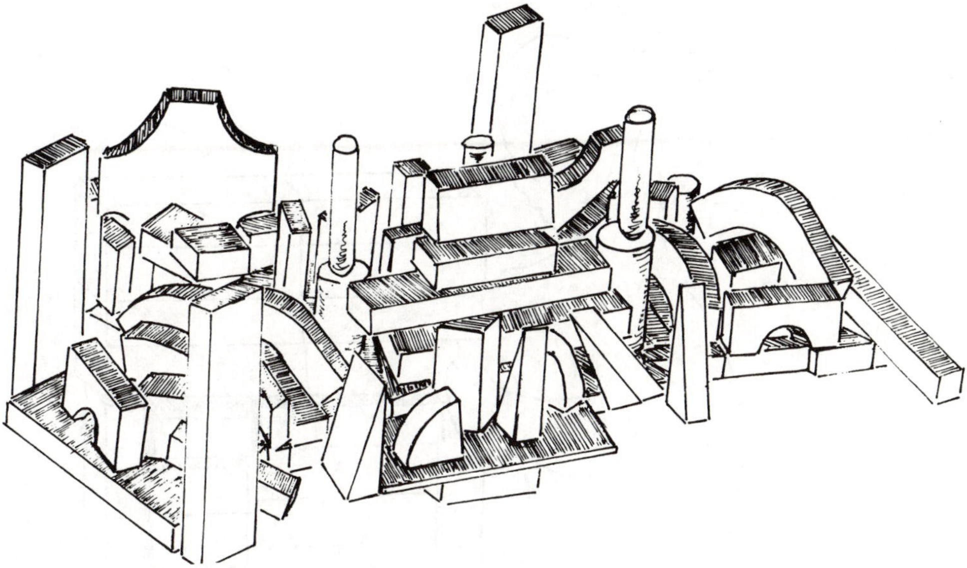

Figure 4.3

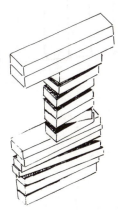

Figure 4.4

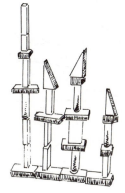

Figure 4.6

Figure 4.5

Figure 4.7

Repetition

Repetition appears to be an important feature of materials mastery. As each block form is discovered, there is much practising, refining and variation within the familiar. A particular block form may be constructed so often that the procedure becomes effortless. Each block form and its method of construction represents what Bruner (1973, p. 4), in discussing early skilled action, has termed a behaviour 'module'.[8]

Francois (4y. 6m.) demonstrates some reflective awareness of the routinization of building processes when he tells the adult, 'I practised this yesterday'.

Figure 4.8

Figure 4.9

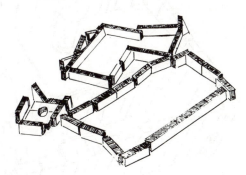

Figure 4.10

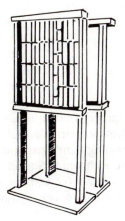

Figure 4.11

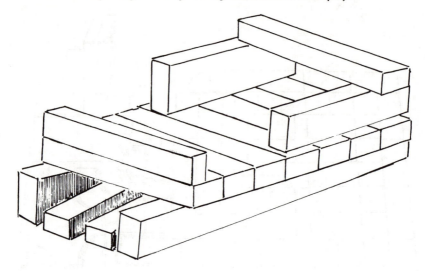

Figure 4.12

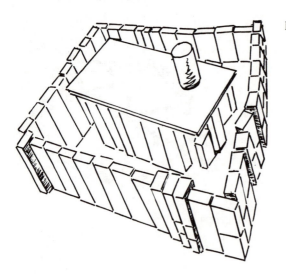

Figure 4.13

The adaptive significance of practising a newly acquired routine, or 'module', is, according to Bruner (*ibid.*), 'To make its performance virtually automatic' and thus leave the mind free for the task of co-ordinating familiar routines into new complex wholes. This is exemplified in the ease with which Sinead, Harry and Rachel put together the basic structure of their car ferry without having to consult each other, and the freedom this gave them to concentrate and collaborate on the novel aspects of the situation.

Figure 4.14

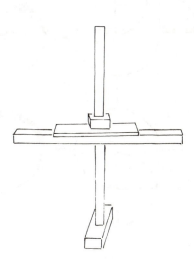

Figure 4.15

Figure 4.16

Stunt-Building

When children have a good grasp of a basic routine or a combination of these, they enjoy taking risks, especially with balance (Figures 3.5, 3.6, 4.14, 4.15 and 4.16). Johnson (1933) referred to this very aptly as 'stunt-building'. The term captures well these high spots in materials mastery.[9]

Visual Harmony

As already indicated in Chapter 3, visual harmony is a particularly striking feature of blockplay. This might be seen as a by-product of striving for structural balance. However, observation of children as they build suggests that this is not the whole explanation. There seems to be, in the early period at least, a rhythmic combining and patterning of movement, shape and space. As they move with the blocks, they often seem unaware of the visual effects being created (Johnson, 1933). Sean (5 y.) made one particular arrangement very rapidly, without seeming to check the visual effects as he added blocks (Figure 4.17). There was a right–left, right–left rhythmic swing to his actions. The arrangement was covered over without a pause, but a definite change to less

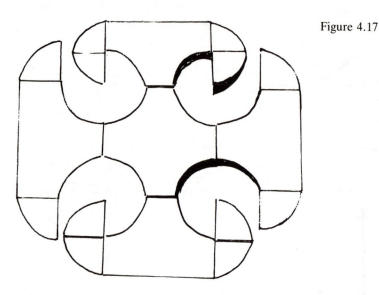

Figure 4.17

rhythmic movement, with a layer of assorted cuboids, in no discernible pattern.

Gradually the dominance of rhythm and bilateral *action* is replaced by a more reflective approach to composition. Children can be seen to try a block in various positions and orientations without releasing until and unless they are satisfied. Sometimes this is to check that what they have in mind is physically possible (Figure 4.18).

Eventually they become sufficiently experienced to be able to visualize the effects they want to create in advance of actually building, to select the appropriate blocks in advance.

Child–Child Observation

A great deal of active observation occurs in the block area, and our records show evidence of children making use of their observations. One child watched for over an hour as other children built. The following day she produced a structure very similar in character and structural complexity to that she had seen built the previous day. Her technique showed she had moved on in her own handling of the material. Over the next few days she practised the new module until it was more her own. This should not be taken as evidence we can demonstrate technique and children will be able to copy.[10] The child in question selected for herself those aspects of the blockplay going on around her she would attend to. She later integrated what she learned from this with knowledge and competence in handling blocks she already possessed to produce her own version.

Our conviction that observation does affect the pace of development stems

Figure 4.18

also from the fact that during the first year of the study, each new intake of 3-year-olds in mixed 3–5 groups started to get to grips with basic structuring principles slightly in advance of the one before. When we compare the early building competence of our pioneer builders, who were starting from scratch in terms of never having seen the blockplay of others, with that of children who regularly actively participate in blockplay as observers, critics, consultants, mathematicians, scientists and co-builders, we can see that there is a gap of between 3 and 6 months. Our own developing understandings must also be considered a contributing factor in this respect.

Early Admission to School

Matterson (1990, p. 152), commenting on the disappointment expressed by nursery group leaders in the blockplay observed in their groups, suggests the premature departure of 4-year-olds to primary schools deprives the 3-year-olds of opportunities to observe the play of more experienced children. Our own records appear to support this suggestion.

One nursery group involved in the study was within a local authority area that had a policy of admitting children to primary school at the age of 4. During the two years of the study, it was very noticeable that blockplay did not develop beyond the basics in this group, despite the fact that similar efforts and resources were used as those in other groups. However, at different times during the study, two children stayed on until the age of 5 at their parents' request. Both were keen on blockplay and had the opportunity to develop this. One of them, Imran (4y. 9m.), produced a representation of a fairwheel (Figure 3.1), which involved an advanced level of materials mastery.

Where premature admission to school is the norm, the effects are two-way. First, the departing 4-year-olds are left with a lot of loose ends, which they may not be given the opportunity to pick up on in their new settings. Second, as already discussed, is the effect of lowering the average age of children in the nursery. Some research has been conducted on the first.[11] Our own study suggests that to complement this, research needs to be done on the second.[12]

Revision

We have noticed how children will often revise their repertoire of basic forms as a warm-up exercise, prior to embarking on a more elaborated construction. Children have also been observed warming up after a period of absence away from blocks. This happened when a group of 6-year-olds, who had not been able to take their blocks with them from their reception class as they moved up the school, were given the opportunity to use them after an interval of about two terms. We wondered if we should see great advances in their use of blocks. In fact, they spent the whole of the time available to them enjoying the feel of the blocks in the construction of towers, rows, floors and walls. One school now has blocks in two of the early-years classrooms and another across the age-range 3–11, in recognition of the need for regular access to enable children to move forward as well as backwards in developing their ideas about blocks and through blocks.

Form and Content

Athey (1990, p. 103) suggests that it is possible to describe a developmental sequence relating to the formal aspects of children's early representations but not to content, as the latter is dependent on first-hand experience. This is an important point and alerts us to the need to organize experiences for children such as outings and, in the case of blocks, *innings*, so that exterior and interior places and spaces can be explored in detail at a leisurely pace, talked about and revisited from time to time. Evidence from the present study supports an interactive view of the relationship between form and content development. It seems that both form and content become more differentiated and more integrated as a combined effect of both age and experience. A child with total command of the material but scant awareness of a house as a *system* of structurally interdependent parts will not build houses that reflect this. The opposite also holds true. (The *form–content* relationship is discussed in detail later in the chapter.)

To summarize so far, competence in making use of the formal properties of the blocks follows a general developmental trend. The dominance of experimental manipulation tends to reduce gradually with age and/or experience with blocks.[13] Children may need to revise before they can go forward again after a time lapse in opportunity to use blocks.

Recent studies[14] that focused on children's use of materials tended to be conducted over a much shorter time-scale than that reported here. Play, in these studies with materials, is reported as being unchallenging and repetitive. When manipulation of materials can be seen, as in the present study, to be part of a developmental continuum, a more positive view of materials and children's activities with them may emerge.

SIMILARITIES AND DIFFERENCES

There were considerable individual differences relating to age, urge and experience of the material, which influenced the overall pace and style with which children explored and experimented with blocks. Starting-points were different for some children.

Tim's first encounter with blocks at 4 years was to make his name, then a line of blocks designated a 'road' followed by a small three-dimensional covered building named a 'stable'.

A child may spontaneously engage in a one-session crash course. *Natalie, another first-timer at 5 years, ran rapidly through the basic forms, until the problems of bridging slowed her down. Within the hour she was attempting to combine towers, rows, and bridges.*

On the other hand, 11-year-olds having an occasional turn with the nursery blocks, at first produced only one- and two-dimensional structures. They needed some time to get the feel of the material. The same was true for adults offered the chance to use blocks in workshop sessions.

Other Differences

Some children develop a very distinctive *style*, which may persist throughout their development in this area. Blockplay regulars can also identify each others' work by their awareness of 'trademarks', such as Jolene's chimneys and Katy's geometric arrangements or the current form an individual is exploring. This may be of a more generalized conceptual nature, such as *enclosure* or a particular idea like *boats*. The study group also had no problems identifying structures from two particular schools. Children from the Roman Catholic school often topped off their buildings with a cross, or incorporated one into their arrangements (Figure 4.19 is 'a cross when you're dying'), and children from the housing estate, where the blocks of flats rest on stilts, often became preoccupied with this form of construction (Figure 4.11). We are aware that

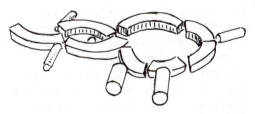

Figure 4.19   Figure 4.20

children whose homes are not on stilts also build this kind of structure and others put crosses on buildings but, because of the frequency of their appearance in these schools, it seemed they may have had particular salience for them.

Drawing with Blocks

Some children adopt a *drawing* technique in some of their representations.[15] They use the *givens* in the blocks: straight lines, curves and angles to create two-dimensional outlines. Sometimes this may be chosen as a strategy because the child is not thinking three-dimensionally. Competence in two-dimensional forms of representation may be developing at the expense of three-dimensional. This would bear out the arguments of Eisner, set out in the previous chapter. Does this reflect an over-emphasis in the home and school on the acquisition of skills more closely identified with literacy? Sometimes, however, the chosen subject-matter, combined with the medium of blocks, makes outlining the only choice. Imran chose this technique for his fairwheel and Marie for her elephant (Figure 4.20).

Different Child, Different Emphasis

Our records show some children finding more interest and challenge in exploring and varying certain of the basic block forms while seeming to pay only token attention to others. Matthews (1984, 1987) and Athey (1980, 1981, 1990), in separate studies of early representations, have identified and described the development of basic mental structures, or schema, in young children. It seems from these accounts that children become absorbed in systematically exploring particular basic ideas. Different materials and situations are seized on by young children according to their usefulness at a particular time in serving particular cognitive concerns. They may be used consistently for a period then ignored by the same child for days, weeks or months and returned to once again, depending on what the material or situation offers in relation to the prevailing cognitive concerns of the *individual* child.

This has important implications for the resourcing and management of early-years settings. Children need a wide range of representational materials to choose from. Casual evidence from classrooms arranged as a series of self-service resource areas suggests that children do very well at matching resources to present need. In the case of blocks it did seem as if they were used selectively by individuals to explore some ideas more than others.

Placing blocks horizontally in single straight lines was observed far less frequently than the building of vertical lines that stand erect from the two-dimensional plane. Adults and children returned repeatedly to create this form. One reason for this apparent fascination may be as Golomb (1972,

p. 390) suggests in relation to the medium of clay: erect verticality has no equivalence in drawing and can therefore be regarded as an 'invention' particular to three-dimensional media. By the same token vertical enclosure and envelopment are also block inventions.

Children often return to forms already mastered, to try out a novel or more complex variant, such as the stacking of vertical enclosures. Sometimes, when it looks as if a particular form has dropped out of the child's repertoire, it reappears in combination with the latest discovery.

Special Ability

Reifel and Greenfield (1982, p. 228) suggest that some of the arrangements produced by children with blocks are 'creative masterpieces of the highest order'. Some children seem to have a special ability to use the *givens* in the blocks, to compose them into visually harmonious block sculptures, unimaginable to the rest of us. Sometimes it is a little more difficult to follow the line of development of these children than for others. Sebastian (4 y. 3 m.) had no difficulty in adapting his complex road systems to the space available (Figure 4.21). No one in his nursery school seems able to remember him not being able to do this. His mother told us he frequently played with a wooden train set.

Katy (Figures 3.14, 5.3 and 5.12) was seldom observed making simple lines, rows, towers, etc. We do know, however, that she played with blocks at home. In a study of the blockplay of ten 4-year-olds, Hulson and Reich (1931) could find no conclusive evidence of a relationship between frequency of block use at home, frequency of use at school and the children's performance when individually invited to construct whatever they wanted with one hundred assorted unit blocks. It may be that there are other influences at work of which we are unaware, or that some children do have a very special flair. Further study is needed to see what we can discover about such children, which may be of benefit to them and other children.

Setting

There is evidence that *setting* has an influence on more general lines of development. Guanella (1934) and Elkins (1980) each record increased interest in using blocks in the making of horizontal grids, e.g. road and rail systems, at age 4–6, than in the more structurally complex three-dimensional houses, etc. Grid arrangements in blockplay, according to the literature and our own records, are often characterized by numbers of children working side by side and often co-operating on the same network. Social concerns may interact at this age with block activity to facilitate the emergence of this kind of play where children are free to interact with each other. However, where space

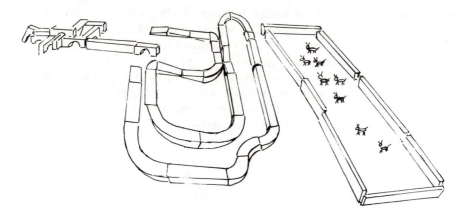

Figure 4.21

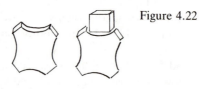

Figure 4.22

permits only two children to work comfortably in the block area at a time, as in one of our study classrooms, the children of 4–6 seem to by-pass grids and concentrate on building in three dimensions, which happens to need less space. At a later date, when they were able to take their blocks into the playground, grids and larger teams working together on them soon emerged. Gibson (1979) suggests that children discover through studying the situation actively what each context *affords*. Here we see children adapting knowledge of blocks to spaces and spaces to blocks.

USING THE LANGUAGE OF BLOCKS

A good working knowledge of blocks puts at the child's disposal a symbol system similar to written and spoken language, dance, music, painting and drawing, in its generative power (Reifel and Greenfield, 1982; Reifel, 1984). Just as a word can convey many different meanings, depending on its re- lationship to other words in a sentence, so basic block forms can be arranged in relation to each other to give an infinite number of different meanings. Through blocks the child can explore and represent, in original block crea- tions, both the actual and the possible worlds of objects, events and ideas.

Means and Ends

We are often asked whether there is a *representational stage* in blockplay. What we discovered was that, just as in the use of spoken and written language, children do not wait until they have the full kit, so to speak, before attempting to represent what they have in mind. They simply adapt what they do have to a wide range of purposes.

We would agree with Reifel and Greenfield (1982) that a child's level of skill in using blocks determines *how* rather than *what* is represented. Blocks are adapted to particular ideas and ideas to blocks. The children's level of materials mastery affects the form the representation takes, and what they know about the object being represented affects the way in which they try to use the material.[16]

Sometimes a single block is given a name to indicate its function: a baby, a house, a chair, a table. At others, a physical correspondence between the shape of a single block and a real-world object is recognized.

On several occasions children have been heard brainstorming ideas about particular blocks. On one occasion an eliptical curve called forth the following list from a child: rainbow, hat, a mouth, an eyebrow and a nose. For good measure someone else contributed 'ribs' and demonstrated with two eliptical curves. When different ideas share a similar form, they are said to be *isomorphic*.

Anna (4 y.) suggested the quarter circle looked like a shark's fin. She also suggested that the cross, when rotated, looked like a person. 'This is the face (the centre) and these are the arms and legs.' A few days later she had refined this, by placing an eighth between the 'arms' for the face (Figure 4.22).

Sometimes there is an association with movement.

Tom (4 y.) cruised around the room with his 'fighter jet', formed from two wedges.

Two girls (5 y.) followed each other in a turn-taking game of miming a series of musical instruments, using one or two half-unit blocks. These included harmonica, flute and violin.

Words attached to certain features, such as 'door' or 'chimney', may be used to identify an otherwise indeterminate pile (Figure 4.23, called 'A house with an aeroplane in the sky').

Multi-Referentiality

The relative uncommittedness of blocks as objects and the basic lines, surfaces and enclosures that can be formed with them, allow for the assimilation of a wide range of content to these. Smith (1978, p. 15) discusses this characteristic of blocks and basic forms in terms of their 'multi-referentiality'.

Children's brainstorming with a single block illustrates the way in which they use the same form to refer to very different ideas. They also use combinations of blocks in the same way.

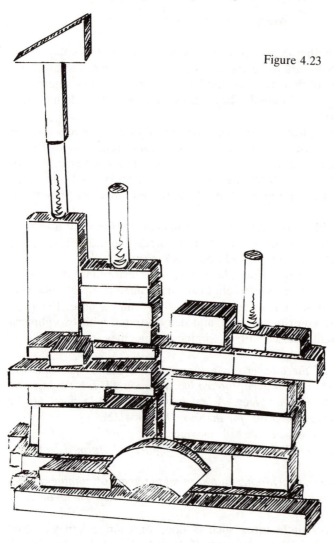

Figure 4.23

Crysantha's (5 y.) module (Figure 4.24) was a four-block enclosure, used by her on one occasion to represent beds inside the house she built, a shower cubicle and a pond in the garden.

Sometimes, with very slight alteration, the same basic arrangement is adapted to different content. *Nitin (3 y. 6 m., Figure 4.25) started with a Y-shape and called it 'something from the alphabet'. After a few moment's reflection this was changed to 'a star' and then 'a tree'.*

The reverse of this sometimes happens and similar meaning is given to different forms, not necessarily by the same child. *Figure 4.26 shows different ways of representing a 'bed'.*

Figure 4.24

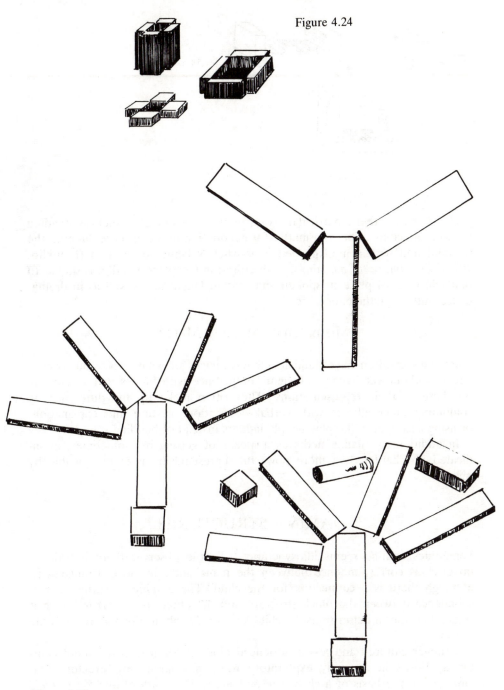

Figure 4.25

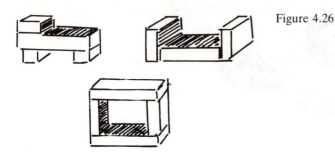

Figure 4.26

However, whether a particular arrangement is accepted by others as standing for what it claims to be, is a matter for negotiation between those fluent in the medium and with some knowledge of what is being referred to (Franklin, 1973). Negotiation of meanings, as discussed in Chapters 3 and 6, is similar to that which takes place in spoken and written language, as well as in drama, dance, music, mathematics, etc.

Mismatch or Mix and Match?

Sometimes children have detailed mental images of what they want to construct, without yet having sufficient competence with blocks to rely entirely on these in their representations. They often make up the difference by combining block effects with verbal description, gesture and explanation, or using accessories like play-people ladders instead of building stairs.

In addition to mixing media as a means of getting by, sometimes, as indicated in Chapter 3, a more powerful representation is made possible by mixing.

NAMING STRUCTURES

Sometimes naming seems idiosyncratic.[17] To the observer there is little or no obvious correspondence between the name and the block arrangement, although there is a connection for the child. The *graphic* or surface correspondence between the block structure and the object (or such) to which it refers, becomes a better fit as the child learns more about the material and the object.

Younger children and less experienced older children who set about combining blocks in a purely exploratory way, may name any structure that emerges on the basis of a chance resemblance. *The result of one 5-year-old's first contact with the unit blocks was called 'A three telescope in an eyeball' (Figure 4.27).*

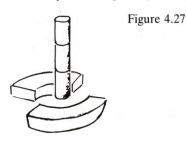

Figure 4.27

Sometimes a child may announce an intention to make something specific before starting: a house, a Buddhist temple, London Bridge, the Pompidou Centre or even a 'person'. For some this seems to be a device for getting started and may be triggered by browsing through a book. Sometimes children who have become used to being asked what they are making or have made adopt the labelling convention as part of the activity, even though the particular label may not be personally significant. Renaming occurs for a variety of reasons. It is a strategy that may come into play as the child constantly adjusts to both inner and outer constraints, including those of the material itself. Sometimes it seems as if, carried along by the rhythm of placing blocks into pleasing arrangements, the child names and renames the emerging structure as it reminds the builder of this, then that. Where observational records show that this is a characteristic of a child's present blockplay it seems it may be inappropriate to over-emphasize the need for prior planning.

This pattern of naming is termed 'transient' by Zervigon-Hakes (1984, p. 43). It incorporates a visual dimension with word association. The process is similar to the 'chaining' that characterizes the way in which young children latch onto a word in a conversation and carry it off into a different context (Wood, McMahon and Cranstoun, 1980, p. 55).

Last there are structures that have their identity decided before building starts, as with the car ferry described at the beginning of this chapter. The same idea is sustained throughout and there can be little doubt that, in this instance, the name helps the children to organize their thinking and action.

There are many children who do not make announcements before starting or name their structures on completion but who can be seen to be working to a plan. Signs like gathering a certain number and kind of blocks before starting are often an indication that some prior planning has taken place.

Advanced Non-Figurative Representation

Some children are more interested in the creation of abstract block sculpture and patterning than in representing the known world. These children also work to plan – a fact we may simply not recognize because they are working from totally original ideas. Many children who work in this way would have difficulty in expressing their ideas verbally either before or after the event, as the High

Scope approach[18] would require them to do. The ideas they wish to express are nonverbal. Failure to recognize this could put at risk their very individual approach to the medium. As discussed in Chapter 3, knowledge of personal styles is important in tuning in to the intentions of different children.

SUMMARY AND CONCLUSIONS

Analysis of our observational data (see Appendix III) relating to the changing character of the blockplay of 3–7-year-olds is broadly consistent with that described by previous researchers.[19] A working knowledge of blocks is acquired through the interacting processes of *differentiation* and *integration*. The findings indicate the importance of observing the activities of children with materials *over time* before coming to conclusions about the value of the material or the quality of a child's play. In the early period of blockplay, the need to come to terms with the materials dominates. The acquisition of a basic repertoire of building techniques, which can be described in terms of Bruner's *modules* and Piaget's *schemas*, encourages and enables the child to use blocks in the creation of symbolic representations and abstract sculpturing, which become more detailed and structurally integrated as children get older and their real-world imagery and skill in using blocks develops.

Visual harmony, at first related to repetition and movement, is a striking characteristic of blockplay. Later, children deliberately strive for this in their structures, with some children preferring to develop their blockplay along abstract sculpturing lines rather than in figurative representation.

It can be seen from the descriptions offered here of the development of blockplay that this involves mathematical, scientific, technical and problem-solving competence. These aspects of blockplay are expanded on separately in further chapters. Later chapters also deal with the influence of the physical and social settings.

In summarizing the relationship between what the child brings from within the self to blockplay and the part played by the environment, Johnson (1933) says[20] 'No adult could have planned a didactic method which could have stimulated children to this sort of activity, but also no such building is found unless favorable conditions are made for it.'

NOTES

1. Franklin (1973, p. 5).
2. The blockplay of infants has been recorded by Vereecken (1961) and Forman (1982).
3. Bruce (1987, p. 13); Read (this volume, Chapter 1).
4. These aspects of blocks were brought home forcefully when two equivalent sets of unit blocks were in use in a school and had become intermingled. One set belonged to the school, the other, a gift from *community playthings*, was shared by the project schools. When the time came for another school to have the use of the project blocks,

the children insisted on helping the research assistant to sort them once again into two sets. She had begun the operation on a simple one-for-one division of the blocks. 'You can't do it like that', she was told. 'You have to feel the ends.' And 'They're different woods.' The end faces of one complete set had a very slightly furry feel. One set was made from maple, the other from beech, although this had never been pointed out to the children.

5. Johnson (1928, 1933) and Guanella (1934) were the primary sources of reference for our study of developmental aspects of blockplay. The methods of study employed by Johnson and Guanella are discussed in detail in Chapter 8. The terms used in the Froebel Blockplay Study are adopted from Guanella (1934). Description of the basic characteristics of blockplay is consistent across numerous accounts: Krotzsch (1917, cited in Guanella, 1934); Parry (1978); Amor (1980); and Elkins (1980).

6. There appear to be inner-determined *lower limits* to the child's combinatorial skill with blocks. A blockplay landmark, the bridging of two separate blocks with a third, is possible in some circumstances at about 3 years. According to Gesell (1952, p. 117) a child of 3, in a test situation, can bridge a gap between two small cubes with a third when this is demonstrated. Johnson (1933) describes bridging, i.e. vertical enclosure, with what we call half units, occurring in the spontaneous blockplay of some 3-year-olds after a year of blockplay experience. Our observations indicate that bridging with longer-length blocks is often beyond the scope of 4-year-old *beginners* (Figure 7.18). Since envelopment is an extension of the process of bridging, a 3-year-old would be unlikely to reproduce it, even if it were modelled.

7. See Chapter 3, this volume, for discussion of children's exploration of general conceptual concerns.

8. Bruner (1973, p. 4); Piaget (1969, p. ix). The Brunerian notion of behaviour *modules* overlaps with that of *schema*. It is concerned with the way in which action is organized into chunks, each of which may incorporate several general ideas, i.e. *schema*. In the present volume the term *modularization* is used to refer to the behaviour chunks into which *blockplay* can be analysed. This is to differentiate it from the generalizable Piagetian *schema*. The concepts of *modularization* and *schema* fit with ideas discussed by Conolly (1975); Dillon-Goodson (1982); Matthews (1984, 1987); and Athey (1980, 1981, 1990); relating to action as a cognitive process. Actions are linked in increasingly complex hierarchies.

9. Reprinted in Provenzo and Brett (1983, p. 115).

10. Bruner (1974, p. 18) distinguishes 'imitation' from 'observational learning'.

11. Barrett (1986); Ghaye and Pascal (1988); and Cleave and Brown (1989).

12. Mounts and Roopnarine (1987) found from observational study that in construction play in mixed groups of 3- and 4-year-olds, the older children had chance to refine skills. It is suggested this had a facilitative effect on the play patterns of the 3-year-olds by causing them to make adjustments in accordance with the levels of their more mature partners. It is argued that mixed age-groups may also encourage children to decentre as they make contact with others who are either more or less competent than themselves and present ideas different from their own. Four-year-olds in mixed groups were no worse off than 4-year-olds who were separately age-grouped and may have gained on dimensions such as decentration. Azmitia (1988) compared the social-cognitive play patterns in same-age and mixed-age early-childhood settings and found the learning of younger children was enhanced when they worked with an older, more experienced partner, with the benefits increasing over time. Contributing factors were increased use by the children of planning, discussion, observational learning and/or guidance.

13. Several studies, including those of Johnson (1933) and Guanella (1934), have attempted to establish whether aspects of children's ability to use blocks are age related. Hulson and Reich (1931) found a range of competence within the group of 4-year-olds they studied; Moyer and von Haller (1956) found individual differences in the design of

structures to be as great within age-groups as between them; Guanella (1934) found a tendency for the constructions of older children to be bigger than those of younger children; Guanella (*ibid.*) and Reifel and Greenfield (1982) found that forms became more integrated with age. Reifel and Greenfield (*ibid.*) also found an increase in dimensionality with age. Bailey (1933, p. 121) attempted to draw up an age-related scale of block construction to 'evaluate constructive and manipulative ability in nursery and kindergarten children'. Buhler (1945) offers a developmental outline of children's use of blocks. Gesell (1952) uses age-related block-building tasks to assess a child's 'adaptive behaviour' (tool use). He describes the child's spontaneous performance and on the test that follows in a clinical situation. He draws attention to the fact that a child may produce a copy of a model before this is seen in spontaneous play and suggests that this does not necessarily mean the child cannot do this without the help of the model. The test simply calls forth behaviour for which the child is 'functionally mature' (*ibid.* p. 114). Franklin (1973) also comments on the lag between the spontaneous occurrence of an activity and the propensity for children to perform many tasks on demand.

14. Reviewed by Clark (1988); and Macauley (1990).

15. Golomb (1972) also noted the use of drawing techniques in her study of children's use of clay.

16. Reifel and Greenfield (1982) and Reifel (1984) studied the development of correspondence between a block symbol and what it refers to. Children of 4 and 6 were read the story of Little Red-Cap (Little Red Riding Hood), then invited to re–create it using table blocks. Progression was found to be age related in terms of levels of structural integration and dimensionality. Complexity of subject-matter affected *how* rather than *what* was attempted. Other texts useful in the interpretation of this aspect of blockplay include Guanella (1934); Smith (1978); Zervigon-Hakes (1984); Matthews (1984, 1987); and Athey (1981, 1990).

17. These observations are consistent with those of Zervigon-Hakes (1984).

18. Hohmann, Banet and Weikart (1979, p. 59) describe the structuring of the High Scope session around a routine of 'plan', 'do' and 'review'. The session begins with children individually stating their plan of action to the group. These are acted on and, finally, each child reports back to the group on how the plan worked out.

19. For details of earlier research, see notes 5 and 13.

20. Reprinted in Provenzo and Brett (1983, p. 156).

5
BEING MATHEMATICAL
Froebel Blockplay Research Group

> The child can certainly be interested in seriating for the sake of seriating, and classifying for the sake of classifying, etc., when the occasion presents itself. However, on the whole it is when he has events or phenomena to explain or goals to reach in an intriguing situation that operations are most exercised.
>
> (Piaget and Garcia, 1971, p. 26)

These observations about mathematics education have been emphasized in many reports since the above passage was written. Cockroft (1982, p. 84) suggests that in the context of practical activities children can be enabled to consider the mathematical ideas contained in them. More recently, in summing up a survey of mathematics teaching and learning in nursery and primary schools, HMI (DES, 1989b) noted that good work in mathematics was characteristically that which had a purpose meaningful for the children.

When children interact with blocks they produce the kind of intriguing situations suggested in our opening quotation. Sometimes these can be in pursuit of practical goals, such as the building of beds for teddy bears (Figure 5.1), a house or garage. Equally often, intriguing situations present themselves during the course of what might best be called the children's focused doodling with the material. In this context they often become spontaneously engrossed in seriating for its own sake (Figure 5.2) as well as classifying, exploring topological relationships, lines, angles and surfaces, part–whole relationships, sequence, aspects of number, area and volume. When children are free to invent such arrangements, they seem to gain as much satisfaction from organizing their blocks in these non-utilitarian ways as when pursuing more definite goals. The appeal often seems to be both mathematical and aesthetic (Figures 5.3 and 5.12).

In this chapter, examples are offered of children's natural capacity for

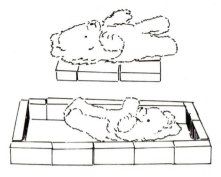

Figure 5.1

Figure 5.2

Figure 5.3

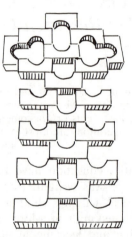

engaging in mathematical action at the experiential level, driven sometimes by need, often by curiosity only, to check out possibilities. We see how they begin to create rules based on their developing mathematical understandings, which can be adapted to different purposes.

The chapter is constructed around an account of a morning's blockplay of 5-year-old Edward. This is interwoven with the blockplay of other children, from his own group and elsewhere, to help flesh out the theoretical points·being made. Edward's blockplay was chosen because of its representative character. Edward, like all children, is unique.

A MORNING'S BLOCKPLAY: EDWARD AND OTHERS

Edward (5 y.) is using blocks to build a 'car'. In the process he combines the ideas of enclosure and covering an area. He starts with an outline approximately

Figure 5.4

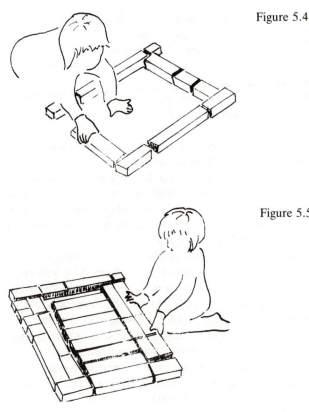

Figure 5.5

2.5 × 1m. This defines the outer limits of his construction. He then begins to fill in the enclosed space that results from this, with unit cuboids varying in length and width. His purpose is to create an unbroken edge-to-edge surface. He has made similar arrangements on several recent occasions. His very publicly announced intention each time is to make a 'fantastic car for a wicked game' in which everyone is invited to participate 'when it's ready'. The finished car is yet to be seen, or the game to be played. Alternative intriguing situations seem to abound and he becomes totally immersed in problem-solving. His work is often accompanied by an intermittent hum.

We can compare Edward's current preoccupation with creating areas of blocks to other areal arrangements and note the differences and similarities.

Sinead (4 y. 11 m.) also combines enclosure with filling in, but on a smaller scale (Figures 5.4 and 5.5). She systematically uses insights about equivalence to solve some of her problems and also indicates an emerging understanding of the relationship of blocks to spaces; Seema (4 y. 6 m.) tackles an upright variant (Figure 4.11); Alia (4 y. 2 m.) places a single eighth block (marked X) on the floor and proceeds to use a technique of wrapping blocks around this to create an ever-increasing area of blocks (Figure 4.8). The long eighths and long quarter cause her to reconsider some of her earlier placements. Having started in the middle, the challenge for Alia becomes that of 'squaring off'.

Interestingly, the tiling of floors and laying of paving stones in real-world contexts works from the inside out. However, the tiler and the paver have the option of cutting material to fit at the edges!

David (4 y. 5 m.), like Sinead, uses the mathematical relationships between the blocks to create a very regular arrangement (Figure 4.7), with a partially bounded edge.

There are challenges to the children's understanding of the situation which-ever strategy they employ in creating continuous surfaces.

Edward, Sinead, Alia and Seema each played around in their different settings and on different occasions with areal themes and variations for several weeks, modifying and refining their understandings and techniques. There seem to be developmental differences between children in their tendencies to consider solutions to problems as being either *within the blocks*, sometimes indicated by a child commanding the blocks to 'behave!' or describing them as 'naughty' and 'stupid', or *within themselves*, sometimes indicated by reflective pauses in the action and statements such as Crysantha's 'that's not right' when she stacked the arch blocks to make a tunnel.[1] Although the child's devel-opment influences his or her approach to problem-solving, other influences mean that standardization of technique in arranging blocks is only a limited possibility. For example, from the point of view of the adult anxious to see 'results', there may seem more obvious ways of creating a regular-shaped area of blocks than some of those we have been considering. However, in the actual blockplay situation, there is no guarantee which particular sized blocks will be free at any time. There are also differences depending on whether a child is working in the horizontal or vertical plane. Unintended gaps between blocks in the making of horizontal lines, which can occur by accident or lack of precision in placing blocks, does not happen when blocks are stacked vertically, because of the influence of gravity. On the other hand, gravity brings other problems to vertical building.

We also need to bear in mind that the production of an area of blocks, or any other block form, may be *incidental* to the child's main purpose, which could have been an interest in the notion of *decreasing* an area of unoccupied space (Figure 5.5) or *increasing* an area of blocks (Figure 4.8). It may be important for the development of flexibility in problem-solving in any symbol system that alternative strategies are explored. This idea is discussed further in Chapter 8.

UNIT BLOCKS

A set of unit blocks (Figure 4.1) has an internal logic that challenges the young child to explore, experiment and problem solve. First, there are units of length

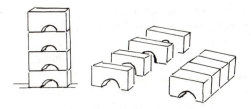

Figure 5.6

that can be added, multiplied or divided. Second, there are dissected shapes and volumes that can be fitted together.

Immediate Feedback

Part of the attraction and value of unit blocks is that the design enables children to judge, as they go along, the appropriateness of their own actions, relative to their intentions. Feedback following the positioning of a block is immediate. This, combined with ease of making changes, encourages feelings of being in control and of competence.

Unit Blocks, Montessori and Cuisenaire

The use of feedback to inform action positively is a characteristic of children's play with unit blocks. The same principle applies in relation to Montessori apparatus but the similarity ends there. Unit blocks are intended to be used in an open-ended way. Children are encouraged to discover that action with the blocks can be varied. Ideas can either be centred on the blocks or lead away from them according to the child's own purpose. An item of Montessori equipment presents a single problem with one right answer.

The mathematical relationships of unit blocks are discovered by the children in pursuit of their own creative ideas. This, coupled with their open-endedness, puts unit blocks effectively in the category of 'raw material'. This is very different from a piece of Montessori apparatus or the coloured rods designed by Georges Cuisenaire, which are intended to be used to promote the discovery of particular mathematical concepts embodied in the material.[2]

Chrysantha (5 y.) announces she is going to make a train tunnel. She collects a number of arch blocks and stacks them vertically. She considers the effect. 'That's not right,' she mutters. She knows from her understanding of tunnels that what she wants is one continuous arch. After some reflection, she slowly re-orders them horizontally, one behind the other, then pushes them together (Figure 5.6).

Shakti (4 y. 5 m.) is organizing his blocks in a bilateral arrangement. He needs a second cylinder equivalent to the one he has already placed on the right-hand side of his arrangement. The one he selects turns out to be taller than the first so he discards it and resumes his search. A third cylinder is drawn out of the block bin and compared to the first. This, too, is found to be taller. He frowns, considering the problem, then quickly retrieves the second cylinder, checks it against the third, confirms that they are the same shape and length, discards the first and places the two matching ones at opposite ends of his structure.

In writing about the 'mathematical mind', Wood (1988, p. 199) comments: 'The disposition to correct oneself is not an attribute of personality or ability. When children know, albeit intuitively, what *looks*, *sounds* or *feels* right, we have reason to be confident that they will self-correct and self-instruct.'

Exploration of the physical properties of the blocks and relationships between them go hand in hand with the pursuit of particular goals. Sub-routines, such as sorting and matching; connecting blocks; forming parallel lines, counting or pairing one for one; forming right angles and enclosures; and fitting and filling are gradually co-ordinated, resulting in ever-increasing complexity.

MODULES AND SCHEMAS

Bruner (1973, p. 4) suggests that young children have a predisposition to organize their actions into subroutines or chunks and he uses the term *modularization* to describe the process. They practise a *module* until they know it off by heart and can run it off almost automatically. The purpose of modularization, according to Bruner, is to leave the mind free for dealing with newer elements of the situation.

The notion of modularization links with that of *schema*, the Piagetian term for a generalizable repeatable pattern of behaviour which is not tied to specific contexts. A module in blockplay is analogous to the 'primitives' in the computer language LOGO.[3] Primitives are subroutines that can be used to build up new and more complex wholes or programs.

In blockplay, a sign that a particular routine is well established occurs when children collect the exact shape, size and number of blocks required to carry it out. Sometimes they even preassemble subsections of a larger arrangement (Figures 5.7, 5.9 and 10.1).

PATTERNING

Modules or schema are particularly apparent in patterning that uses *translation*. The child uses one or more blocks, then repeats this along a straight line. *Reflection* and *rotation* may also be involved (Figures 3.4, 3.10, 3.11, 3.15, 5.8, 5.9, 5.10, 5.11 and 5.12). Genni (4y. 5m.) recorded her own repeat block pattern (Figure 8.2).

At first, this regular patterning seems to be dependent on visual and kinaesthetic feedback, but gradually as children become more reflective in arranging their blocks, it is increasingly governed by rules based on mathematical relationships.

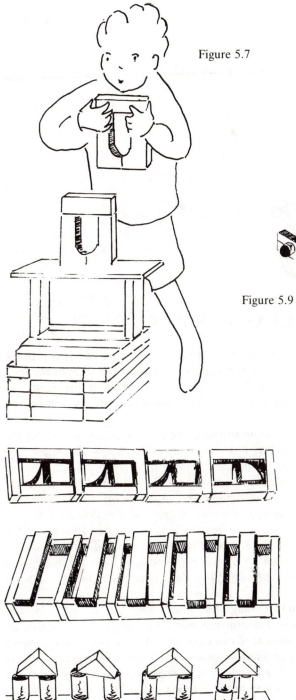

Figure 5.7

Figure 5.9

Figure 5.8

Figure 5.10

Figure 5.11

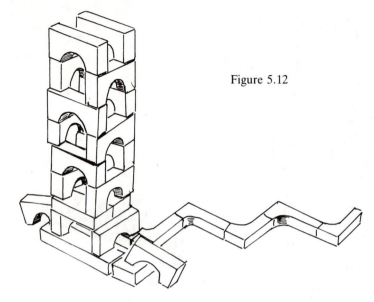

Figure 5.12

CREATING RULES

Other aspects of blockplay also become increasingly regularized. This process of regularization takes the creation of block forms beyond the level of reliance on sensory feedback, i.e. doing it by 'eye' or feel. This is the result of increasing competence in using internalized representations as sources of reference and reflection.

Edward has shown remarkable persistence, despite or perhaps because of the problems. Over several sessions he has tried to come to grips with some of the principles involved in blocking in an area, defined by a rectangular enclosure. One of his many difficulties is in constructing the initial outline. Although he has invented the rule that a block on one side of his arrangement should be paired with an equivalent block on the opposite side to keep them matched for length, sloppy positioning of blocks causes the lines to gently zigzag and confound his strategy. A view from the top of a stepstool (a move suggested by the teacher) helps him to identify this problem. This is a good moment for a reminder from the adult about the need to align blocks so that they connect 'end to end', without gaps.

Ellie (5 y. 6 m.) hit a similar snag. *She found one side of the 2 × 1 m rectangular enclosure she was constructing wandering diagonally towards its opposite number, and complained: 'I can't get this line straight. It keeps going in.' Edmund (5 y. 9 m.) pondered a moment, before commenting: 'It is straight . . . it's straight across.' He mimed a diagonal by raising his right arm and sweeping it across his body and to the left. 'It's got to be straight down, like this other side.' 'Parallel' is mimed with both arms.*

Although Ellie sees the effect she is creating is not what she intended, she is not at this point aware of a unitary cause. She is more concerned about where she wants to be than how to get there. She makes local adjustments that simply push the problem onto the next block in line. Edmund, on the other hand, standing back from the problem, reflected on it and correctly diagnosed the cause. A solution is less likely to be hit or miss with the help of Edmund's insight.[4]

This is the first time Ellie has tried anything on this scale. The blocks are in the playground. There is plenty of ground space that seems to have influenced the emphasis on building in the two-dimensional plane for several of the children, including Ellie.

When she builds indoors, where there is much less floorspace, she plans her work on a smaller scale and often constructs three-dimensional, roofed structures with integral windows to represent shops (Figure 3.8) and houses. She has had the time and experience to formulate rules that can be generalized to similar circumstances.

One of her earlier three-dimensional houses involved her in an attempt to make integral windows on three adjacent walls. She had great difficulty in maintaining the same overall height for all three walls. At one point she had two out of the three with matching walls and windows, with the third finishing several rows of blocks higher. Stephanie pointed this out to her: 'Hey, Ellie . . . low, low, high'. Ellie's solution to this novel situation, as with her current problem, was localized. She began to take down the low wall adjacent to the higher one. When the adult asked what she had in mind, Ellie said she had to take it down to build it again, 'only high this time'. Having dismantled one of the two lower walls, she was left with two parallel walls, one higher than the other, and could not make up her mind whether they were any longer related. 'How can I do it?' she wondered aloud and, without waiting for advice, announced: 'I know! Take 'em all down and no one's got to use 'em (blocks) 'cos I'm going to build it all again.' Whereupon she dismantled the remaining walls and started again.

Only after several more attempts on different occasions and some reflecting discussion with an adult did she regularize aspects of her house and shop construction. She combined her knowledge of blocks and houses with the more general ideas of continuity of lines and surfaces, which go round corners and eventually meet up with themselves.

In doing this, she found that a board, which corresponds to the blocks in length and width, could be used as a template[5] for her groundplan, by simply building her first course of blocks around its inside edge.

Ellie's use of a board as a way of standardizing the shape and area of the floor and roof guaranteed that when the walls had been raised to the desired height a second matching board would make a roof of exactly the right size. She demonstrated understanding of the spatial, shape and size relationships of the floor to roof, as well as the order in which she must proceed. She anticipated the steps she would take by collecting her floor and roof boards before starting.

Dan (4 y. 5 m., Figure 4.13) is also developing a routine for building roofed enclosures. He likes to start with a generous supply of matching blocks. The ones he prefers are half units, standing on end. He once explained that this was an easier way to make walls than by laying blocks one on top of the other. Through this labour-saving building strategy, Dan is perhaps on the way to recognizing that the same area can be created with different combinations and orientations of blocks, i.e. conservation of area.

After collecting his blocks he builds one side, forms the first right angle by eye, builds along for a few blocks, then checks for shape and size by holding above his construction the board he intends using as the roof.

He is taking the first steps towards standardizing a method for the checking of angles. This strategy indicates some recognition of the relationship between right angles formed with the blocks and the given right angles forming the corners of the board. His use of the board as a template could be regarded as a prototypical set-square.

The latest refinement to this routine is to gain the co-operation of another child, or an adult, to hold the roof board above the walls while he takes a sighting from above, to check for irregularities. Another strategy is to start his first wall with a narrow cylinder. He says this is to remind him of the direction to build in.

In effect he has created a reference point, from which he can take bearings. He calls it a 'marker'. No one is quite sure whether he invented the term or not, but it seems most apt.

MATHEMATICAL RELATIONSHIPS

According to Piaget,[6] the theories children formulate to guide their actions are based on two kinds of knowledge. The first is knowledge about the physical properties of objects. In the case of blocks, this means such things as hardness and weight and how they behave under various conditions. The second is what Piaget calls *logico-mathematical* knowledge. This is the world of abstract ideas, such as *sameness* and *difference*, *two* and *second*. These are not physical characteristics of individual objects but ideas that go beyond what is observable in the physical world. They are generalizable and can refer to height, weight, colour, texture, quantity and any other physical attributes of objects when *in our minds* we put two or more objects into a relationship with each other.

The earlier example of Shakti's search for a matching pair of cylinders illustrates the idea of sameness related to both the shape and length of the blocks.

When an accident occurred to someone's structure, causing several blocks to be dislodged, the builder said: 'It doesn't matter. If you look at the gaps, you know how to mend it.'

Here the child was relating particular empty spaces to particular solids.

Figure 5.13(a,b,c) illustrate a building sequence that started with a general

Figure 5.13

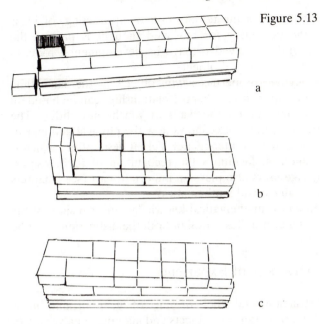

a

b

c

exploration of the blocks, with Paul (4 y. 5 m.) standing blocks next to each other to see whether they 'measured' each other, i.e. were of the same proportions.

A development of this was to use a unit as a standard against which to count off how many of each different-size block 'measured' the unit. Next he began systematically applying the information he had abstracted during his investigation in creating a volumetric arrangement.

The challenge was to make up successive rows, matched for length, with a different-size block for each row. We know he wasn't doing this by eye because of the problem he got into with his top row and the way in which he eventually tried to solve it.

Abstract, generalizable ideas, such as *equivalence* and *sameness*, have the power to extend the boundaries of what we can think about, enabling us to create new possibilities. Things that are not of the same kind may have in common the fact that they are the same weight or colour. A biscuit and an elephant can theoretically be put into *the same class of objects*, if the class is 'things that don't grow on trees'. Mathematics is often described as the search for relationships and pattern.

Play with Objects

How do we acquire such powerful ideas as 'sameness', 'difference' and 'two' or 'second'? Although Piaget's term *logico-mathematical knowledge* is not in everyday usage in mathematics education, the prefix *logico* is a helpful reminder that mathematics involves the teasing out, or abstracting, of ideas by reasoning. Although the possibility for reasoned thought is part of the human condition, it is generally believed to have its developmental roots in early exploratory and playful handling of objects.

Children discover the *physical* properties *within* objects at the same time they are discovering relationships *between* them. Relationships can be based on what objects have in common, or on the ways in which they differ. The example of Paul's activities with the blocks shows how the physical and logico-mathematical aspects of the situation inter-relate. Verbal description, which is rooted in shared understandings, facilitates the recognition of relationships; thus interaction with language users also plays an important part (see Chapters 3 and 6 for discussion of language and mathematics).

Physical knowledge and logico-mathematical knowledge are two sides of the same coin. Blockplay offers a useful illustration of both the distinctions and the interactions between the two.

Diversity of Experience

Logico-mathematical abstraction and the forming of generalizable ideas depends on the handling of a wide range of objects and materials in a variety of contexts. Blocks are just one example. Sometimes children need to experience the same objects and materials in different contexts and, at others, the same contexts with different objects and materials.

All objects and materials have something unique to contribute to the totality of children's development as mathematicians. As objects, blocks are figu-ratively neutral. This characteristic allows children the mental space to explore some fundamental mathematical ideas, which they put into practice in their block creations.

In order to create likenesses with the environment, the child must analyse the chosen form into chunks and create correspondences to these with blocks. This involves detailed mental imaging where the object to be represented is not available to refer to.

From Simple to Complex Relationships

The development of mathematical thinking involves the understanding of increasingly more complex relationships, such as the understanding that no matter how the number of objects in a set is spatially arranged, the number of objects in the set stays the same. This is what, in classical Piagetian ter-minology, is called *conservation* or *invariance* of number. When children play regularly with blocks, they intuitively employ conservation. We often heard children saying words to the effect that they are going to 'break up' their construction and use the same blocks 'to make something different'. This is obviously far from a formal understanding of the concept, but it is clear that the children's experience of the recycling of blocks will contribute to the

Figure 5.14

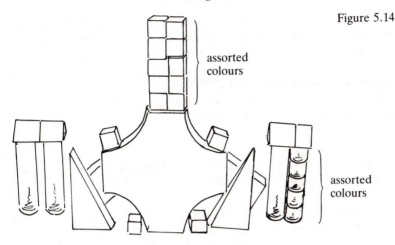

assorted
colours

assorted
colours

development of the abstract idea, especially as they begin to use counting strategies to regulate their building, which we saw Edward doing as he tried to keep the opposite sides of his rectangle even with each other.

Sometimes an arrangement looks deceptively simple but, on analysing it, we can see that it involves the co-ordination of numerous logico-mathematical and physical knowledge elements.

Stephanie (5 y. 6 m., Figure 5.14) has used a subset 'small cylinders' from the class of objects 'cylinders' to make up a column as tall as the one adjacent to it, which, in turn, is as tall as the two columns on the left-hand side of her arrangement. In doing this she has managed to maintain overall height and shape in her columns, despite the presence of other potentially confounding variables, such as the colour and length of individual cylinders. At the same time she has maintained the reflected symmetry of her design as well as attending to the building process itself.

Stephanie was having to make do with oddments of blocks as there were few unit blocks left for her to use. Plenty of previous experience under more enabling conditions may have made it more likely that she would be able to improvise successfully.

It is possible to get by in solving many practical problems by relying heavily on sensory feedback, without there necessarily being any deduction involved. However, once the number of elements in the situation to be tackled increases, there is a greater need for reflective thinking. In these circumstances, children can benefit from having a more experienced partner working alongside them to help them use the mathematical understandings they do have to work towards a solution.

On the present occasion, for example, Edward has finished blocking in his rectangle. All, that is, except for a small gap in the centre. 'Cover it over and that can be the drain, because you must have drains in pavements,' someone suggests. 'This is a car,' says Edward through gritted teeth. The gap is smaller than any block in the set. He forces an eighth in and immediately sees the knock-on effect as blocks shift out of alignment. He quietly hums a snatch of 'Thinkabout', and another, getting louder. Now in full song, which could be either bravado or a sign that he is really enjoying this last little teaser, he removes the eighth and thoughtfully mimes chopping it in two. In doing so he demonstrates his understanding of cutting and dividing to make smaller. Next he mimes sawing it with appropriate sound effects. He catches the teacher's eye and says: 'It's only a joke!'

> Teacher: *Too big is it? Let's have a look.*
> Edward: *It will go in this way.* (He demonstrates that the eighth will slot into the gap when standing on end and protruding from the surface.) *That spoils it. It's got to be flat like the rest.*

Together, with the benefit of an overview, Edward and the adult spot several other small gaps that interrupt the continuity of the surface, near to the problem gap: [Teacher]: 'You know about not leaving cracks between the blocks, don't you? That they have to touch each other on all sides? Try getting rid of the cracks and see if that helps.'

The idea of gaps as well as blocks taking up space has not yet been abstracted by Edward, much less the idea that lots of little gaps separated by blocks can become one big gap. This problem has similarities to that Crysantha tackled in creating a tunnel from arch blocks (Figure 5.6).

Sinead (Figure 5.5) seems to have a more mature grasp of the general principle involved. She is systematically matching blocks for equivalence throughout the creation of this arrangement and knows she does not need to squeeze any more blocks in or take any out. She pushes gently along one side of her arrangement towards the centre and the gaps in the surface of her arrangement are eliminated.

Edward needs more experience of handling objects such as blocks to help him more clearly understand the relationship between positive and negative – or occupied and unoccupied – space. Packing away a set of blocks offers particularly valuable opportunities, especially when shared with others, of pondering the mysteries of *volume*. The same collection of blocks can be randomly stored as a mini-mountain that rises above the storage container or systematically packed to fit exactly into it. Connections can also be made, with the help of adults, between different areas of experience. Children frequently have to 'shove up' to make room for one more on the carpet at story time. For the present, Edward realizes from past experience that closing the gaps one by one *might* work. On this occasion it does.

Eureka!

'I've done it! Fantastic!' He is radiant. Alessandros comes over to look: 'It's beautiful,' he says. 'I know,' says Edward. He prowls around and over his rectangular surface for several minutes, surveying his achievement and savouring its wholeness.

MATHEMATICS AND AESTHETICS

Alessandros wasn't the only child to comment at one time or another on the aesthetic aspects of an arrangement. Many children spontaneously expressed pleasure at the 'decoration' made by Yuseff (5 y., Figure 9.1) and, although Dan was desperate to use Elizabeth's blocks, he could not bring himself to dismantle her 'snake' (Figure III.6) in order to do so even though he had her permission. *'It will make me so sad,' he said, 'it's really clever.'* An adult mathematician might have used the term *elegant* to describe Elizabeth's use of rotated quarter-circle curves to represent a snake. It seems that St Thomas Aquinas, writing in the thirteenth century, was right when he stated: 'The senses delight in things duly proportioned' (cited in Bergamini, 1972, p. 88).

Jane Read in Chapter 1 describes the blocks that form part of the series of Gifts designed by Froebel and the kinds of representation they were designed to encourage. These included 'forms of knowledge', by which was meant mathematical ideas, and 'forms of beauty' in which pattern and symmetry predominate. Both forms could be represented using the same blocks.

Frank Lloyd Wright, the American pioneer of the modern school of building design, has written of the profound effect play with Froebel's Gifts in early childhood had on his later development as an architect. He writes euphorically of 'That early kindergarten experience with the straight line; the flat plane; the square; the triangle; the circle!' He describes his discovery of the potential of these shapes to generate yet more shapes when combined with each other – in other words, the 'grammar' of blockplay – and he concludes by saying 'These primary forms and figures were the secret of all effects . . . which were ever got into the architecture of the world' (cited in Manson, 1954, p. 15).

A fine example of the fusion of mathematics and aesthetics is the Guggenheim Museum in New York, designed by Wright, which consists of a gently spiralling interior ramp rising from a base of a mere one hundred feet in diameter and yielding over a quarter of a mile of continuous display space for works of art (Bergamini, 1972, p. 102). This has been described as one of the 'most magical spatial experiences. . . . At any moment one is in intimate proximity to a small group of works yet in the presence of the entire exhibition' (Trachtenberg and Hymen, 1986, pp. 536–7).

We share with Froebel and other educators, such as Johnson and Guanella, the view that aesthetics is of central importance to the child in blockplay. The visual harmony that seems to be a characteristic of children's block creations is in part due to the design of the blocks, which can be seen to contribute to an emerging awareness of the inter-relatedness of mathematics and art/art and mathematics in terms of line, form, the control of space in the arrangement of shapes and forms, ratio, proportion and pattern and the relationship of parts to wholes. These are exemplified in many of the sketches.

Katy (4y. 6m., Figure 5.3) spent a period of several weeks creating increasingly more complex patterns with the same two shapes. Note particularly the generation of new shapes within this highly original arrangement.

Sebastian (4 y.) was very attracted to the narrow wedge block. 'Feel that,' he once said, running a finger down the slope of a narrow wedge, 'I love it.'

Frank Lloyd Wright mentions 'The smooth shapely maple blocks with which to build, the sense of which never leaves the fingers: so form becomes feeling' (cited in Manson, 1954, p. 15). Sebastian frequently used the wedges to create undulating, flowing lines of blocks.

Isaacson (1989, p. 54) suggests that mathematics *as an arts subject* is 'a vehicle for the development of creativity' that overlaps and interacts with mathematics as a utilitarian subject and vice versa. If, as educators, we can provide for and stimulate the development of the aesthetic component in mathematics for its own sake, it is probable, according to Isaacson, that some useful mathematics will be learnt in the process. Our observations of blockplay lend support to Isaacson's argument that both the aesthetic and the utilitarian should be included in our planning of the mathematics curriculum. There is much to be gained and nothing to lose.

Marking Time

It is almost the end of the morning. Edward has worked through playtime, maintaining his commitment to getting his basic form exactly the way he wants it:

Edward: *Right! Now I'll just do the rest of it, then we'll have a really wicked game.*
  (The original idea of the 'car' has reasserted itself.)
Teacher: *You haven't time for more building and a game. It's tidying up in five minutes.* (Edward appears to ignore this and carries on selecting blocks. Seconds later, he appears in front of his teacher.)
Edward: *How many minutes was that? Five?* (He has five narrow cylinders gathered to his chest.) *These are your minutes, right?* (He places them in a line, counting as he puts each one down.) *One, two, three, four, five.*
(The teacher goes along with him): *D'you want me to take one away every time a minute is used up?*
Edward: *Yes. Let me see your watch.* (The teacher indicates the minute hand. Together they watch the passing of one minute. As the hand sweeps past the twelve, Edward jumps and punches the air with a fist. *Yeah!* he shouts, before laying flat one of his cylinders.) *1 – 2 – 3 – 4 minutes to go, everyone!* (He counts his remaining 'minutes' and continues marking time in this way, subtracting a block for each minute as it passes and counting the remainder, until all the cylinders are flat. He becomes so absorbed with his tally he completely forgets the object of the exercise and, once again, doesn't finish his 'car' or use it in a game.) *It doesn't matter. I can build it again, or I might build a computer.*

SUMMARY AND CONCLUSIONS

In writing this chapter we could have chosen to present a list of the mathematical ideas that can be explored in blockplay and systematically described and discussed these. Instead, we have presented our account in a form we hope communicates something of the feel of children being mathematical *as part of the blockplay process*. In particular, we were concerned to illustrate the way in which competence develops, with children driven by curiosity to study mathematical relations, to reflect on their problems and eventually come up with increasingly regularized but flexible methods of dealing with them.

The children's positive and confident approach to mathematics is perhaps captured at its best in their creative geometry and pattern-making.

Any aspect of mathematics can crop up at any time. We have learnt how important it is for adults to have a good grasp of the mathematics involved, otherwise many opportunities for helping children to move forward in their thinking are lost.

The processes of lifting mathematical ideas out of particular contexts and making them more general is the subject of the next chapter.

NOTES

1. Donaldson (1978) and De Loache and Brown (1987) discuss research into the development of reflective problem-solving through the use of internal representations.

2. Bruce (1976) compares the Montessori method with a Piagetian-based conceptualization of the early-childhood curriculum. De Vries and Kohlberg (1987) discuss and evaluate Montessori apparatus and Cuisenaire materials from the constructivist viewpoint. They contrast Montessori's notion of sensory absorption as a mechanism for learning with intelligent construction.

3. The analogy is borrowed from Noss (1983, p. 6), who likened the building system, Lego, to LOGO primitives.

4. See note 1.

5. Children's own invented templates should not be confused with those commercially available as drawing aids. These pre-empt discovery in early-years teaching and learning.

6. In this section we have made use of the interpretations of Piagetian theory offered by Williams and Kamii (1986) and De Vries and Kohlberg (1987).

6
SPEAKING MATHEMATICS
Froebel Blockplay Research Group

First, we shall consider the role of language in mathematics teaching and learning and how appropriately we interact with children in the block area from a mathematics point of view. Then we shall share some ideas about organizing for continuity in mathematics education, especially looking at the transition from informal mathematics to that involving formal written symbolism.

LANGUAGE AND MATHEMATICS

In the last chapter we saw children discovering mathematical relationships through play with blocks and using knowledge of these relationships as tools in problem-solving. We saw that, in addition to the exploratory handling of objects, language was an important factor in enabling children to make logico-mathematical abstractions.

Daniel (4 y.) places four wide cylinders in a group, then puts a narrow cylinder on top of each one. The arrangement is more in the nature of a creative doodle than the result of prior planning. He looks at it for a moment, then with great pleasure sums it up: 'Look, four to four!'

Daniel's knowledge of number and number words makes it easier for him to ignore the respective shape and size of his two sets and to discover their numerical equivalence. The word 'to' expresses the spatial proximity of the sets. In just three words he has described the mathematically salient details of his arrangement. This illustrates the power of language and its role as an aid to reflection and abstraction and a means of communicating mathematical ideas.

The inter-relationship between the development of mathematical ideas and language has been discussed by various writers. Choat (1978), in the Piagetian tradition, suggests that knowledge is abstracted as a result of action. Words play an important part in enabling individuals to incorporate incoming ideas resulting from action with what they already know. Words facilitate the adaptation of existing ideas in the light of new experience. Choat emphasizes that, without the underlying knowledge to which it refers, a word will not be understood, and without the word further development of an idea will be difficult. Knowledge and words that describe this are two sides of the same coin.

According to Walkerdine (1982), many teachers consider that children will first develop understandings by their own acts and then be given the appropriate terms. It seems from research carried out by Gelman and Gallistel (1983) into children's understanding of number that they do not wait to be given words to match their developing concepts but will adapt whatever language they already have to their present purposes.

Gelman and Gallistel (*ibid.*) found children from 2 to 4 years of age spontaneously using the cognitive principle of one-to-one correspondence, which is the basis of counting, as a problem-solving strategy. These children structured the 'counting' process by using words to 'tag' each object in sequence. As words to count with, according to these researchers, children will adopt 'whatever usable list becomes available' (*ibid.* p. 194). They recorded instances of children who used the alphabet in place of the usual number-word sequence. There were also children who used conventional number words but in the wrong order. However, in all instances the one-to-one principle was applied. Only one number name or letter was given to each object and the same name was never used twice in any particular count sequence. The cognitive principle of one-to-one correspondence apparently searches for an appropriate list (*ibid.*).

Implications for Teaching and Learning

This evidence that children actively seek words as mathematical tools has important implications for mathematics education. Rather than seeing the development of mathematical ideas as a two-step process, with action and abstraction preceding language, they should be viewed as an integrated process. The adult role then becomes one of helping the child develop both the understandings and the corresponding language through shared activity. This includes what Wood (1988, p. 210) calls the 'shared construction of experiences', i.e. processes such as counting and adding and the terms that describe these are worked out by agreement, starting with the knowledge and the linguistic tools the child already has.

In blockplay, for example, children bring all their existing powers of description to the mathematics of the situation.

Amanda (4 y.) described the enclosure she had built as 'a wall you can get inside'. Akash (3 y. 4 m.) described a plywood slat as a 'line one' to differentiate it from a block. Kelly (3 y. 3 m.) described her three-block stack as a 'tall'. It was clear in the context that she was referring to the verticality of her arrangement.

Negotiating Terms

Terms may need to be renegotiated to bring them more into line with conventional terminology. Sometimes the move towards more conventional terminology will be gradual, sometimes it will be a simple trade-in of one word for another. Sometimes it will be necessary to make clear when a term in everyday use is being used in a mathematical sense. We speak of the block 'area' meaning the space where blocks can be found and played with. When we speak of an area of blocks we are speaking the language of mathematics. Wood (1988, p. 193) cites an example of a child whose understanding of the word 'volume' was 'what is on the knob of the television set'.

In reviewing 'good work' in mathematics across the primary age-range, HMI (DES, 1989b) drew attention to the emphasis teachers gave to language in their work with 4- and 5-year-olds. They comment favourably on the practice of gathering the whole class together to follow up and discuss ideas the children have explored informally in the course of their activities. In these sessions ideas could be refined and children could begin 'to recognise the need for precision in the use of mathematical language' (*ibid*. p. 2). From the experience of studying blockplay and our reading of research on the teaching of mathematics, we would want to add that this kind of gathering together probably has greatest effect in small rather than whole-class groups, for whom the discussion has some personal relevance.[1]

In the following section we describe our attempts to adapt some of these ideas about the role of language in mathematics teaching and learning and the language of mathematics to the context of blockplay.

Every Block Has a Name

'Pass me some more blocks called . . .' the speaker (4 y.), who was using unit blocks for the first time, paused and looked at the block he was holding '. . . these', he finished.

At an early stage in our study of blockplay we became acutely aware of the linguistic poverty of some of our interactions with the children, particularly when we were reduced to waving blocks in the air and asking for 'two more blocks like this'. The children, for the most part, used familiar, concrete images in differentiating the blocks: pants/underpants/knickers were the words used to denote the 'T' block; sausages/rolling-pins/chimneys denoted narrow cylinders; lagers denoted wide cylinders; rainbow/turnaround/eyebrow/trunk/lips denoted quarter eliptical curves; cheeses denoted quarter circles and/or wedges; and holy cross/hospital sign denoted the cross block.

Children were indicating recognition of a correspondence between a block and some other object with which they were familiar. They were also communicating perfectly clearly in the context. If someone asked for a rolling-pin, no one listening suspected they were baking, if the request was made in the block area.

Limitations of Personal Imagery

The problem with this kind of familiar, concrete imagery is that its meaning is *embedded* (Donaldson, 1978, p. 76) in lived experience. Concrete images used as representations of mathematical ideas are not readily transferred from one context to another and can cause confusion if this happens.

In order to transfer ideas from one context to another, general words are needed, i.e. those that have no *particular* real-world associations. Words such as 'cylinder' and 'cylindrical', for example, act as terms of reference by means of which new experience can be related to knowledge already held, e.g. sausages, cans of lager, chimney pots and rolling-pins can all be filed under the word 'cylindrical'. Through the use of general terms we are enabled to focus on the characteristics all objects bearing the same descriptive label have in common. These general descriptive terms make it easier for ideas to be adapted in the light of new experience, e.g. some cylindrical-shaped objects are tubular while others are solid; cylinders can be wide, narrow, tall, short, plain or coloured, light or heavy.

Jolene (4 y.), whose father was a roofer, was particularly attracted to cylinders and referred to them initially as 'chimneys'. There was a display of geometric shapes and forms in the classroom as part of a curriculum focus on this aspect of mathematics and there were frequent discussions between adults and children about the names of the various shapes. On several occasions, Jolene was heard practising 'Cyn . . . cyn . . . cynDILLA'. Some weeks later, she presented an arrangement that incorporated a wide assortment of cylindrical blocks with the words 'Look, I've used cylinders'. The adult helped her describe each of the cylinders to enable her to reflect on both their sameness and differences.

Such conversations help children to internalize their representations so that, when confronted with the problem of finding the right block to fit exactly into a particular hole, they don't have to try different blocks physically but can run through the possibilities mentally, before acting.

An abstraction expressed in general terms also makes it possible for the individual, who already understands the general principle, to imagine, for example, what a 'cylindrical-shaped vase' would look like, without ever having seen one.

With general words at our disposal, we do not necessarily have to abandon our homely, concrete images. In fact for many of us, the word cylinder will always be synonymous with a rolling-pin. It is this image that flashes onto our mental screens rather than the pure, abstracted form when we hear the general word. However, there will be occasions when the old images let us down, as those of us for whom a fraction is a slice of apple know only too well. We used general terms such as 'quarter' to enable children to reflect on those features essential to an understanding of the concept: quarter units, which are cuboid; long quarter units (also cuboid); quarter circles (solid); and quarter-circle curves and quarter-eliptical curves. The emergence of the idea of a quarter as a fourth part of *anything* is what we hope will eventually result from such labelling.

We spent many months naming a set of unit blocks. We felt there should be a more generalizable vocabulary available for the children to take on board as it became more useful to them. We also needed a common language of blocks in order to share experiences and observations.

Form rather than Function

The main criterion guiding our choice of terms was *form* rather than *function* (Figure 4.1). This was to facilitate logico-mathematical abstraction. We wanted to avoid, as far as possible, a vocabulary that might unduly influence both our own perceptions of the child's purpose and the uses to which the blocks might be put if such terms as the 'cross-roads' block and the 'bridge' block were adopted.

Initially, we chose *length* as our primary reference point in naming the rectangular blocks, which constitute the core of a set, at the expense of volume. In this we were unthinkingly adopting the Piagetian orthodoxy that indicates volume as a later developing concept. Subsequent research[2] suggests this is not universally so and that much depends on experience.

As we became aware of this we revised the names of some of the blocks to take account of volume. What we had called the narrow quarter became the long eighth and similarly the narrow half became the long quarter.

We are open minded about whether it is more useful to regard the shortest or the longest cuboid as the *unit*, as the term has particular connotations in relation to place value and, if blocks are to continue to play an important role throughout the primary years, the use and meaning of the term in different contexts may have to be clarified.

The advice we would offer to other early-years educators who might consider conducting a similar, block-naming exercise would be to do this in consultation with colleagues across the school so that continuity with extension can be achieved through shared terms and meanings.

As a group of educators we developed a shared vocabulary by struggle and negotiation. We each brought our own experience, priorities and preconceptions to the task. This mirrors exactly the condition of the children as they grope for words to express their developing understandings and the processes we need to engage in with them in order for them to learn to translate the language of everyday discourse into the language of mathematics.

The process is summarized by a group of mathematics teachers:

> The history of mathematics is full of examples of creative mathematicians struggling to hammer out agreed usages, in the course of working on unsolved problems.

Expressions which achieve a clear sense for a given group at a particular time, emerge out of the language of struggle. An agreed solution to a problem creates a space within which it is possible to operate. Ambiguities are pushed aside, at least for a time, and for that group which participates in the agreement. It is the common fate of such agreements eventually to be undermined, abandoned or supplanted, in the process of arriving at fresh solutions to problems.

(Association of Teachers of Mathematics, 1980, p. 19)

To date, we can report that most children we have observed mix selected bits of the block vocabulary we devised with their own terms. Particular words serve merely to label blocks in many cases and cannot be taken as a sign, when used by a child, of understanding of the abstraction it represents. It would be unwise, for example, without some additional evidence, to assume that a child correctly designating a block 'an eighth' was doing more than merely name it.

CONTINUITY WITH EXTENSION

The idea of negotiating the way forward with children in mathematics education is bound up with the educational principle of finding the right degree of cognitive challenge to provide stretch without strain, bearing in mind present levels of competence and knowledge. Watt (1987, p. 10) expresses this succinctly as allowing for 'continuity with extension'. This theme is developed in the next section.

Translating Ideas

In order to distinguish competence at the level of informal, practical mathematics from that at the formal level that employs technical language and symbolism, Piaget used the analogy of being able to sing in tune without having a theory of singing or being able to read music (cited in DeVries and Kohlberg, 1987, p. 207).

Research carried out by Hughes (1986) and an HMI report (DES, 1989c) on the state of mathematics teaching and learning suggest that there is plenty of evidence of children successfully employing mathematics at the informal, practical level. There is also evidence that significant numbers of individuals experience difficulty in making connections between this active maths-as-you-go and that which uses formal symbolism. This includes spoken and written words, such as we discussed in the earlier part of the chapter, as well as written numerals, letters of the alphabet and the signs for operations, such as adding, subtracting, multiplying and dividing.

An example, taken from Hughes (1986, p. 46), illustrates the point. The child, Amanda (3 y. 11 m.), seems baffled when asked 'how many is two and one?' However, when Hughes offers her a further 'sum' involving *bricks*,[3] 'How many is one brick and one more brick?' she has no difficulty. The sum is then repeated in numerical terms only, and again Amanda is stuck. Hughes explored several possible explanations for the type of breakdown illustrated in this example, which persists for so many individuals and interferes with their development as mathematicians. Amanda obviously understands the mathematical idea 'one' when it is presented in a meaningful context. The conclusion Hughes came to was that the problem is not one of breakdown in reasoning but in communication.

Embedded and Disembedded Representations

The difference in the two ways of representing the problem to Amanda is that one is 'embedded' in a context that makes 'human sense' to her while the other uses context-free generalizations or 'dis-embedded' terminology (Donaldson, 1978, p. 76).

This disembedded terminology started life, like Jolene's cylinders, in the tangible world of sausages and chimneys. Soundly based mathematics education enables individuals to develop alternative ways of packaging the same mathematical ideas and develop competence in packing, unpacking and repacking them.

Both Hughes (1986, p. 152) and Papert (1980, p. 54) emphasize that the translating of ideas from embedded to disembedded representations and vice versa also needs to have some relevance for the learner.

In the blockplay sequence that follows, we see the ideas of equivalence and 'one more', which are initially embedded in the construction of a 'see-saw' balance, being preserved while the way in which they are represented becomes progressively disembedded.

Caveta (3 y. 5 m.) centres a unit on top of a quarter unit. 'See-saw,' she says. She places another quarter on one end, causing the unit to dip. She smiles at a watching adult, then turns her attention back to the see-saw. She stares hard at the down side, then looks again at the adult, who asks: 'Is it stuck? See if you can make it come up.'

So far, Caveta's interest is in the way the blocks behave. In the last chapter we differentiated between this kind of physical knowledge and logico-mathematical knowledge. The emphasis alternates from one to the other as the sequence progresses.

Caveta seems as if about to remove the quarter unit but has second thoughts and, instead, places a second quarter on the opposite end, bringing both sides into balance once more. 'Same-same,' she says, delightedly pointing to one end then the other. She follows up this sequence by holding both hands in front of her, curling up all but her two index fingers, which are stiffly extended, and says: 'one-one'. The sequence is repeated three times more, with Caveta adding a block each time to both sides of her see-saw and keeping a corresponding finger tally. The adult chips in by helping her to count the fingers when she stumbles over this in declaring each new total.

In the last chapter we saw how Edward created a tally system with blocks for recording the passage of time. This was an instance of a disembedded idea being translated into a concrete representation. Caveta, on the other hand, 'translates' from the concrete situation to increasingly more disembedded representations of this, as she numbers the fingers that stand for the blocks on her see-saw.

The term 'translate' is adopted by Hughes (1986, p. 44) to suggest the linguistic/communicative characteristics of the processes involved in shifting from embedded to disembedded terminology and symbolism and vice versa.

Pimm (1981, p. 139) suggests that numbers act 'as a kind of filter, dispensing with all but the essential elements involved'. Caveta shows us this filtering process, as she dispenses with all but the elements expressing numerosity.

The power of numbers lies in the way they can generalize. This goes even beyond the power of generalizations such as 'cylindrical'. Numbers also have power as elements of a *transformational* system of symbols and signs, i.e. there is a 'grammar' of number just as there is of spoken and written language and blockplay. The meaning of numbers changes depending on how they are placed in relation to each other.

The adult also recorded the mathematical sequence created by Caveta, using a mixture of personal symbols and conventional written numerals and signs.

Conventional written numerals and signs, which indicate what is being done, are among the most disembedded of mathematical representations. In appearance they are far removed from the real world they describe and for this reason are potentially the most baffling and mysterious aspect of mathematics for the novice. The teaching and learning of conventional mathematical notation needs to mesh with earlier concrete experiences and with the language, imagery and symbolism already in use to express mathematical ideas.

Caveta was interested in watching how the written record was made by the adult, who explained the meaning of the signs and symbols. Other children watched and joined in with a chorus of 'I'm three' and 'I'm four' as they recognized the written numerals.

Through the intrinsically motivating blockplay setting and the opportunities offered for interaction with a mature partner as well as with peers, Caveta was enabled to extend her understandings as a mathematician, free from anxiety.

TRANSITIONAL OBJECTS

Papert (1980, p. 11) has described how gears, which were part of his early childhood 'landscape', became for him 'objects to think with', which facilitated translation from 'doing' to abstract symbolizing. He sees the computer serving a similar function. This notion of objects to think with and as facilitators in translation from one mode of representing to another, i.e. *transitional objects*, was taken up by Hughes (1986) in his study of children's ability to handle number. He devised games involving translation and explored the capacities of 4-year-olds for simple computer programming, with very promising results.

Our experience suggests that blocks are similarly material to think with. Like the games devised by Hughes, and Papert's Turtle Geometry, they can facilitate the translation of ideas from embedded to disembedded representations and vice versa. The important dimension seems to be, as Papert suggests with his gears, that blocks are part of the 'landscape' from which children construct their understandings. Acquiring skill in creating and interpreting both embedded and disembedded representations is, like anything else, according to Papert (1980, p. vii), 'Easy if you can assimilate it to your collection of models. . . . What an individual can learn, and how he learns it, depends on what models he has available'.

For the remainder of this chapter we will try to justify our description of blocks as transitional objects.

RECORDING BLOCKPLAY

As part of our recording of the study, we have routinely made on-the-spot sketches of children's constructions. Individual adults devised their own style of symbolizing the different blocks and block forms. The children have taken enormous interest in this process and often advise and direct the adult. There is further discussion of the dialogue we had with children concerning two-dimensional symbolic representations of their structures in Chapters 3 and 8.

To become our advisers, they needed to be able to 'read' a sketch. This involved the recognition of a correspondence between the two-dimensional symbolic representation of a block or block form and its three-dimensional equivalent. As with spoken language, some negotiation is necessary for a two-dimensional symbol to be understood and accepted.

Sometimes, to help the adult, children described the temporal sequence of building. This involved them in mental reconstruction of the sequence and translation of this into speech. They checked the number of blocks represented on the sketch corresponded to those in the round. In other words, they translated meanings from the model to the drawing and they checked back from drawing to model.

It has been but a small step for many children to begin recording their structures for themselves. Even some of the 3-year-olds attempted it where recording of this kind was practised by adults. At this point we want to stress the voluntary nature of the children's translations of mathematical ideas from one mode to another.

From one Dimension to Another

The business of translating a three-dimensional structure to a two-dimensional drawing is a problem in its own right. As already noted in other chapters, this was something the children actively explored. Multiple transformations are needed when copying from a model in a different medium (Shapiro, 1978). The

Figure 6.1

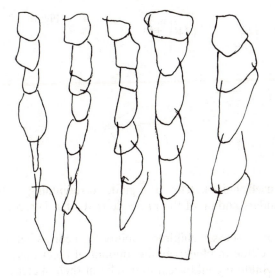

processes involved are to do with part–whole visual analysis of what is to be copied and strategies for constructing correspondences in the new medium (*ibid.* p. 157). The question of scale crops up regularly.

Patricia (5 y.) was struggling with the problem of getting her sketch onto the given page: 'I'll have to start again, I've done it too big.'

Marie (4 y.) was not yet at this stage. She had been watching the nursery nurse make a sketch of her structure and announced that she was going to make her own drawing. Independently, she hit on the idea of drawing with her pencil around blocks of equivalent proportions to those in her building. In using blocks as templates in this way, she was saying, in effect, 'Let the face of the block stand for the whole block'. Once she was launched on the process, she quickly realized that she would not be able to fit her drawing onto the A4-size paper she had started with. She changed to a large sheet of brushwork paper, which eventually needed several extensions. At this point in the development of her ideas about drawing her block structure, Marie was more concerned with getting the shape and numbers of blocks right than with considerations of scale. She also needed help in orientating the blocks she was using as templates to correspond with the orientation of the corresponding blocks in her building.

These actions may well encourage greater awareness of the different faces of a rectangular cuboid and the processes of translation.

Pictographs and Tallies

In many of their representations the children have made a pictographic record .in which an attempt is made to draw a likeness to what is there (Figure 8.2). Others have made a pictographic *tally*, which maintains the general outline of the structure while using a mark as token for a block (Figures 6.1 and 6.2).[4]

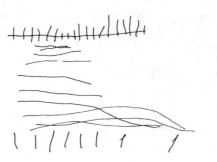

Figure 6.2

Some children have used their sketches as a guide to rebuilding on the following day, indicating understanding of the principle that what is recorded can be 'read'.

Hughes (1986, p. 58) discusses children's ability to record small numbers of objects, using tallies. Often in blockplay the amount of blocks used was far in excess of what most children could accurately tally in their sketches on a one-to-one basis, but in principle many did attempt to employ a tally system. In using tallies we can see a move towards a less embedded representation, in which numerosity and relative position take precedence over other features of the situation.

Photographs and Picture Books

The children are not only developing as producers of two-dimensional translations of their three-dimensional work: we also shared images with them in many forms. Photographic transparencies of their block structures were shown to them through a small hand-held viewer as well as on a screen through a slide projector. In this way, two-dimensional images of their three-dimensional structures can be shown scaled up or down in size, from life size to miniscule.

We also viewed video-recordings of blockplay alongside the children. This and the use of colour slides and photographs were found to be most effective in stimulating lively discussion, both between children and between adults and children.

Two-dimensional silhouettes of blocks were pasted onto shelves in some groups to serve as a guide to storage. Children soon learnt to understand the solid forms to which they referred. An illustrated vocabulary of blocks was produced as an aid to identification and to help children to think about the blocks they might need when planning a particular structure. Picture-story books and information books about buildings, structures, processes, shape and form also became part of our evolving blockplay tradition.

Cross-cultural images abound in books on architecture and even the 3-year-olds, with some interest in blockplay, have been intrigued by the multitude of shapes and patterns to be found in pictured buildings. Some books have become particular favourites, with children referring to them before and during blockplay as well as at other times. In these instances, children are discovering relationships between pictures and blocks.

Distancing and Decentering

We found that video-recordings, photographs, transparencies and illustrated books can be considered, along with spoken language, as means of enabling children to distance themselves from their actions so as to engage in the reflective thinking that is essential for abstraction and the elaboration of existing ideas. This kind of representation lends itself particularly well to small-group discussion in which children can put forward their comments and perhaps hear confirmation of their ideas from other children. Alternatively they may hear views that run contrary to their own, which may enable them to modify their ideas. Considering ideas from different viewpoints, or 'decentering' (Donaldson, 1978, p. 17), is an important mechanism in the development and elaboration of ideas (see Chapter 7).

The selecting, which is an inevitable part of creating a two-dimensional representation, may help the children focus on particular elements in the situation.

CONVENTIONAL SYMBOLS AND SIGNS

We have already noted that conventional signs, such as written numerals, are the most disembedded way of representing mathematical ideas. Consequently they are also the most likely aspect of mathematics to cause shock to the learner. How might this be avoided? Caveta, whom we observed earlier, was being enabled to discover something about written numbers as an extension of her own work by observing the adult's use of numbers in labelling her sketch. Could we create situations where this can happen more often?

Our collaboration with the children during the study has brought home to us the potency of the adult in education. As an example we look again at the adult practice of recording block structures. The children wanted to know everything about this process, including our use of numbers and symbols to stand for blocks. Figure 6.3 shows how one child (5 y. 4 m.) adapted the adult's system for her own use.

This links with what is known about early literacy. It may also be that if children see adults using the written signs and symbols of formal mathematics as an everyday event and can see this as both purposeful and rewarding, they will take a positive and active interest in becoming fluent speakers and writers of mathematics.

The burgeoning of formal symbolic representation occurs after children have left their nursery and reception classes. We would not therefore expect to see much evidence of this occurring in relation to early blockplay. We believe there is scope for such development in later years and this has been an

Figure 6.3

important consideration for some members of the group who now offer blocks across the primary age-range.

Drafting

Banta (1980) describes her experiences of providing blocks for children from 3 to 9 years of age. On the basis of observation, she divides blockplay into eight stages. These follow the general lines of development described in Chapter 4 but go further to include older children. From 6 to 9 years, children fall into her eighth or *drafting* stage of blockplay. This occurs when, often in collaboration, children plan their work on paper before they start. This would seem an ideal opportunity for making use of signs and symbols. Of the drafting stage, Banta (*ibid.* p. 17) says: 'This is a powerful argument for leaving blocks in the classroom long past kindergarten. Who knows what possibilities there are for further learning if these activities are available over longer periods of time under teachers who are understanding and who study how children progress developmentally.'

SUMMARY AND CONCLUSIONS

We have considered the role of spoken language in relation to the development and representation of mathematical ideas. This led into a discussion of the need for continuity and progression in mathematics education. It was suggested that meanings and processes have to be constructed through partnership between adults and children. Links are forged enabling children to understand and make use of the relationships between mathematics embedded in practical situations and that represented in the disembedded symbolism of formal mathematics.

The children have taught us that they will use both embedded and disembedded representations as appropriate to their present purposes in situations when it makes sense to them. Children have found their own important reasons to describe, draw and tally as part of their blockplay.

Further research is needed to discover whether the more disembedded representations can be developed through the drafting of building plans and whether this could even be regarded as a precursor to such activities as computer programming.

Blocks are, we suggested, transitional material, allowing for ideas to develop in complexity and for the assimilation of new ideas. As part of the landscape of early childhood, they can help bridge the gap between the known and the unknown, the embedded and the disembedded. In writing about mathematics education, Wood (1988, p. 207) suggests that 'a well constructed ideal curriculum would, of course, offer a common base of mathematical experiences, which if genuinely shared by teachers and pupils would provide a common point of reference and a source of analogies'.

The disembedding process should, in theory, support the development of generalization. We need to keep this under review in our record-keeping from the point of view of planning the curriculum, of evaluating it and of assessing the children's educational needs.

In putting spoken language into sharp focus in the present chapter, we are aware of an apparent contradiction to some of the ideas put forward in Chapters 2 and 3, which focused on nonverbal aspects of blockplay. The two are not mutually exclusive and can be reconciled if we think of spoken language as a tool of blockplay that works through the formal art/mathematical elements of the situation. By enabling children to reflect on these, language assists *in the development of blockplay*.

NOTES

1. Wood (1988, pp. 193, 197) examines the case for one-to-one interviewing and dialogue in mathematics teaching and learning.
2. See Hughes and Rogers (1979) and Mortimore *et al.* (1988, p. 192). These sources indicate that practical experience as well as age makes a difference in children's understanding of volume.

3. Hughes was studying number, not blockplay, although 'bricks' were used in his experiments.

4. The terms 'pictograph' and 'pictographic tally' are taken from Hughes (1986, pp. 57–8).

7

CHILDREN BEING SCIENTIFIC AND SOLVING PROBLEMS
Froebel Blockplay Research Group

INTRODUCTION

In Chapter 4 the process of *differentiation* was described and discussed as the means by which children acquire an increasingly detailed knowledge of the material. In Chapter 5 we elaborated on this by differentiating between the two kinds of knowledge that can be gained by exploring and playing with blocks. Using Piagetian terminology, these were defined as *physical* knowledge (which relates to the physical properties of the blocks) and *logico-mathematical* knowledge (which goes beyond the physical to consider pattern and relationships *between* blocks).

The present chapter begins by focusing on the actual *processes* of exploration and experimentation that lead to learning about the material and considers some of the mechanisms that move the process along.

In terms of curriculum content, the examples in the first part of the chapter indicate the difficulty in separating physical from logico-mathematical ideas when we look at them in the holistic context of blockplay. Something of the same problem occurred when we looked at children being mathematical. The two forms of knowledge are in continuous interaction. Despite this, we have attempted in this chapter to identify some of the scientific/physical-knowledge content engaging the children's minds in the examples offered.

In the second part of the chapter we look at the way in which knowledge of the material is brought together with other knowledge and competences in solving problems to do with the many aspects of blockplay. These include not only such questions as 'What shall I build and how shall I build it?' but also those to do with the physical and social setting of blockplay.

Finally, the role of the adult and of language in problem-solving are discussed.

Figure 7.2

Figure 7.1   Figure 7.3

BEING SCIENTIFIC

In our study of blockplay, as mentioned in Chapter 4, a great deal of time was spent by the under-6s in constructive but non-constructional uses of blocks. They observed the effects of their actions and conducted open-ended experiments to check their ideas. Even when they are engaged in creating a figurative representation, children often pause to examine an aspect of their work, as if to say, 'Hello, how did that happen?' They may take time out from pursuing their main purpose to explore the unexpected, as James (4 y.) did when he spotted the stair-like formation unintentionally created at the corner of his 'block of flats'. After much experimenting he produced a second, similar structure (Figure 7.1). Another child, who had been observing, commented that the opposite end looked like 'upside-down stairs'. Everyone present was pleased with that and there was much inverting of heads to check.

A great deal of involved watching of others building, as on this occasion, was also recorded. In fact, the amount surprised us, largely because we had never before considered young children as scientific childwatchers and blockwatchers and here they were doing it as co-equals with adults!

Children need to know about blocks in order to have command of them and so be able to use them at will to fulfil a variety of functions. The interesting fact is that they go well beyond this instrumental view of materials mastery in their investigation of the blocks and a wide range of mathematical and scientific

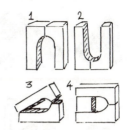

Figure 7.4   Figure 7.5

ideas. They observe, question, toss ideas around and test some of them out (Figures 4.14, 7.2 and 7.3).

Children find exploration and investigation intrinsically rewarding and bring to it an approach that is self-motivated, playful, open-ended, creative, innovative and risk-taking. The driving forces seems to be 'what if . . .' and 'I wonder'.

Limited Adult View

The importance of allowing children to share the initiative with adults about what is to be learnt and how, and sometimes to lead the way in this, comes across in the following examples, which demonstrated to us the limited and therefore limiting view of the material we adults bring to the situation.

A child (4 y. 7 m.) is experimenting with balance, using a unit block and a chair. The unit block acts as the lever. He places it on the seat and manipulates it through the gap between the backrest and the seat, so that it projects further and further into empty space over the back edge of the seat. When it begins to teeter he stops, checks that it won't fall, and fetches a half unit that he places on the end of the lever still resting on the seat, to act as a counter-balance. A second half unit is then carefully placed on the free end. There is a thrilling moment as the lever dips, ever so slightly. A second unit is now lowered onto the two half units, so that chair and balance arrangement are now structurally linked. Another chair is placed just less than a unit's width away and the experiment is replicated. As a final touch, he links the two chairs to each other with unit blocks, effectively knitting chairs and blocks into one complex whole (Figure 7.4).

Varying the Orientation

A child (3 y. 7 m.) experimentally manipulates two 'L' blocks and observes the effect of placing them in different positions (Figure 7.5).

Another child (4 y. 4 m.) starts with a 'T' block she carefully tips to one side. She finds to her delight that it will stand in this position. The move is repeated with a second 'T' block, perhaps to check that the first time wasn't a freak

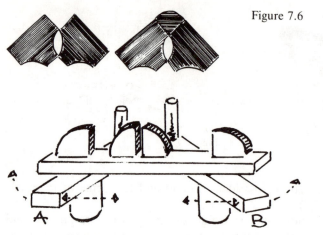

Figure 7.6

Figure 7.7

occurrence. She studies the two blocks, then takes the second and rearranges it so that it forms a reflection of the first, with inside corners touching. After a few seconds spent observing the two blocks, she adds a quarter circle, to make an entirely new geometric form (Figure 7.6).

As children perform spatial transformations with the blocks, they not only create aesthetically pleasing arrangements but are also engaging in experience that will contribute to their developing ability to recognize the same thing from different angles, and also to visualize the effect of moving something along (translation) or through different angles (reflection and rotation) without *actually* having to move anything. (There are several more examples in Chapters 3 and 5.)

Competence of this kind has obvious advantages in some problem-solving situations: arranging a room, planning a painting, packing a suitcase, reading a map in reverse, designing a bicycle spanner, or an engine to fit the engine space of a car.

Variable Geometry

Someone (4 y.) discovered (Figure 7.7) that they could vary the geometry of a construction by gently rotating blocks A and B either away from each other, towards each other, or parallel to the left, right or centre. Everyday objects that employ variable geometry include deck-chairs, folding beds, swing-wing aeroplanes, gate-leg tables, collapsible music stands and lock-gates.

Stunt-Building

Stunt-building, illustrated and discussed in earlier chapters, is an entirely useless activity in functional building terms. The knitting together of blocks and chairs is a prime example. When constructing a house or a road system to

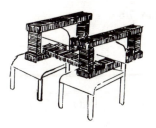

Figure 7.4

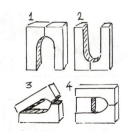

Figure 7.5

ideas. They observe, question, toss ideas around and test some of them out (Figures 4.14, 7.2 and 7.3).

Children find exploration and investigation intrinsically rewarding and bring to it an approach that is self-motivated, playful, open-ended, creative, innovative and risk-taking. The driving forces seems to be 'what if . . .' and 'I wonder'.

Limited Adult View

The importance of allowing children to share the initiative with adults about what is to be learnt and how, and sometimes to lead the way in this, comes across in the following examples, which demonstrated to us the limited and therefore limiting view of the material we adults bring to the situation.

A child (4 y. 7 m.) is experimenting with balance, using a unit block and a chair. The unit block acts as the lever. He places it on the seat and manipulates it through the gap between the backrest and the seat, so that it projects further and further into empty space over the back edge of the seat. When it begins to teeter he stops, checks that it won't fall, and fetches a half unit that he places on the end of the lever still resting on the seat, to act as a counter-balance. A second half unit is then carefully placed on the free end. There is a thrilling moment as the lever dips, ever so slightly. A second unit is now lowered onto the two half units, so that chair and balance arrangement are now structurally linked. Another chair is placed just less than a unit's width away and the experiment is replicated. As a final touch, he links the two chairs to each other with unit blocks, effectively knitting chairs and blocks into one complex whole (Figure 7.4).

Varying the Orientation

A child (3 y. 7 m.) experimentally manipulates two 'L' blocks and observes the effect of placing them in different positions (Figure 7.5).

Another child (4 y. 4 m.) starts with a 'T' block she carefully tips to one side. She finds to her delight that it will stand in this position. The move is repeated with a second 'T' block, perhaps to check that the first time wasn't a freak

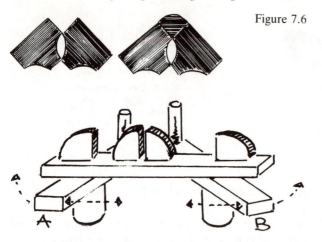

Figure 7.6

Figure 7.7

occurrence. She studies the two blocks, then takes the second and rearranges it so that it forms a reflection of the first, with inside corners touching. After a few seconds spent observing the two blocks, she adds a quarter circle, to make an entirely new geometric form (Figure 7.6).

As children perform spatial transformations with the blocks, they not only create aesthetically pleasing arrangements but are also engaging in experience that will contribute to their developing ability to recognize the same thing from different angles, and also to visualize the effect of moving something along (translation) or through different angles (reflection and rotation) without *actually* having to move anything. (There are several more examples in Chapters 3 and 5.)

Competence of this kind has obvious advantages in some problem-solving situations: arranging a room, planning a painting, packing a suitcase, reading a map in reverse, designing a bicycle spanner, or an engine to fit the engine space of a car.

Variable Geometry

Someone (4 y.) discovered (Figure 7.7) that they could vary the geometry of a construction by gently rotating blocks A and B either away from each other, towards each other, or parallel to the left, right or centre. Everyday objects that employ variable geometry include deck-chairs, folding beds, swing-wing aeroplanes, gate-leg tables, collapsible music stands and lock-gates.

Stunt-Building

Stunt-building, illustrated and discussed in earlier chapters, is an entirely useless activity in functional building terms. The knitting together of blocks and chairs is a prime example. When constructing a house or a road system to

Figure 7.8

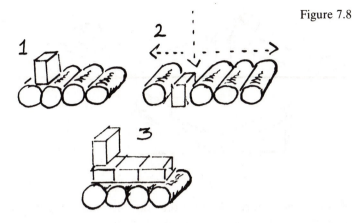

serve the purposes of a game, children do not want to put their plans at risk for a moment. However, in stunt-building risk is central. Through risk-taking they discover the limits of the material and extend their understandings. Stunt-building falls into the category of behaviour Tina Bruce refers to as 'wallowing' in a situation. It results in a greater range of knowledge and strategies that can be applied to solving problems at higher levels of structural complexity within the context of blockplay and possibly beyond.

OWNERSHIP OF IDEAS

As well as observing and experimenting, the children also spent a great deal of time *volunteering* comments, descriptions and explanations of their activity. In this they indicated both a sense of autonomy as learners and of ownership of their experiences and discoveries. One way to safeguard these is to keep blockplay itself open ended. The development of understanding of scientific ideas, methodology and the attributes of the scientific mind could be put at risk if we ignore children's own interests, methodologies and theories.

Our own role could be characterized as one of 'wait and see' (Milloy, 1987, p. 15), in which the adult tries to help children to capitalize on ideas as they emerge. It is doubtful in any case whether we could succeed in interesting children in gratuitously introduced curriculum content such as conservation of energy, transfer of potential to kinetic energy and the resolution of forces (Figure 7.8) that the children were experiencing at an intuitive level as they tried to work out how to make a lorry with blocks.

WONDERING

Eisner (1982, p. 51) describes the process of working with materials as partly 'heuristic', i.e. one of discovery. Smith (1978, p. 21) suggests that in learning

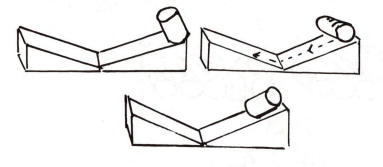

Figure 7.9

concepts of materials, children do what they do, the material does what it does and the children accommodate to the consequences.

In this section we consider the question of what it is that causes an individual's thinking to shift from what 'is' to questions such as 'I wonder *why* that is?' and 'I wonder whether it *always* is?' (Figure 7.9).

Nathan Isaacs (1930) suggests that when *children* ask themselves or someone else 'Why?' such and such is so, this represents a more significant learning situation than if the adult had addressed the same question to the child. The adult asks the question on the assumption the child will see the point of it. The child may, as yet, see nothing odd or contradictory about the situation and is puzzled by the questioning. Until something makes them stop and think, things are what they are and they do what they do.

In the sort of open-ended exploration and experimentation we have been looking at, the process is often driven along by continuous visual feedback. Sometimes a particular move works. When it doesn't, there is often no attempt to find out why but instead something else is tried. However, there are occasions when children can be seen to stop in their tracks and start to think about something in a way that enables them to update their theories.

Children's Theories 1: Blocks Change their Shape

A child (5 y. 3 m.) takes two wedges from the storage tray en bloc *(Figure 7.10(a)). He splits the pair and places them back to back on the floor and registers surprise that, instead of meeting back to back to form a tent shape, they meet at the bottom edge then go off at an angle from each other leaving a V-shaped gap between them (Figure 7.10(b)).*

This is a common problem with wedges (Figure 7.11) and is often treated as if it cannot be helped.

The child who is for the first time thinking about it tries putting them together again to form a cuboid, as he found them, and finds they don't go together any more in quite the same way (Figure 7.10(c)). 'They're magic,' he says. This is where hypothesis testing often starts in the early years. A great deal of exploratory manipulation follows. 'Turn them round,' he is advised by someone.

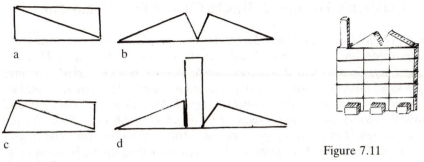

c   d

Figure 7.11

Figure 7.10

'That's what I am doing,' he replies and he is, non-stop. 'Here, let me show you.' His adviser takes over – and gets it wrong! Soon everyone is fiddling about with narrow wedges. For some it's 'easy-peasy', others are not so sure.

Occasionally the blocks fall into the desired alignment by chance. That doesn't stop our researcher. He wants to understand so that he can get it right every time. He is no longer interested in the construction he started, having become totally absorbed in solving this particular problem.

On this occasion he doesn't tease out the source of his difficulty and it is obvious from his remarks that he is not entirely convinced that the blocks don't change their shape. This would be consistent with his general attitude to blocks, which is one of caution, if not suspicion. He still seems to regard them as having a life of their own, and only half trusts them to stay put when he has arranged them. He usually takes the precaution of 'screwing' or tapping them into place with an imaginary screwdriver or hammer made from an 'L' block, which never actually strikes the block, but is more a symbol of defiance.

Blocks are excellent material for setting off the sort of inquiry we have just been following. Each block has several faces, edges and corners that remain in the same *spatial relationship* to each other despite successive *spatial transformations* of the whole block, such as we saw at the beginning of this chapter as children experimented in reorientating particular blocks. A block may be rotated from top to bottom, right to left, front to back or the reverse of these.

The result of such spatial transformations can be either to create or reduce compatibility between two identical blocks. When children *inadvertently* rotate blocks, as in the case of the wedges, before placing them together, their expectations are often contradicted.

They may explain the contradiction to themselves as a *physical* change in the blocks, about which they can do nothing. Alternatively, it may occur to them to check out the possibility that the change is reversible. Through their experiments, children learn what are the constants and what can be changed.

The blocks that appear to have a particular capacity to tease are the eliptical and circular curves, the wedges and the 'L' block. This may be something to do with the fact that they are parts of dissected wholes children have an intuitive urge to reunite.

Children's Theories 2: Blocks Change their Behaviour

A group of children have taken the blocks into the playground and chosen the worst possible site on which to build – a sharply inclined surface. They are extremely surprised to find themselves unable to stack blocks, a skill they have had for some time. 'Stay up!' someone is heard to shout. 'Are these our blocks?' asks another. 'They might be Froebel's.' 'Yes, I think they are.' They ask and are told the blocks are the usual ones. 'I know what it is. It's this floor. It's not smooth enough. I'm going to get a board.' They all follow suit. The boards appear to make very little difference. 'We need something to make them stick, like Sellotape or something.' 'Cement would be best.' 'No, then you can't use them again.' 'All right, then, screw them together, then take out the screws at packing-up time.'

Drawing on the work of a group of Piagetian researchers working in Geneva in the late 1970s, Duckworth (1979, p. 308) describes a theory that suggests that, when faced with a problem, children's behaviour alternates between 'trying to achieve a certain result and trying to understand the situation'. The examples of the wedge blocks and the blocks that wouldn't balance seem to bear this out.

These researchers suggest that there are 'three lines of access' that determine how an individual approaches a *particular* problem and arrives at understandings in relation to it. These lines of access are to do with the following:

1. *Perception* The way things *look* at the moment, compared to what they can be recalled looking like at other times (e.g. being able to visualize wedges back to back).
2. *Action* As we act we are reminded of earlier actions (e.g. twisting and turning things to get them the right way round).
3. *Conceptual* The ideas, words, formulae we already have may provide a way in (e.g. 'straight up', 'back to back' and 'a bit like a square').

In problem-solving these three lines of access interact to help bring about understandings (*ibid.*).

THE ROLE OF THE ADULT

One of the problems with the 'wondering' approach to science is that, as educators, we can never be entirely certain what ideas will crop up and when. Sometimes this means our immediate contribution falls short of what is needed to help children move forward. When considering how to help children organize their inquiries, we need to know which directions are likely to lead to enlightenment and which are likely to lead them into dead-ends, or even astray.

From experience, it seems a good strategy to start with, to hold back, observe and listen. In this way, we can often learn what we need to know in order to tune in more accurately to the ideas and theories the children are exploring. We also give ourselves thinking time in which to plan and time a response.

Sometimes children need help in structuring their inquiry. The number of variables to be checked and eliminated in the playground building episode, in order to arrive at the cause of the problem, was more than could be handled by the children without help. In the case of the wedges, the problem was compounded by the child's difficulty in telling the two wedge blocks apart. He couldn't remember from one manipulation to the next which block he had just fiddled with. It was also difficult to see whether one or both needed to be adjusted, when guided only by eye. Talk of angles would, in the circumstance, have been unhelpful, since the illusive angle also happened to be a 'right' angle. There was a possibility, on this occasion, of leaving an impression that all other angles are 'wrong'. At the time the adult had no suggestions to offer that would help advance the child's thinking. However, after reflecting on it, she was able to share an idea with him on a subsequent occasion. This was to introduce a perpendicular in the shape of a quarter unit, on end, as a reference point, against which each wedge in turn could be manipulated until the desired position was reached. The final move was to slip out the quarter unit perpendicular and slide the wedges together (Figure 7.10(d)).

This strategy offered by the adult was, on this occasion, aimed less at illuminating the abstract principle and more at helping the child to move to a position of control. An important aspect of the teaching–learning situation is the need for adults to try to identify with the problem from the individual learner's point of view, in order to negotiate a way forward.

There is no risk of curbing children's initiative as learners if we are aware of what they already know and where they are trying to get to with it. We know that the child with the wedges had begun to think about them in new ways (Duckworth, 1979, p. 304). He indicated by his behaviour and comments where he was in understanding the situation and where he wanted to be but couldn't quite get to. With adult help and contributions from his peers, he was enabled to move onto a slightly more mature level of understanding. Vygotsky (1978, p. 87) has identified two levels of learning: (1) the level of *actual* development; and (2) the level of *potential* development.

The level of *actual* development is what the child *can do* already. The level of *potential* development is what the child can *nearly* do but needs help with. It eventually becomes the *actual* level of development when the child can do it alone. There is further discussion of these two levels of learning and the implications for the adult role when we take a closer look at aspects of problem-solving later in the chapter.

CONTENT

In discussing the importance of content, Duckworth (1972) suggests that new ideas and questions occur to those who already have a fund of ideas at their disposal. Intelligence develops, she argues, as existing ideas are extended and co-ordinated into more complex wholes. Athey (1990, p. 203) stresses the importance of first-hand experience in providing the 'content, or "stuff" of thought'. Forms of thought, i.e. schemas, are fed by experience.

From long-term observation it is possible to forecast some of the scientific or 'physical knowledge' content likely to be a regular, spontaneous focus in blockplay for individuals or groups of children. We have seen children studying the properties of the material, balance, levers, the effects of movement, inclined planes, static and dynamic forces, cause and effect relations, structures and systems. Some examples of the way in which these ideas were spontaneously explored and represented by the children were offered earlier in the chapter. This 'pool of probabilities' (Milloy, 1987, p. 15) suggests an agenda on which to base our reading for our own professional development so that we are equipped to help children conduct their inquiries as these occur during the course of children's blockplay.

The scientific and other ideas that emerge in the course of spontaneous play can sometimes be followed up away from the block area to be developed as topics in their own right. This seems a logical and reasonable extension, so long as the 'disembedding' (Donaldson, 1978, pp. 93–4) of the idea from its original blockplay setting doesn't strip it of all meaning for the children. When contexts are linked through joint action and dialogue, there may be a greater chance of transferable skills and understandings being developed.

We have seen children on numerous occasions transferring ideas from one area to another and developing them further. In one group, some children built a den from blocks in the garden. In the process they disturbed an ants' nest and attempted to build 'cages' from blocks to contain the escaping ants. The non-deterrent effect on the ants caused the children to stop and watch how the ants tackled an obstacle such as a block. Soon, instead of cages, there was an assault course for ants, consisting of wedges, bridges and walls. The children tracked ants as they crawled over, under, around and between cracks.

'What about a cylinder?' suggested the adult. Before adding the cylinder, there was some speculation about what the ants would do when they found the cylinder in the way. In this the children were reflecting on both their knowledge of blocks and their observations of ant behaviour so far. When the adult recalled that, as a little girl, her mother had thrown the biscuits away because ants had managed to crawl into the biscuit tin even with the lid on, there was discussion of the kind of structure that would be needed to stop ants from getting in or out.

By being helped to co-ordinate the three lines of access outlined earlier (perception, action and ideas) from *both* areas of experience, the children increased the range and complexity of their learning.

Because of what is basically a 'developmental approach' to the curriculum,[1] we did not gratuitously 'introduce' content to the block area and would advise against the adoption of an instrumental view of blockplay, i.e. using blocks as a service area for content-based teaching, particularly of science and maths. The

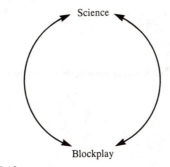

Figure 7.12

content children assimilate to their blockplay interacts with structuring problems and structuring problems interact with content as the above examples demonstrate. The two serve each other in what Kamii and De Vries (1977, p. 387) refer to as a 'relationship of circular causality'. This is explained as one in which A, e.g. science, contributes to the development of B, e.g. blockplay, and B in turn contributes to the development of 'A' and so on (Figure 7.12).

SOLVING PROBLEMS

Exploration and experimentation overlap a great deal with problem-solving in blockplay. The theoretical distinction between the two kinds of action is that one is open-ended inquiry conducted for its own sake while the other is goal directed. However, as we have seen, during the course of experimental investigation, problems arise and may take over as the focus, while problem-solving itself often involves investigation.

Exploration and Problem-Solving

Sutton-Smith (1975, p. 198) expresses the view that it is the very 'uselessness' of play, such as the exploratory manipulation of blocks and stunt-building, that gives it value. He argues that the effect of not having to produce a useful result, because there are no external pressures to do so, is to free the individual to act creatively and to be innovative. The more variety individuals can get into their acts, the more strategies they can call on when behaviour has to be directed at solving particular problems. Viewed in this light, play can be seen as 'variability training' and, suggests Sutton-Smith, is of the utmost importance in those societies that demand adaptability from their members (*ibid.* p. 214).

There have been a number of experimental studies aimed at testing such arguments.[2] Taken together, the findings give no clear indications one way or the other. There is a strong suggestion that methodological problems have so far confused the issue. No one, so far as we know, has done any long-term, naturalistic investigation in this area.

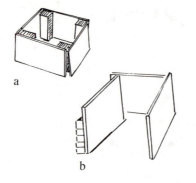

Figure 7.13

a

b

Our own study shows a direct link between exploratory activity with blocks, i.e. materials-mastery play, and the ability to use them with increasing fluency and *flair* in creating representations covering a wide range of content. This involves a great deal of problem-solving as children work out which aspects of the object or experience they want to represent can be done with blocks, and how.

In this sense, the exploratory handling of blocks can be described as variability training, within the blockplay context. It may be that more generalized effects can be claimed for mixed-media play. Or perhaps it can be argued that the greater the facility with blocks, or any other representational medium, the more powerful they become as material to think with. The representations that can be made with blocks enable the child to reflect on events and experiences.

It is probable that any general links that may exist between exploration, play and problem-solving are more complex and indirect than is implied by experimental research aimed at establishing direct causal connections over a very brief period.

An interesting line of inquiry would be to follow up children who seem to have a flair for setting and solving problems. Insights may be gained relating to other characteristics of these individuals: How did they get that way? Do they have things in common? Does this special competence persist? What becomes of them as they go through the formal education system and out the other end?

CLASSIC CONSTRUCTIONAL PROBLEMS

There are a number of challenges that regularly seem to crop up in blockplay.

Instant Walls

Some children discover that building boards can be a substitute for blocks in creating walls and high-sided enclosures and experiment with different ways of supporting these. During the course of their investigations they discover that a prefabricated wall is not necessarily a short cut!

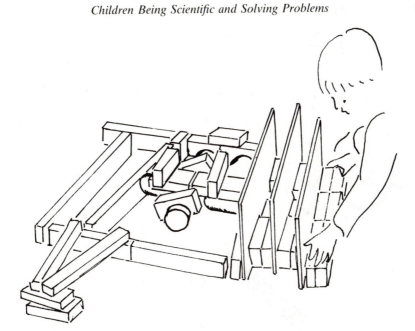

Figure 7.14

Figure 7.15

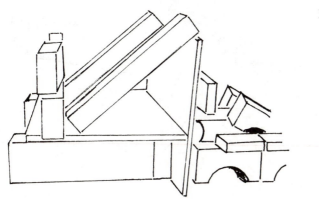

Roslynne (3 y. 9 m.) used supports at the corners (Figure 7.13(a)) but found this very vulnerable to sudden movement and another child, who found a board was not self-supporting, built a wall of blocks for it to lean on, making it extra stable (Figure 7.13 (b)).

Edmund (6 y.) produced a complete portfolio of ideas on one occasion. One of his less satisfactory solutions – his own evaluation – involved the buttressing of buttresses (Figures 7.14 and 7.15). This led to further thought culminating in the invention of the flying buttress, an effective and economical design we have since seen in other groups.

Figure 7.16

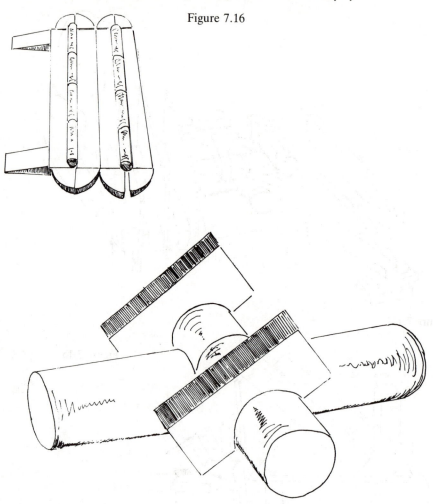

Figure 7.17

Cylinders

Various ways were found to stop cylinders from rolling out of control including a prototypical wheel clamp (Figures 7.8, 7.16 and 7.17).

Tied Spaces

Many individuals have initial problems in working out the optimum sequence of moves in joining two blocks across an empty space with a third, to create what is in effect a tied space, i.e. bridge or vertical enclosure. There are several moves involved that, to the novice, appear to cancel each other out. A col-

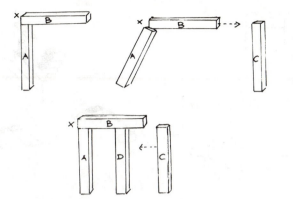

Figure 7.18

league likens this to the dilemma facing children on the playground slide where two contradictory ideas have to be reconciled: one to hold on tightly so as not to fall, the other to let go.

When Daniel (4 y., Figure 7.18) starts constructing a vertical enclosure by forming a right angle with blocks A and B at point X, he realizes he will have to let go of B and that his arrangement so far will collapse. He cannot advance while holding on to B or by letting it go. He changes strategy and starts with the two uprights A and C spaced well apart. Again an angle is formed at X but this time it doesn't reach across. He gives B a tug towards C. The result is disintegration at X.

A third attempt involves a half-way house strategy. Block D is introduced and placed between A and C. It supports B, which still doesn't reach across to C, but now he discovers he has a hand free to move C to where he wants it.

Sometimes children ask an adult to hold together the two blocks forming the first right angle while they fetch the third.

Many children discover the strategy of starting with a block on the floor as a spacer for positioning the two uprights. They have to remember whether the uprights go on the ends of the spacer block, or to either side of it (Figure 7.19(a,b)).

While a spacer solves one aspect of the bridging problem, it creates a problem for through traffic. Anita considers it, prompted by a remark from an adult (Figure 7.19(c,d)).

Stair-Building

Stair-building seems particularly puzzling and children come back to it repeatedly. One 6-year-old was overheard saying to another: 'Not stairs again! You know you can't do them.'

Here, again, there are aspects of the situation that sometimes appear to contradict each other.

Lance (3 y. 7 m.) has built a door above floor level and now wants to build

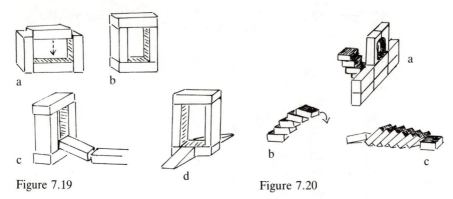

Figure 7.19

Figure 7.20

stairs to reach it. He places a block against the wall and finds he can't build another step the way he thinks it should go because the wall is in the way. So he builds the steps going the other way . . . which he knows isn't right either (Figure 7.20(a)).

Children's choice of corbelling, i.e. the strategy of placing each successive block so that it overhangs the previous one, for stair-building was striking in its near universality and persistence even with many 6-year-olds.[3]

Elaine (6 y.) practises stair-building using the corbelling technique and finds a flight of four blocks to be the limit after which the stair collapses (Figure 7.20(b)). The higher the rise, the greater the risk. An alternative strategy is tried (Figure 7.20(c)). While this arrangement cannot fall, it cannot rise either.

It is through the resolution of such apparent contradictions as children face in these and other situations that learning occurs.

CLASSROOMS AS ECOSYSTEMS

The study of *systems* is an area of science and technology that can be effectively and meaningfully dealt with in the early years by including the buildings and other spaces we inhabit. A classroom is an ecosystem of related and inter-related parts and dimensions. The parts are to do with physical aspects of the situation, such as materials, work surfaces, spaces and boundaries. The dimensions are concerned with social and strategic aspects, such as which activities make good neighbours. As ecosystems, classrooms offer meaningful contexts within which adults and children can consider and resolve many real-world problems.

Mini-Systems

Within the larger classroom system, there are mini-systems, or 'micro-environments' (Hutt *et al.*, 1988, p. 98), such as the block area, which also provide contexts for real-world problem-solving of a similar kind to those at the whole-classroom level. This aspect of blockplay is a core theme of Chapters 9 and 10.

A few examples of children solving practical problems relating to physical aspects of the block area are offered here as illustration: the longest blocks (the unit) are difficult to stand on end on carpeted surfaces. Investigation of alternatives leads some children to move to uncarpeted areas (which may in turn produce a problem by obstructing a traffic lane). Alternatively, they may create a smooth surface with boards or even build a block floor on top of the carpet. Children building towers often begin with a unit or half unit placed flat as a base to ensure evenness. When there was no room on the carpet for the drawer container in which play people were stored, someone had the idea of propping up the drawer, fully extended from its cabinet, with two unit blocks. This ensured that everyone could see to the back of the drawer and there was no danger of it crashing to the ground. Hollow blocks have been used to raise the height of the builder, when placing blocks onto tall structures. A hollow block stair was produced for the purpose on one occasion and chairs have undergone collective review between adults and children in terms of their safety as building platforms (Figure 10.5). Numerous strategies for carrying multiples of blocks were also devised.

These examples suggest that, given opportunity and encouragement, children are natural improvisers and should be taken seriously as our partners in the business of organizing for blockplay as well as in classrooms generally. It makes a great deal of sense in terms of *relevance* to nurture positively the wider view of problem-solving indicated here rather than that which focuses only on problems that arise in play, important though these are in stretching children's resourcefulness. In taking the wider view, it is possible to imagine the demise of the imported 'design brief' in technology teaching in the early years, as groups of adults and children become more aware of the part they can play *as insiders* in creating better classroom environments.[4]

THE PROBLEM-SOLVING PROCESS

When a child is committed to a definite objective, the steps to achieving it are systematic.[5] This includes elements of planning, making and monitoring, and evaluation. To emphasize the way in which these interact, the process can be represented diagrammatically (Figure 7.21).

Planning

With young children planning and action occur simultaneously, but gradually planning in advance of action begins to emerge, especially where adults model the process in their own problem-solving by doing this aloud and encouraging children actively to think ahead and to articulate their observations and ideas.

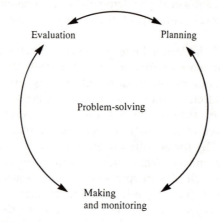

Figure 7.21

Monitoring

As they follow their plan through they need to continue to observe and to use feedback from their own actions and those of others in order to keep the plan on course. They need to be able to judge when a strategy is not working out and have others available they can try. This is where knowledge gained on other occasions, through their open-ended inquiry of the material and what it can be made to do, becomes important.

In self-monitoring, children often apply to themselves the kinds of remarks, cautions, hints, strategies and comments they have heard applied by others. They can often be heard muttering to themselves such things as 'Will this work?', 'Now what does this look like?', 'Let's have a look what blocks we've got for tables', 'Is this going to be too many? Don't want it to be collapsing up', 'I could leave this difficult bit while I sort the easy bits out first', 'Do I need walls? Not if I'm not going to give them any neighbours. That's all right then. They haven't got any neighbours.'

Private or 'egocentric' speech (Piaget, 1926) has many uses in early child-hood, one of which, according to Vygotsky (1978, pp. 25–6) is self-monitoring and self-guiding of the kind just described. Vygotsky and other researchers[6] offer evidence that private speech is not only a natural but a *necessary* accompaniment to problem-solving that, in later years, becomes inner speech. He sees speech and problem-solving as part of 'one and the same complex psychological function' (*ibid.* p. 25–6) *with speech increasing as the difficulty of the task increases.* This is often when there is no adult or other person around who might help. In this situation the child assumes two roles, that of the self and a guiding other. *Competence in engaging in dialogue with the self needs a social context in which to develop.* Children need to know what someone more

Figure 7.22

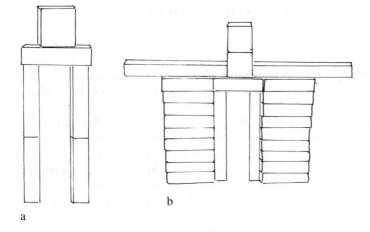

b

a

experienced would advise in the circumstances and for this they need opportunities to interact with more experienced partners. This aspect of problem-solving is developed later in the chapter.

Evaluation

Adults are often invited to contribute to this part of the process when they are asked to 'come and look'. It is important for children and adults to be able to take (and give) feedback that gets away from bland statements of approval. If we manage to pitch it right by using our knowledge of individuals, further planning, action, monitoring and adjusting may occur.

This happened when Clare (4 y. 3 m.) pronounced her 'man' to be finished (Figure 7.22(a)). 'How will he eat his dinner?' asked the teacher. Clare considered this and eventually came up with an idea she tried out (Figure 7.22(b)).

Nitin (4 y.) announced he had made a car park. The teacher thought it rather a token affair and tackled this by asking if she might drive her car in as she wanted to do a bit of shopping. The response was electrifying. Entrances and exits were created, with a barrier 'Where you put money in for a ticket to park'. The exit had reverse ramps to stop cars escaping without paying for a ticket.

Real-world considerations are a powerful evaluative tool for the child in blockplay. They seem to have the effect of allowing children to stand back and to stretch their thinking and planning skills.

Children often evaluate their own structures when these are used in imaginative play, in combination with other items such as farm animals, cars, play people, etc. In such a context flaws in their design and construction become apparent and lead to some rethinking and rebuilding.

Self-evaluation, questions posed by the adult and by other children enabled individuals, partners and groups to think about what they were doing in new ways and eventually achieve success.

SOCIAL INTERACTION

The interpersonal aspects of the situation give rise to problems of a social kind: gaining adequate space and materials without infringing the rights of others; gaining the help of others when two hands are not enough; gaining access to a project under way; persuading someone to be a play partner; negotiating plans; or negotiating roles – architect or hod-carrier.

The problem-solving process is no different here from that which applies to the physical world. However, feedback from humans is not always immediate nor as predictable, and is often ambiguous (Block, 1984, p. 194).

If we value the concept of people working together to solve humanity's problems, it is particularly important for adults to be aware of how children are coping socially and to take steps to enable children to acquire social competence. Play partnering, described by Tina Bruce in Chapter 2 and discussed further in this section, is one way in which the adult can act as guide and social mediator. Children who are new to the situation may have a particular need to have positive strategies modelled for them and often need direct adult support to begin with.

In the block area, we regarded interaction between adults and children and children with each other as part of the whole. Partnership and co-operation between children develop as they come to recognize and appreciate each other's strengths and weaknesses. The actively observing non-builder as well as other builders often asks questions, offers comments and advice that, as we have seen, may cause the builder to stop and reflect.

Through social interaction children become aware of differing viewpoints and the value of considering alternative views. This applies particularly to the identification of problems and in problem-solving. Viewpoint has important *literal* meaning in blockplay and this must make it a particularly powerful context in which the cognitive process of decentering can be nourished. In blockplay, children and adults can *literally* check what something looks like from another's angle, by taking up that position. To decentre, the individual must be able to make internal representations of alternative viewpoints in order to evaluate and choose between them.

The interpersonal context of blockplay also seems positively to encourage some children to describe and explain spontaneously their activity to those around. Perhaps this helps them clarify their ideas. The effect on others is to provide openings for discussion and conversation.

Private Speech

In an earlier section, the important relationship between private speech and problem-solving was discussed. Interaction between adults and children is the source of private speech. From this we can perhaps appreciate the significance for subsequent development of sessions spent building *with* someone, where the activity is shared between a child and a more experienced partner.

Build with Me

Earlier we looked briefly at the *actual* and *potential* levels of learning described by Vygotsky (1978). This has given rise to an approach to the teaching–learning situation that casts the child in the role of 'apprentice' to a more experienced partner. Liz Waterland (1985) has explored this approach in her book, *Read with Me*, from which our present heading has been adapted. An important principle of this approach, applied to learning to read, is that children are offered the freedom to select what they want to read. The adult role is to *accept* what children *can do*; to *help* when they *nearly can*; and to *take over* when they *can't*. This, says Waterland, is how 'natural learning' takes place (*ibid.* p. 47).[8] There is continuous retuning of adult input to match the ever-changing levels of competence the child brings to the situation.

In blockplay children have the freedom to select what they want to build. As with reading, this freedom is somewhat hollow if it is not backed by the understanding that they will not be left to struggle alone with the bits they can nearly do and be forced to give up when they come to bits that they cannot do. Tina Bruce points out in Chapter 2 that this approach leaves them exactly where they are in their learning. Arguably they could be worse off because of the damage to their feelings of confidence and independence.

We offer an example of what was achieved by one child when the adult adopted the apprenticeship approach to problem-solving in the block area.

The children are examining a spider's web outdoors. Ricci (4y. 6m.) is captivated and he draws it. He then decides to make one with blocks using his drawing as a general guide. He has an excellent knowledge of blocks and his first steps involve negotiating for those he thinks he is going to need. His teacher records that she had to 'talk him through' construction of the concentric enclosures (Figure 7.23).

In tackling the radials, he runs out of the longest blocks: 'I need more big blocks.' The adult offers an idea: 'Could you make that length by joining some of the shorter ones?'

Given her knowledge of the child, his previous experience and her understanding of what he was trying to achieve in the medium, the adult was able to give the right degree of help at the right moment for him to succeed. She did it in a way that supported play 'without dominating it' and avoided 'damaging the process of self-regulation' (Bruce, 1987, p. 81).

This kind of adult–child partnership is important in providing an enabling model to draw on in private speech, to be used when the adult or other source of help is not available. This is another important mechanism in children's development that helps them to move from one level of learning to another.

Special Needs

We have discussed the implications of the interactive dimensions of development in problem-solving. Language has been seen to play a key role in this.

Figure 7.23

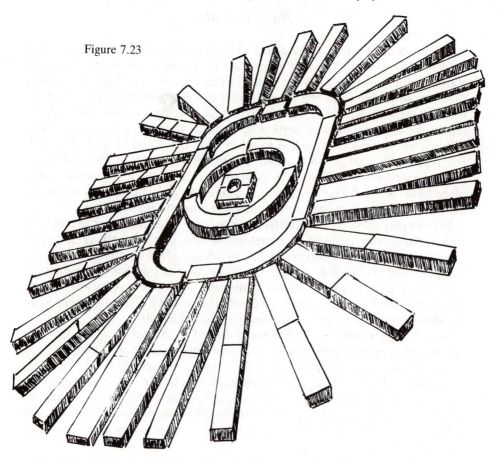

What does this mean for children with little or no speech and hearing? And what about the needs of children who are surrounded by others speaking an unfamiliar language?

Extra effort is needed to ensure that *all* children have the same opportunity to engage with more mature partners as well as independently, in speculating and reflecting on what was, what is and what might be.

According to Wood and Wood (1986, pp. 27–30), adult effectiveness in teaching–learning situations, regardless of any special conditions affecting the child, can be assessed in terms of the extent to which the adult retunes to the child as the interaction unfolds. Added to this there is the need to give 'postural, facial and other non-verbal cues' to help get messages across. This means allowing time for children to pay attention to the communicative aspects of the situation as well as to the job in hand. Perhaps we all need to question how well we would acquit ourselves in helping a deaf or bilingual child new to English to make a spider's web, if they wanted to.

Sharing Control

When adults try to retune the level of their contribution to the child's ever-changing levels of learning, control of interactions is shared between teacher and learner. Adult questioning, on the other hand, has the effect of reducing child initiative by controlling the discussion and determining what must be attended to. Wood and Wood (1983, p. 150) have demonstrated in several research studies that questioning is a marked feature of adult contributions when interacting with children.

According to these researchers, the level of our questioning is also often very basic and not of the sort that stretches children's thinking or enables them to make a contribution. Often our questions concern things children know we know the answers to. The more complex, speculating, reflecting, 'wondering' kinds of questions, which characterize our more thoughtful interactions, enable control to be shared on a more equitable basis. However, a particularly important finding of the Wood and Wood research (*ibid.*) was that if the overall level of questioning is high, even this type of question will fail to inspire.

There are important implications for early childhood educators, especially in relation to science, problem-solving and mathematics where, at first glance, questioning might seem an obvious way of guiding inquiry. In our study we can honestly say that we did not know the answers to many of the questions we asked the children, especially about how they managed to achieve particular arrangements with particular blocks. We were, in a sense, the novices and they the experts. However, we can't dodge the fact that we probably fit the description of over-use of questioning.

Instead of asking questions, Wood and Wood (*ibid.* p. 116) suggest we might try making a contribution. This is what Patricia (5 y.) did when she saw that a doorway had been superimposed onto a solid wall instead of being built into it: 'You'll bust your head on that door.' An adult might have asked, 'Are doors really like that?' Wood and Wood (*ibid.*) found that children responded to adult's own attempts to reason and speculate in their presence. The idea seems to be to invite comment and further speculation. By this means, they say, we may be able to use talk to encourage children's thinking and reasoning and avoid the deadening effect of questioning.

SUMMARY AND CONCLUSIONS

In this chapter we have presented a view of children initiating their own research into matters that interest and puzzle them. We have seen them apply their learning in attempts to solve problems they have encountered as they have gone about their affairs, or have deliberately set themselves. There are many parallels between the ideas discussed in this chapter and Tina Bruce's description of the processes involved in our own adult research into blockplay.

Everything that has been said about children in this chapter applies equally to the conduct of our own inquiries.

In both there are elements of 'wait and see', curiosity, uncertainty and risk-taking, which are based on previous learning. It is no coincidence that there is this degree of internal consistency in the relationship between the processes of research as practised by adults and that of the children they teach. They are based on the common philosophies and principles of early childhood education Tina Bruce outlines in the Introduction.[9]

As in our attempts to rationalize our thinking about mathematics and block-play, we have been at pains in this chapter to discuss science and problem-solving only in the meaningful context of blockplay. At this stage in the discussion it is legitimate to ask what, in broad terms, we have in mind when we provide for children to develop their scientific and problem-solving dispositions. By what criteria might we assess development in these respects as they relate to blockplay – and do they have wider implications?

From our records we drew several dimensions that seemed to us to have both 'educational' and human value – perhaps they are the same thing? To conclude the chapter we offer them here:

- The competence of individuals as observers, reflected in their capacity to act with increasing deliberateness and reflective awareness of the effects being created and of themselves as agents in this.
- Open-minded curiosity, characterized by both verbal questioning and active inquiry, imagination, originality and flexibility.
- The capacity for independence of thought and action allied to an awareness of relatedness to others; willingness to co-operate with others, to be comfortable both as follower and leader.
- A healthy pride in achievement, allied to a willingness to engage in constructive self-appraisal and to accept the constructive appraisal of others; to have the confidence and understandings to take calculated risks.
- A willingness to engage in the constructive appraisal of the achievements of others.
- Competence in distancing, decentering and negotiating.
- Competence in describing, interpreting and recording experience and ideas.
- Competence in problem-solving, indicated by evidence of ideas being carried through, using feedback to maintain a plan on course and awareness of when something is or isn't working or when a change of strategy is needed.
- Awareness of and increasing competence in the use of reference material.
- An increase in range and differentiation of the content assimilated to blockplay, for example, mathematics, science, art, geography, history, ecology and sociology.

These are dimensions that could be assessed across the curriculum and not simply confined to blockplay or to children. In applying them generally, we can judge the extent to which competencies and understandings are becoming generalized. According to whether they are or not, we may need also to evaluate our provision and in particular the character of our interactions.

NOTES

1. See Blenkin and Kelly (1987); Bruce (1987).

2. Smith and Simon (1984) offer a comprehensive review of experimental problem-solving studies that have attempted to establish whether there are links between play with objects, creativity and problem-solving. Hughes (1981), in a similar experiment to those described by Smith and Simon (1984), concluded that different kinds of play with different kinds of materials may affect development in different ways.

3. Johnson (1933, p. 147) comments on the difficulty children below the age of 5 have in making a solid stair from a row of gradually decreasing, or increasing, stacks; Shotwell (1979) reports that, although 3-year-olds were able to build a stair using increasing or decreasing length Cuisenaire rods, they could not transfer the process to cubes, even when offered a model to copy. It was at first thought that the problem was caused by the spatial complexity of co-ordinating both stacks and rows. Children who did solve it were over the age of 5 and used counting, addition and subtraction. The few solid stairs recorded in our study were done by eye. During eighteen months of record-keeping from the beginning of the study, no record was made of a stair more than three blocks high being systematically built from a row of towers.

4. Support for this view of problem-solving can be found in Easen and Green (1987) and Moyles (1989).

5. This is not to be confused with the institutionalized routine of the High Scope curriculum.

6. For a review of studies into private speech, see Berk (1985).

7. Goetz and Baer (1973) and Goetz (1981) found that increased versatility in using blocks was encouraged by the adult's use of 'descriptive' responses to new forms; Hitz and Driscoll (1988) review research on 'praise' and conclude that the aim in offering feedback should be to foster autonomy, positive self-esteem, a willingness to take risks and an acceptance of self and others.

8. At no time does Waterland suggest that shared reading is the only strategy to be employed in the teaching of reading.

9. See also Bruce (1987).

8
RECORD-KEEPING AND CONTINUITY
Froebel Blockplay Research Group

The audio cassette-recorder has been running, with the children's permission, and I have been taking photographs. 'I've just been thinking,' says Edmund (6 y.), 'wouldn't it be good if you could take talking pictures – then you wouldn't have to have a camera and a cassette-recorder . . . (pause) . . . and if they could move as well . . . (pause) . . . that's it, talking pictures that move.' 'Edmund has just invented the video camera,' I write in my notes.

TWO RECORD-KEEPING PERSPECTIVES

Two overlapping aspects of record-keeping are considered in this chapter: first, there is the contribution record-keeping can and must contribute empirically to the *verification of good practice* in early childhood education as defined from a developmental perspective (Bruce, 1987; Blenkin and Kelly, 1988); second, there is record-keeping itself as an essential element of good, everyday professional practice.

Verification of Good Practice

In her Introduction, Tina Bruce makes clear the educational principles guiding the blockplay project. They apply generally to all aspects of early childhood education and provide the broad frames of reference that influence planning, conduct and evaluation of the curriculum. Factual accounts of all these aspects of curriculum are needed if we are to demonstrate, on its own terms, the effectiveness of this particular approach. This means, among other things, that we need to develop evaluative measures consistent with the principles that guide our planning and conduct of the curriculum. To illustrate this we can take a dimension of children's play that has been a focus in a number of evaluation studies in early childhood education. This is the relative import- ance of *duration* of concentration,[1] as a measure of the amount of 'cognitive stretch'[2] in an activity (Sylva, Roy and Painter, 1980, p. 50), and in judging the quality of the play material itself.

Our records of blockplay support other evidence in the literature that dura- tion of attention is an unreliable measure of concentration and commitment when taken on its own.

Salmaan enters the block area. He rapidly arranges a square eighth block to either side of a quarter unit to form a T shape. 'An owl,' he says, before moving on.

This episode lasted less than two minutes, including time to select the required blocks. However, the sureness with which he composed his owl, a new arrangement for him, suggested this was a coming together of block knowledge and a developing impression of owls distilled from picture books, television and perhaps a trip to the zoo. Here, 'duration of play' as a measured observable is an irrelevance and a distraction, as it ignores the time taken to develop and co-ordinate his ideas to this point.

Times recorded for blockplay ranged from Salmaan's scant two minutes to over two hours – if we exclude those play sequences that carry over for several days. Averaging out would have produced nonsense statistics in terms of providing frames of reference for evaluating either play or provision. Averages can even be counterproductive in the assessment of the lived experiences of individual children. Duration of concentration seems neither a valid nor useful measure of play. It isolates individual episodes from the totality of the child's experience. Only those who have regular contact with a child over time, such as parents and the child's full-time classroom educators, can possibly gauge the part–whole significance of individual play bouts. Professional researchers who have tended to deal only in a variety of *sampling* techniques need to take this fact of life on board.

Observational Record-Keeping

Observational record-keeping is a characteristic of the early childhood educa- tion tradition and is exemplified in the work of Susan Isaacs (1930, 1933) and Harriet Johnson (1929, 1933). It is one of the means through which we create our representations of teaching–learning processes, enabling us to reflect on and refine our theories and practice.

Harriet Johnson

There are a number of not entirely coincidental parallels between the work of Harriet Johnson (1929) and that of the Froebel Blockplay Project. Johnson (*ibid.* p. 154) asks: 'What does growth demand of education? Can we find out facts about how children gain control of their bodies and the materials in the environment which will throw light on educational method?'

Both Johnson, as teacher, and her research colleague, Guanella (1934), wrote pioneering accounts of blockplay distilled from the mass of classroom records routinely kept by the staff in Johnson's nursery school. They were to serve several purposes and these, together with the record-keeping procedures, were kept continuously under review.

One particularly important purpose was the detection of common developmental patterns as well as that unique to each child. In parallel with this was a concern to trace any relationships there might be between observed behaviours and a range of environmental variables on both individuals and the group. These included materials, setting and the presence and behaviours of adults and children. It was central to Johnson's purpose that these issues were studied by educators in the educational setting. It is by this means that educational theory develops, hand in hand with theories of development.[3]

Everyday Professional Practice

Observational record-keeping is seen here as an integral part of our day-to-day teaching and learning processes. Observation and reflective evaluation illuminate and inform our planning and interactions relating to both individuals and groups. It is through this aspect of record-keeping that we are able to judge the significance of the parts to the whole in the case of individual children. The broad general aims with which we concluded Chapter 7 were formulated from this perspective.

STRATEGIES AND PRINCIPLES

In her school, Harriet Johnson employed a variety of data-collecting/recording strategies. Minimal factual data were recorded daily, including what and with whom the child had played. These routinely recorded facts were augmented with anecdotal records gathered on the wing. The simple strategy of using tear-off pads combined with a rule of only one subject to a page meant that notes were relatively easy to collate from day to day, week to week and month to month. Once a month each child was the focus of everyone's record-keeping for a day.

The development of the underlying philosophy of the school's record-keeping was shared with those in direct contact with the children in school. It was they who, in consultation with Johnson, drew attention to the importance of recording the 'everyday and consecutive' as opposed to the 'unusual manifestations' (Johnson, 1928, p. 160).

This point needs to be qualified in terms of the different purposes our record-keeping is intended to serve. In the Froebel Blockplay Project we were attempting through our records to establish a baseline of information about general patterns of development in blockplay and the influences on this. In this context the necessity of being able to recognize the everyday and consecutive and *its relationship to the whole* becomes obvious. It may be that because the everyday and consecutive have tended to be neglected in classroom record-keeping in the past twenty years or so that there was very little evidence with which to counter some of the criticisms contained in recent evaluation studies.[4] These tended to emphasize the everyday but seldom the consecutive. The result is that we get very little impression from these sources of a *developmental continuum* in children's use of materials.

Obviously the level of detail advocated here cannot and need not apply to our entire record-keeping output. Eventually, when we feel more secure in our understanding of blockplay, it will not apply to our record-keeping in this area either and we can then turn our searchlight onto some other aspect of our early childhood practice.

Another important decision made by Johnson (1928, p. 160) and her colleagues was to set record-keeping in an interpersonal context: 'We came early to the realization that we did not wish our diary notes to deal with children as single units but as members of a group...we had the evaluation of our environment in mind in developing a method of record keeping.'

It is salutary to note that, although the context of education is interpersonal,[5] the unit of measurement in evaluating the education offered is usually the performance of the individual child.

Professional Development

Gaining insights into effective record-keeping is a developmental process for individuals as well as within and between groups of educators. The interacting processes of differentiation and integration, which characterize the development of blockplay, apply equally to the development of observational record-keeping.

Means

Like Johnson, we need to explore different means of recording our observations: in written language; in drawings; and in video- and audio-recording and photography. Each one of these can be further differentiated – written records, for example, can be explored in terms of checklists, narrative, diary, etc. We need also to explore combinations of these different means.

Data-Collecting

What we record, if the subject is new to us, needs, as Johnson (1929, p. 160) suggests, to be the 'everyday and consecutive'. At this early stage we are not in a position to pick out the significant from the insignificant. Gradually our recording becomes more discriminate and differentiated and we become better able to recognize some behaviour as part of a pattern common to many individuals and many situations (Athey, 1980, p. 5). As we learn to do this with reasonable confidence, we are better able to read off less usual occurrences (Johnson, 1928) and those aspects that, according to our value system, we judge to be significant indicators that the child and/or the group are thriving.

Patterns, Relationships and Explanations

Time and opportunity are needed to use our records to reflect on possible relationships between behaviours observed, what each child brings to the situation and the physical and interpersonal aspects of the educational setting. We also need time and opportunity to discover any commonalities and differences that might exist between children and between content areas of the curriculum (Athey, 1980, 1990). Through our record-keeping we began to appreciate the links between maths and science, maths and art. We need time and opportunity to discover whether children are representing the same ideas through different media and at different levels of 'embeddedness' (Donaldson, 1978, p. 89). We need time and opportunity to search for explanations in both the psychological and pedagogical literature as well as in discussion with children, colleagues and parents (Athey, 1990). Finally, we need time and opportunity to reflect on how we might integrate our records into systems that view curriculum planning, implementation and evaluation as a whole.[6]

THE FROEBEL BLOCKPLAY PROJECT

The above summary of record-keeping as both professional development and developmental process is based on a review of issues relating to record-keeping that emerged during our study of blockplay: means, focus, interpretation/ evaluation and use of findings. In the following account, our own record-keeping experience may appear a much smoother, logically developing process than it actually was. The reality was characterized by unevenness and on-the-spot improvisation. Emphasis tended to shift back and forth between concerns about record-keeping format, behaviour categories, curriculum content, terminology, etc. – depending on individual or group concerns at any particular time.

Interaction

The blockplay project was an interactive experience on several levels. First, the keeping of records with a shared focus but based on our individual classroom experiences enabled us as a group of educators to share and consider each other's points of view. Sometimes these coincided and at others there were differences. Both confirmation and dissonance were powerful incentives to go on looking and recording. We developed our record-keeping and blockplay practices as we went along, helped by our contact with each other to update continually our understandings.

At a second, equally important level, we were engaging in the same processes with the children. As participant observers, engaged in action research, we were simultaneously monitoring and taking part in what was happening during play, using feedback from our child partner's behaviour to influence the course of events. A simple example is that of encouraging children *literally* to stand back from their actions in order to reflect on the effects being created by these actions. In Chapter 2 Tina Bruce has described other kinds of interactions that occurred between children and adults. The most important and exciting aspect of this kind of action research is that there can be no absolute distinction between observer and observed.

In observing each other in playful interaction, adults and children change each other's behaviour. This affects all aspects of record-keeping, planning, implementing and evaluating.

Finally, there were continuous cycles of interaction between the development of our record-keeping and the focal point of the study, i.e. blockplay itself. The way in which we recorded our impressions began to affect directly what was happening in blockplay itself. The two became increasingly more inter-related and tuned to each other as we learnt more about each.

The establishment of theoretical and factual frames of reference in relation to blockplay is the main context of our discussion of record-keeping. Some attempt will be made towards the end of the chapter to indicate how the insights gained at this level of record-keeping could be translated into frames of reference for everyday and longer-term curriculum planning, implementation, assessment of individuals and evaluation of provision.

'What Are We Looking for?'

An open-ended brief to observe and record can result in a mass of undifferentiated and possibly unrelated observations. However, starting-points are not easy to decide on in uncharted territory, as blockplay was for project participants.

We were typical as a group of early childhood educators in wanting to keep records that were not so simple that they told us nothing useful later on (and might even put children in the wrong light), or so complex that we all suffered burn-out in keeping such records. We did not want to be so exhausted from record writing that we should never have the time or inclination to refer to them later, especially if they took a long time to read through, collate and analyse.

Formats

Creating a straightforward, easy-to-share recording format for blockplay took most of the first year of the project. We looked at a range of local-authority proforma – those used in various recent research projects – as well as consulting the blockplay research literature and general readings in the field of early childhood education.

Record-keeping is an area that seems to be particularly sensitive to the recorder's need to feel a sense of ownership of the format used. The Task Group on Assessment and Testing Report (DES, 1987) suggests that record-keeping is at the heart of the teaching process. It is also close to the heart of the teacher. Putting one's observations and understandings on the record for all to see exposes not only the child but also the keeper of the record. This is not an entirely cognitive experience. It takes some courage to step outside the anonymity afforded by checklists.

Checklists

Before thinking of using a checklist, we usually want to be sure it is capable of giving us the information we want. As a precondition to using a checklist, therefore, we need to consider who is being checked against what criteria, or what criteria are being checked against whom and *on what theoretical basis*.

Although checklists do have a modest part to play in some aspects of planning, evaluation and assessment, in some areas of the curriculum, they did not prove either a useful or popular record-keeping strategy in relation to blockplay.

As a means of recording behaviour, checklists are problematic for many early childhood educators because they tend to carve swathes through notions of wholeness. They make those behaviours on the list appear, by inference, to be more important than those left out. In checking children against lists of behaviours, there is a danger of our becoming more concerned with what it appears children can't do than what they can. Items may take on the status of *norms*. They may also stunt the development of thinking about those areas on which the checklist is based. Finally, there is the added risk, where they are used as a matter of routine, of them becoming the basis of our planning and teaching.

Despite all of these misgivings we tried at one stage to create a check-list based on developmental changes that occur in blockplay. In design this attempted to mitigate the problems just mentioned. The idea was to give ourselves a fall-back strategy, which would enable us to maintain our records on days when we might be pushed for time. Everyone gave it a try; some gave up sooner than others. Although we were not teaching to the broad descriptive categories on which the checklist was based, we felt the record they offered was seriously impoverished in contrast to the richness of blockplay itself. The consensus seemed to be that it was better to have gaps in the record than to give a poor account of individual children's play and of blockplay itself.

Rather than checklists we felt the need for general conceptual frameworks about how blockplay develops and under what conditions, as well as learning about what blockplay affords the child in terms of material to think with and material to think about. Such frameworks would allow for flexible planning, evaluation and assessment.

Initially, just to set the ball rolling, we used a home-made illustrated chart, based on the work of Johnson and Guanella, outlining the development of blockplay from simple to complex forms. We soon outgrew it, but this does not diminish the important part it played in the development of our record-keeping. Tina Bruce describes in Appendix I how this same pattern occurred in relation to the research proposal, which changed as the research progressed. Starting-points are obviously not to be confused with points of arrival.

Other broad categories of behaviour/issues that were used informally to help in the structuring of observation and record-keeping in different phases of the study were talk, problem-solving strategies, non-specific uses of blocks, gender effects (e.g. are there any observable differences?) and social aspects, etc. Categories not only provide frames of reference for observation but they also reflect areas of interest and concern and assist in the physical management of record-keeping, especially at the stage of collating and analysing. We would want to emphasize the need for these frames of reference to be broadly based, otherwise the range of data recorded becomes seriously limited. In contrasting narrowly defined behaviour categories with more broadly based ones, we can draw on a blockplay analogy. The difference between the two is like that between a set of Richter Anchor Blocks (described by Jane Read in Chapter 1) with their stamped-on windows and doors and the more open-ended unit blocks. One limits creativity and the other invites it.

Planning Diagrams

In planning for blockplay, both within the whole curriculum framework and in its own right as a subset of the whole curriculum, planning diagrams could be used to indicate purposes, procedures and links to other curriculum areas. As with checklists, this presupposes a good working knowledge of blockplay that, in our case, had to be established first. Abundant examples of the setting out of such planning diagrams can be found in the literature.[7]

Target-Child Observations

The method we settled on for guiding our working knowledge of blockplay was, in general principle, that of target-child observation and recording, developed by Sylva, Roy and Painter (1980). At first we tried to use the techniques described by Sylva, Roy and Painter in a relatively unadapted way. However, we found watching the seconds so as to mark the passing of each minute of a ten-minute observation profoundly distracting. Before long, we were ignoring our carefully constructed grids to the extent that they might just as well have been blank sheets of paper.

Child's initials	Gender	Age	Date	Observer initials	School/

Time	Activity	Language	Social
Starting time/time of any changes in the situation, incidents etc/finishing time	Written description of action and/or sketches	Arrows can be used for cross-referencing to other columns	Alone, Small-group Large-group Associative Collaborative

Figure 8.1 (Adapted from *Target Child* observation strategies (Sylva et al, 1980))

Narrative

Narrative took over – the way it does! As a research tool, narrative records offer a very richly textured account of behaviour in context. At first glance narrative may seem cumbersome as an everyday classroom tool. However, after much observation and recording virtually everything that happened, some basic facts about blockplay began to emerge. This meant we improved at homing in on the salient aspects of the situation. As a result, our ability to express our observations succinctly, without losing important detail, also developed. This same point was made by teachers who helped pilot the Primary Language Record developed by the former Inner London Education Authority, which also uses narrative (Barr *et al.*, 1990).

Early on, we also discovered the importance of including sketches as part of the record. The physical format we arrived at allowed ample space for this (Figure 8.1). This suited some participants, who used the columns. Others liked to use it because it was recognizable as a recording sheet but preferred to write anywhere on it, ignoring the columns, while the rest preferred plain paper or whatever was handy at the time. One member of the group collated her rough classroom notes and photographs onto the record sheet when she had time to look back over them.

Whatever the physical format adopted by individuals, the procedures were common to the whole group. These were to focus on the child's actions, manner of performing them, the consequences and any language used, together with brief details of the part played by others, if any, in the sequence – adults (this might be the observer) as well as children. Times of starting and finishing were also recorded.

Sketching

Sketching also became an important dimension of record-keeping in this particular study and was to have a profound effect on the course of blockplay in some groups, where this was taken up by the children.

In sketching constructions, viewpoint became a critical factor. Constructions not only looked different from different angles but were also often differently structured from front to back or left to right.

On one occasion, the adult commented on how difficult it was to sketch a particular construction. Jessica (4 y. 5 m.) jumped from her perch on top of a stack of hollow blocks. 'Let me see,' she said, going over to where the adult was sitting. She glanced from sketch to construction from the adult's position. Then she returned to her perch. 'Come up here,' she said. 'You can see more better.'

Sometimes several sketches were made including, occasionally, bird's-eye views. Sometimes, as Katy once pointed out to an adult: *'You don't need to draw two sides, because they are the same.'*

Individually we began to develop our own symbols to denote particular blocks rather than drawing the block itself each time.

Video-Recordings and Photographs

In one school, video-recording became the established form of record-keeping, and in all the schools photography played a major role. Whatever form is used, it is important to date recordings and keep brief notes to enable these to be blended with other records.

Running Records

All these strategies in record-keeping were used in busy classrooms and did not involve removing children to unnatural or less familiar settings. They were in the nature of 'running records', which attempted to tackle the problem so dominant in record-keeping of losing the moment in the hurly-burly of events. As we studied blockplay our record-keeping gradually began to match the model of a 'good record' suggested by Harlen (1983, p. 5). This should contain sufficient detail to provide the kinds of information required, should not take more time than it is worth and, in addition to its accumulated value, should inform as it is being made. The information we gained on the development of blockplay, its role in the curriculum and how to facilitate this are some of the issues we elaborate on in discussing the spin-off from our action research and the ways in which this experience has been assimilated into our general practice.

TRANSLATION TO GENERAL PRACTICE

It is not easy to keep good records of some aspects of the early childhood curriculum, and blockplay is one of them. As we began our study we quickly began to see why three-dimensional media are seriously under-represented, in terms of what we objectively know about them from both everyday practice and research.

Confidence and Independence

There were also difficulties for all of us at first in terms of our confidence in ourselves as record-keepers. With practice and encouraged by the insight we were gaining about many aspects of our work as early childhood educators, different groups gained sufficient confidence and independence to transfer and adapt record-keeping strategies developed in the block area to other areas of the curriculum. Where this happened, similar questions arose initially to those we had considered in relation to blockplay: 'what do we want to know about this activity and how do we record it?' Other groups worked on the integration of blockplay record-keeping into existing systems.

Reflective Evaluation and Assessment

Johnson (1928, p. 154) makes the important point that 'the act of recording does not in itself bring wisdom'. Just as children's block structures and other forms of representation enable them to reflect on their experiences, so the observations we record enable us to reflect on ours. During the project, adults and children sometimes engaged in shared reflecting; at other times this was done separately, when we discussed the recorded observations, studied photographs, slides and videos. The adults linked their reflections to research literature and theory, which included general current readings in education. The children were enabled to make links to and from the block area through the setting up of interest tables and in the provision of books and pictures and by means of shared outings to observe and sketch in the school neighbourhood and sometimes further afield.

One school now involves children from 3 to 11 years in regularly choosing samples of their work from across the curriculum, which they or others have recorded on their behalf, to be added to a personal record of achievement. This invites *self-assessment* and *comparison with the self over time*. It is also a means by which adults and children can *jointly* reflect on the concerns and developments represented by the records.

Where records are cumulative and sequential, the adults' narrative accounts of the episodes depicted in photographs and drawings help to set them in context for the children – reminiscent of the way in which older members of families invoke the past for younger members through the family album.

Effects on Provision for Blockplay

The records we made during our intensive study provided us with bases on which we can now evaluate our regular blockplay provision. Colleagues in the project group tend to agree with Johnson (1928, p. 111) when she suggests that play with blocks is a 'central and co-ordinating feature' of the whole curriculum. In this it functions very much like drawing, painting, written and spoken language and its use and development needs to be encouraged and facilitated.

A topic approach to blockplay itself has been found to be an irrelevance. Like written and spoken language and drawing, it does not need an external agenda or *theme* to be grafted on to it. This is what we need to reflect in our planning, conduct and evaluation of blockplay.

It is likely, however, that children who are fluent in the language of blocks will try to reflect any particular shared curriculum focus in their blockplay. One group was engaged for a whole term in building a freshwater pond, and many of the concerns relating to this became the subject of the children's spontaneous play in the block area. Another group focusing on the general idea of 'transport' and 'transporting' found children exploring aspects of this interest through road-building and consideration of different ways of shifting blocks at clearing-away time.

If the match between what children do falls short of what we know can happen in the block area we are, as a result of our experience, more likely to re-examine our own contribution, as a first step, than to consider the problem as starting with the child.

Tuning in to Individuals

We can now assess the development of children in this area, using general dimensions such as those listed at the end of Chapter 7. These are very similar to the dimensions that form the learning continuum suggested in the *Primary Language Record* (Barrs *et al.*, 1990, pp. 6–7).

As we have indicated in various chapters, the range of content children assimilate to their blockplay is very wide. Once a holistic understanding of blockplay was established among the adults in some groups, strategies for differentiating 'content' within the written narrative framework began to develop. One of these was briefly to indicate content on a corner of the record sheet: maths, philosophy, science, history, etc. This facilitates the scanning of records when the time comes to collate and interpret them. Athey (1990, p. 81) warns, however, that too much attention to *content* can prevent the perception of similarities in *form* from one area of provision to another. *Form* rather than *content* may sometimes be of greater individual significance in record-keeping.

Process and Product

In a study of the education of 4-year-olds in primary schools, Bennett and Kell (1989, p. 29) indicated a lack of diagnosis by teachers of individual educational need and there was a tendency for assessment to be limited to the *products* of children's work. In terms of blockplay, accurate diagnosis, which would include the processes of problem-solving, can only be gained by active adult participation in the block area. *This has to be part of our planning and resourcing of the curriculum.* From our own before-and-after experience of studying blockplay, we cannot stress this too much.

Our study of blockplay has enabled us to fine-tune our interactions to individual children in the block area. We agree with the suggestion of Wood, Bruner and Ross (1976, p. 97) that educators need two kinds of insight for effective adult–child interaction. First, understanding of the nature of the task confronting the child and, second, knowing the 'performance characteristics' of the child. Without both of these the adult cannot interact in ways specific to the particular child at a particular point in a particular activity. We can use the Vygotskian (1978) notion of *actual* and *potential* levels of learning, discussed in the last chapter, to guide the tuning-in process. What the child can already do with blocks needs to be established as a starting-point; then we can use our knowledge of how blockplay develops to help children consolidate and extend their range. The importance of working with children on the basis of what they *can* do is an important principle to apply to all record-keeping of any child's progress and is particularly important where progress may be slow or uneven. Honig (1990) advises on the importance of thinking in terms of children 'dancing' the developmental ladder, rather than going in a straight line.

Raising the Status of Blockplay

The recording process gave a clear message to the children, parents and colleagues that blockplay was a greatly valued area of the curriculum. In an article entitled 'Put your name on your painting, but the blocks go back on the shelves', Kuschner (1989, p. 49) draws attention to those aspects of the early-years curriculum that often go unrecorded. The implicit messages conveyed by simple classroom management strategies may cause some activities to acquire a lower or higher status than others. Children cannot bring their block structures to us for comment. Planning for blockplay has a *time* as well as a material dimension. Some of our time is needed in the block area where, in addition to supporting and actively participating in play, we can record samples of work for the children.

All the project groups have weekly planning and evaluation meetings, which

Figure 8.2   Figure 8.3

now include consideration of blockplay. Without this, we know only too well that adult cover will be on a hit-and-miss basis.

One group has a meeting at the end of each afternoon, at which some of the day's events and observations are shared and become the basis of follow-up planning. This helps in filling each other in on those aspects of the curriculum that often have no tangible pay-off. Children's school records can be enriched or impoverished depending on our record-keeping strategies. The pay-off for them may be personal profiles that are unrepresentative. At worst these can lead to badly informed expectations, which may in turn become self-fulfilling.

We would agree with Kuschner (*ibid.*) that there is no reason why a descriptive account and perhaps a sketch of a child's blockplay should not be taken home at the end of the day, just as drawings and paintings are. With a photocopier in many schools these days, a duplicate can very easily be made for the school records, if necessary.

Children as Record-Keepers

The record-keeping that helped raise the status of blockplay gained status as an activity in its own right that the children also wished to engage in (Figures 8.2 and 8.3). We have already drawn attention to the opportunity sketching creates for reflection. It seemed to us that the cycle of building and sketching, when engaged in by the children, did lead to greater awareness of different aspects of the situation not only for them but also for ourselves, which led to further individual and collective developments in blockplay.

We found that many of the children were fascinated by the adults' sketches and wanted to join in. This was an entirely unplanned-for and unexpected turn of events. The act of sketching from a model became a means for them, as well

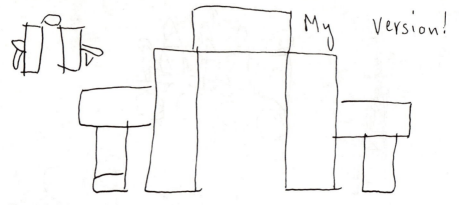

Figure 8.4

as ourselves, to stand back from the act of construction and to consider their work objectively. Some were also able to take on the idea of a sketch as a tangible reminder of structures, perhaps to share with others who hadn't seen the actual building, or to use as a building plan on a subsequent occasion. When the teacher hadn't got her camera, Marie drew a sketch of her caterpillar and was able to use this the following day in building a reconstruction to be photographed.

Clip-boards with wads of paper and pencils attached with long lengths of string were added to blockplay areas in some schools. In others, children were free to fetch drawing materials from the graphics area as they wished. Children drew only if they wanted to. We recognized the importance of letting this aspect of recording find its own level. Some children might have been put off blockplay if they had the impression that drawing was somehow an inevitable accompaniment to playing with blocks. We know from our records that some children are particularly skilled with blocks and a good deal less so with paper and pencil and vice versa. Where children did record their blockplay we gained fresh insights into aspects of representation, as well as adding to our picture of individual children.

One adult records the struggle she had in representing accurately the child's model of a 'person'. She expressed some of her difficulties aloud, and the child who had made it and was also sketching said, 'Don't worry. You can copy mine if you like' (Figure 8.4).

Children appear to have a great deal to contribute as record-keepers, both in creating permanent records of their play and in the processes of assessment described earlier in relation to records of achievement. The encouragement of self-assessment by young children is a relatively new development and it will be interesting to see the kinds of criteria they will use. Will they differ from those used by adults? This is not to suggest that children do not already have opinions about themselves but rather to enable them to discover that their opinions matter to other people. There is a striking parallel here with developments in classroom research in which the viewpoint of the classroom educator is given equal status to that of the professional researcher. The present study is an example of this. If we are to invite children to partner us in assessing their progress, could we not also invite them to partner us in evaluating the curriculum?

CONTINUITY

Record-keeping is a powerful mechanism through which parents, peers and colleagues can be helped to contribute to the achievement of continuity in teaching and learning. They are an extensible line of communication, connecting past, present and future.

Home and School

One school has adopted the blockplay recording sheet for general use and the records are shared with parents. Photographs, slides and video-recordings have also been used to share blockplay with parents. Blocks of the scale and character of unit and hollow blocks are not commonly found in the home. Blocks of any sort may not be available to girls who do not have brothers. 'I wish I had blocks at my house,' said Jade one day. 'What have you got instead, then?' 'Oh, just dolls. Loads of dolls and two baby buggies.'

The response of parents to views of children using blocks has often been that of awe – not simply on account of the creativity being expressed but at the children's commitment to what they are doing. The importance to the child of what is taking place is clear to see without the need for heavy-handed commentary from us.

Many parents express anxiety about the time allowed for play in schools, even where this amounts to very little in relation to that devoted to other things. This is especially so after the age of 4, according to research (Barrett, 1986; Cleave and Brown, 1989).

Modern media, like video and tape–slide presentations, are a gift in promoting play as a curriculum asset. Sharing the records in this way should perhaps be regarded as a duty, especially where activities are involved with nothing tangible to show for the children's efforts *or ours* as professional educators, at the end of the day, week, month, year.

We can only go forward on a whole-school basis in developing play as a holistic activity if parents know what play in school actually looks like and how it got that way, i.e. *the part school plays*.

Partnership with parents, through our record-keeping, helps create links with the child's past, present and future. Teachers come and go for the child, but parents remain constant from teacher to teacher, maintaining the links.

Parents in Classrooms

During the course of the project, parents contributed to observing and record-keeping in a reception class of mainly 6-year-olds, where the teacher was keen that the blockplay, developed the previous year by her group, should continue and be extended. She was aware of the part played by her predecessors, a teacher and nursery nurse team, in that development and regarded it as essential that the same level and quality of input should be made at this later stage.

One of the realities of compulsory schooling is that primary-school teachers have to create their own network of adults prepared to partner them in the classroom, where more than one adult is needed. This teacher had no nursery nurse and so she put the problem to the parents. They had already had an opportunity to consider the role of blockplay in the classroom. This was done through a parents evening attended by members of the study group. Slides were shown and there was discussion of the value of blocks across the curriculum. There was a modest but sufficient response from parents to the idea of becoming actively involved. The proposal was that parents would sometimes enable the teacher to spend time in the block area by standing in for her elsewhere, or would sometimes become participant observers in their own right, keeping whatever form of record they felt most comfortable with.

Joan Sallis (cited in Edwards and Redfern, 1988, p. 120) points out that hidden messages are given about the curriculum when limits are put on what parents can help with in the classroom. By putting blockplay on an equal footing with other curriculum matters and sharing responsibility for it with the teacher, this risk was eliminated.

The information we have on 6-year-olds, reported in Appendix III, was collected from this joint venture between a classroom teacher, parents and children.[8]

The *active* learning environment needs more adults per group than a teacher-centred one. More permanent paid staff to provide a guaranteed generous adult–child ratio are a must in early-years classrooms. Campaigning for this ought not, however, cause us to lose sight of the positive contribution parents can make as classroom partners to both teachers and children. More research needs to be done that looks at the practicalities, advantages and difficulties of parents as classroom partners. It would be especially useful to gain impressions of the lived experience of parents in the classroom from the different participants: children, teachers and parents.

Encouraging parents to participate in the classroom and to share actively in children's play is another way of tackling anxiety about play in the curriculum.

A whole-school approach to parental involvement is advocated by Pugh and De'Ath (1989), who suggest the need for schools to agree a policy outlining purposes and practices.

Peers

Peers also provide continuity from teacher to teacher. Reference to the records can help in organizing the grouping of children so as to support and maintain good partnerships where this is feasible, especially where a high value is set on children learning to play and work collaboratively. This has important implications where a special effort has been made to encourage cross-gender partnerships. Evidence suggests that, if existing partnerships are not positively and consistently encouraged, children revert to same-gender groupings (Sprafkin *et al.*, 1983, p. 188).

Colleagues: Whole-School Approaches

In this chapter we have been at pains to stress wholeness and continuity: the whole child; linking home and school; the wholeness of knowledge; and the whole curriculum, etc. We now focus on the *whole school* (Thomas Report, 1985).

Schooling is often characterized by discontinuity and disjunction (Clark, 1988). In particular, a radical qualitative change occurs in the character of the curriculum, from being developmentally based before 5 to being subject based thereafter. A child may never come across blocks, sand, water, etc., in school again after the age of 4. This gives implicit messages about play and about nursery education we carry for the rest of our lives and perpetuate from generation to generation.

This book stands as a record of one strand of the early childhood educational experience looked at from a developmental–interactionist perspective. It shows children as self-motivated, active learners, pushing themselves and the material to the limits and assimilating an impressive range of *content* to their play. The kind of experiences recorded by the project group can be planned for and co-exist *on equal terms* with more formal aspects of education in the years after 5.

Whole-school discussion of the rationale for play is essential. Resourcing, timetabling, staffing, evaluation and assessment all have to be organized for through *negotiation*, if we are to achieve the 'continuity with extension' Watt calls for (1987, p. 10).

From Discontinuity to Continuity

The process of changing practice from discontinuity to continuity with extension is best regarded as developmental rather than something a short INSET course will see to. Translation into practice of our understandings of play, through our study of blockplay, are still emergent after 3 years.

Application: Records of Achievement

In many schools a portfolio of work is accumulated for record-keeping purposes during the course of each school year and quite often this is given to the child to take home at the end of the year, when its contents have been summarized and entered on the child's school record. As a development of this, one of the project groups, as already mentioned, has devised a plan for holistic *records of achievement* to be compiled jointly by staff and children and made available throughout the year for children, parents and colleagues to share.

Achievements in three-dimensional modelling, such as woodwork, clay, blocks and found materials, etc., will be photographed or recorded in narrative form and sketches. These records will be transferred from class to class as the children move through the school. If necessary they will stored centrally but remain accessible to all those entitled to see them. In this way, a greater *shared* sense of continuity may be achieved.

From the point of view of planning, carrying out and evaluating the curriculum, very valuable data will be available about both teaching and learning in relation to individuals, groups and on a whole-school basis. On leaving the school, children will inherit their primary-school record of achievement from the age of 3 to 11.

ACHIEVEMENT: WHAT IS IT?

These proposals offer exciting possibilities in terms of creating continuity and in their potential for giving status to every area of the curriculum. In turn, this may help change perceptions of what is regarded as achievement. Malkus, Feldman and Gardner (1988, p. 28) suggest that 'mind is organised into relatively separate realms of functioning', each with its own line of development. Examples given are linguistic, musical, logico-mathematical, spatial, bodily kinaesthetic, interpersonal and intrapersonal. One of the strategies employed by these researchers to study this idea is similar to the records of achievement we have been describing, with views of children and parents to be included. This approach is expected to yield a more 'representative and comprehensive view of a child's special skills than would any one, artificially imposed testing procedure' (*ibid.*).

Eisner (1982) argues for the recognition and encouragement of a wider range of representational forms through which meanings can be secured than is offered by the traditional school curriculum, with its emphasis on linguistic and logical forms of expression. Moves such as these could contribute to the broader view of achievement Donaldson (1978, p. 83) suggests is needed if we are to dismantle the 'apartheid' that separates thinkers from doers, intellectuals from technicians, and measures success only in terms of abstract thinking skills. Changes in the value system would involve continued recognition of the importance of intellectual competences but would give equal status to other things (*ibid.*).

There are signs that change is possible. This study of blockplay has caught the imagination of many colleagues who have seen evidence on slides and in photographs of high levels of cognitive competence children bring to their play with blocks as demonstrated by their social interactions, adventurousness, imagination and problem-solving. Both the *Primary Language Record* (Barr *et al.*, 1990, p. 44) and the National Curriculum Council (1989) give equal weight to talking and listening as to reading and writing. Barr *et al.* (1990, p. 44) suggest this is 'potentially very supportive of children whose positive achievements in this area can now be recognised, even where their literacy skills are not so well developed'.

SUMMARY AND CONCLUSIONS

The reasons for record-keeping need to be clarified and agreed at the outset. Methodology must be consistent with our general educational philosophy and conceptual frameworks. Reasons and methods are interdependent and are in continuous interaction, each bringing about change in the other. The development of confidence in record-keeping is assisted by group reflection through discussion but the process of actual record-keeping about real children is deeply personal.

A narrative format, backed by photographs, sketches, video-recordings, etc., offers a richer source of data than checklists in evaluating provision and assessing educational needs. As others have suggested, narrative allows for a holistic view of learners and learning to be gained. Practice in observing and recording makes the process more manageable and the product more effective in fulfilling its purpose.

From our experience we now have some understanding of why blockplay has been under-represented in classroom records and have suggested that this in itself leads to lowered status in the eyes of both adults and children, with inevitable effects on play in the block area. Conversely, where record-keeping becomes one of the means by which adults and children can share in the reflecting processes of thinking about aspects of blockplay, there is a twofold gain: first, in the insights staff develop about blockplay and about individual children, which inform subsequent interactions; and, second, from the impression it gives that activity with blocks is valued.

The contribution of record-keeping in linking home, class and school in the interests of continuity has been explored, together with discussion of the part that records of achievement can play in helping change the value system by which we judge success.

As the Froebel Blockplay Project got into its stride, the importance of blocks as a cross-curricular resource became apparent and along with this the possibility of cross-curricular record-keeping. We found we sometimes needed to look beyond the block area in attempting to discover and understand the patterning of children's behaviour.

There are points of similarity in what we have tried to do and formalized record-keeping systems, such as the observation, sampling and diary format of the *Primary Language Record* (Barr *et al.*, 1990).

Adults in early childhood education often say they feel guilty if they take time out to observe and record. Perhaps we should feel guilty for *not* doing so.

It is unlikely we are doing anything that could be more important than finding out those things that will enable us to engage in more effective teaching and learning. Observing is not time out – especially in the case of the participant observer who becomes part of that which is observed. We become observers and recorders of our own practice.

The record-keeping described has been both process and product of the work of a *group* of people. Our experience has convinced us that our thinking was more rigorous and had greater depth and breadth because we were a group. We stuck at it because we were a group. We are getting somewhere in our thinking and practice because we were a group. Colleagues who find themselves hoeing a lonely row might consider forming a record-keeping collective. This could be within school (ideally, the whole school) or between schools. The consideration of the same point/problem from different points of view can cause our thinking to develop (Nias, 1987).

Perhaps our most significant contribution to the record-keeping debate is the glimpses offered of the potential of record-keeping as a *shared* point of entry for adults and children in the gaining of insight to our own thought processes. As we develop our capacity for self-conscious thought, record-keeping becomes less formidable.

The record-keeping we engaged in together was organic in character, reflecting the different personalities, strengths and resources of individuals and groups. It developed as we developed as an aspect of the action–reflection processes that define action research. Through our records we developed a base from which to operate and grow further.

NOTES

1. For evaluative discussion of duration of attention as a measure of the maturity of play, see Lunzer (1959); Tizard, Phelps and Plewis (1976); and Sylva, Roy and Painter (1980). Lunzer (1959, p. 213) states that 'duration of attention, unless recorded over a very considerable number of sessions is an unreliable guide to the maturity of play'.

2. Sylva, Roy and Painter (1980) rated activities in terms of 'cognitive stretch'. Definitions of this concept were synthesized from examples of play designated by practitioners as 'rich' or 'simple'. Rich play was 'either sequentially organised, or else contained symbolic transformations, often both' (*ibid*. p. 54).

3. Classroom action research, which is carried out as part of everyday teaching/learning processes and seeks to integrate both theory and practice, has been explored and developed in several recent studies into aspects of early childhood education, including Barrett (1986); Ghaye and Pascal (1988); and Athey (1980, 1981 and 1990).

4. Tizard, Phelps and Plewis (1976); Sylva, Roy and Painter (1980); and Hutt *et al.* (1988).

5. The significance of the interpersonal context of learning in early childhood is elaborated on by Bruce (1987, pp. 134–45) and Blenkin and Whitehead (1988, pp. 37–42).

6. Bruce (1987); Blenkin and Kelly (1988); and Blenkin and Whitehead (1988).

7. Early Years Curriculum Group (1989); Katz and Chard (1989).

8. The teacher was Carol Price of Our Lady of Victories Primary School, Putney.

9
THE PHYSICAL SETTING: CREATING A FAVOURABLE ENVIRONMENT
Froebel Blockplay Research Group

In summarizing our account, we would probably want to express this as a process of interaction between maturation and environment. Each aspect is influenced by the other. It is almost impossible to tell at any particular point where the effect of one ends and the other begins.

For this reason we approach the task of sharing insights about the practical aspects of blockplay with some reservation. What we find in one group is as much because it is that group, in that place at that time. The same physical set-up and the same group of adults may interact with different groups of children in different ways, resulting in different outcomes from one term, or one year to the next. No school or group involved in the study would claim that they know 'how to' in any absolute way. This chapter offers some of the more general ideas we developed as we went along.

Our ideas about the creation of a favourable environment for blockplay are presented in two parts. The present chapter deals with the material side of blockplay and the one that follows with interpersonal issues. There is overlap between the two, as in reality there can be no separation.

THE BLOCK AREA

The circumstances under which blocks could be offered differed totally in each of the five schools involved in the study. Initially, no group had an area exclusive to blocks. In resource-based classrooms, children would bring all manner of activity to a multipurpose space. It became obvious that such a set-up was not conducive to the development of sustained and complex blockplay. Some rethinking of spaces, resources and timetables was indicated. Where it was possible to designate space exclusively to blocks this was done. Otherwise blockplay was allotted time and space on a timetabled basis.

Sometimes organizing for blockplay became a focus of discussion and negotiation between adults and children. This is described in the next chapter, where we also discuss the effects of differing amounts of space.

The siting of blockplay, whether permanent or temporary, should be well away from traffic lanes, if possible. A remote corner may seem the ideal from this point of view but may be difficult for adults to keep an eye on, when not actually involved. Staffrooms have been used and a resource room on an occasional basis. These alternative spaces are worth considering as supplementary to any classroom space that is used on a more regular basis. For example, the resource room just mentioned was used as an occasional 'extra' to give the children the opportunity for greater freedom of movement and space to build in than they had in their classroom. There was space for extra blocks to be offered in the resource room and less distraction from other activities. On these occasions, children were able to explore the blocks more exhaustively and conduct more elaborate experiments.

It is clear from the observations made that this 'quality' opportunity, as the headteacher put it, had an enhancing effect on the children's blockplay when they next used blocks in the less spacious conditions of the classroom. They knew more about the material and had greater control of it.

Defining the Block Area

The block area needs to be physically defined in ways that will deter unthinking encroachment into, or from, other areas while, at the same time, allowing for occasional, legitimate stretching of the spatial boundaries. This sometimes happens when children are engaged in setting out elaborate, horizontal grid systems, which seem to gobble up space. Some adult help may be needed, as well as co-operation from peers, in gaining this extra space and ensuring that its temporary annexation for blockplay is respected.

Much problem-solving is involved in tailoring the dimensions of a construction to the space available, and experienced blockplayers learn to gauge this (Figure 4.21).

Melissa (4 y. 4 m.) was constructing a line of blocks that bisected the carpet diagonally, from one corner to that opposite. On reaching the further corner, she hesitated before continuing her line off the carpet and on towards the doorway. She was asked by an adult to stay on the carpet, as people were coming and going through the doorway continuously. She gathered up the overspill blocks and reflected on the situation a moment before saying 'I can turn it round'. She then used her overspill blocks to make a hairpin turn, so that the line was now being extended in the opposite direction.

In the siting of any activity, we inevitably displace something else. Before taking any decisions or moving anything, the wider implications need to be thought through. What are the neighbouring activities likely to be? What would be the best activities to have nearby? There is a possibility of neighbouring activities merging.[1] How do we feel about that? Where blocks are concerned, should hollow blocks and unit blocks share the same space, or have different areas allocated to them?

Building Surfaces

Carpeted areas are comfortable to kneel or sit on and absorb a certain amount of noise from blockplay. A carpet also serves to define the boundaries of the block area. The disadvantage is that the lengthier blocks can be more difficult to balance upright on a carpet. One group removed theirs, but others, in older premises, felt the floors were in too poor a condition to be without carpet. Any floor covering should be firmly anchored to avoid accidents and also to ensure that the building surface doesn't develop corrugations.

Some sets of blocks include building boards, which offer a good flat building surface. We also acquired oddments – laminated chipboard tends not to warp and can sometimes be picked up as offcuts in DIY stores. A rough guide to minimum size for boards as building surfaces would be slightly bigger than a kitchen cupboard door.

Some children like using a board for reasons other than its evenness of surface. They find it easier to organize themselves within the given spatial limits and shape of a board than on the larger expanses of uninterrupted lino or carpet, which may lack any obvious reference points. Other children will use walls and cupboards as reference points for keeping lines straight, or when striking a right angle.

Building boards are also useful where floorspace is at a premium. We have seen very few instances of children crossing the boundary represented by the edge of a board.[2] Sometimes it is possible to 'save' a structure, built on a board, so that it can be shown to parents.

Tables

Several groups occasionally built on tables, usually with smaller-scale unit blocks, Poleidoblocs or similar. Some children prefer this arrangement to the larger-scale floor play. It seems to encourage storying, especially when play people and such are added.

Tables are best positioned away from traffic lanes, as even a slight knock will send structures tumbling. Movement from others using the table also affects the buildings of others. Noise from blocks falling onto laminated table-tops suggests siting away from quiet areas. We have not come up with a satisfactory table covering that muffles sound and does not wrinkle. An old sawn-down domestic table might be better suited to this presentation than conventional early-years furniture.

Despite the problems, observation suggests there were particular benefits to be gained when children and adults played at a table together with blocks. New children and quieter children seem to feel particularly comfortable in sitting around a table with everyone facing inwards and able to observe each other, with the supply of blocks in the centre. However, the more complex building and problem-solving we observed in floor play does not seem to occur in this context until children are much older and using such material as Poleidoblocs.

PRESENTATION OF BLOCKS

As with decisions about space and the siting of blockplay, various means were employed for displaying blocks for use.[3] One person recycled a linen chest spotted in a rubbish skip. This made an excellent block store, provided you were not too tiny – otherwise you might find yourself standing on your head gaining a new perspective on the blocks from inside the linen chest.

Shelves, in one group, had silhouettes of the different-shaped blocks pasted to their surface at intervals, as a guide to their replacement at clearing-away time. Children need initial guidance in using this system, especially the very young ones, who would rather like to have one silhouette per block instead of per category. A refinement to this method is to mark, at the back of the shelves, the height to which blocks should be stacked.

When blocks are stored on shelves, ideally they should be placed so that the different shapes and sizes can be differentiated without having to remove them. When placed end on, all except curved blocks are indistinguishable.

Wheel-mounted block chests, with extra stackable trays, were used by two groups. In this case a bird's-eye view of selection has to be catered for. Where blocks are stacked one on top of another it helps reflective selection if the top block in a stack identifies the blocks beneath it: units on top of units, quarters on quarters. This system was introduced with children as young as 3 years and worked well. As with any system it has to be explained to the children, who gradually pick up the idea as they see adults and other children packing blocks away. They soon discover that if you want a block similar to the one you just used, you return to the same place.

One colleague adopted the practice of having the blocks sorted into stacks at the beginning of the session, according to shape and size. The stacks were arranged around the block area. Once building began, she noticed a distinct tendency for the children to use only (or mostly) the blocks nearest to them. These might be the quarter units *or* the eliptical curves *or* the wedges. This obviously has a knock-on effect on everyone who is using the blocks at the same time. Those children who might want to use a different-shape/size block to those nearest to them often find them already in use. Our video-recordings and some written observations also point to this tendency. Previous research indicates that when children were offered mixed piles of blocks, their structures reflected this mixture. It would be worth bearing all of these observations in mind when planning the presentation of blocks.

TYPES OF BLOCKS

Unit or modular blocks have been described throughout this book (Figure 4.1). We regarded sets of standard unit blocks as the staple building material for children from the age of 3 upwards.[4]

Members of our group varied in the extent to which they made available different-scale unit blocks, but all groups explored the possibilities of smaller-scale table blocks as well as the jumbo hollow blocks.[5] Unit blocks obtained from different suppliers may not be from the same manufacturer and may not be compatible with each other. Dimensions may be slightly different, there may be differences in the way in which the blocks are divided and shaped. Different types of wood may be used, giving a different weight and feel to blocks from different sources. If the supplier is not the manufacturer, it is advisable to check before ordering blocks to add to existing sets that the new ones will be compatible.

Assorted shape, size and colour blocks are used by the children to decorate their buildings and to create small details. Occasionally a small block or combination of these is used in solving a technical problem on a larger-scale construction.

Poleidoblocs[6] are a special case of small-scale blocks. They are precisely proportioned, divided and subdivided. Shape, size, volume and colour correspondences are built in, so that the blocks can also be used as mathematical apparatus. Younger children use them to supplement the larger building blocks and occasionally they are used separately on a table. No attempt was made in our study to use them as mathematical apparatus with younger children, although they can and do explore this aspect informally, as with unit blocks. Also (as with the unit blocks), very pleasing visual harmony can be achieved with them. A group would need several sets if these are to be used as construction material.

Hollow Blocks

These are like jumbo unit blocks in principle.[7] Climb-in-able/on-able structures can be built with them and they often lead to large-group sociodramatic play incorporating props from other areas if this is allowed. In several groups, children created their own house-play areas, transporting the contents of the 'official' home corner to this new setting. Some groups had property boxes containing blankets, suitcases, picnic sets, steering-wheel, etc., for this kind of play.

In one of the primary schools in the study, where blockplay has spread from the nursery class up through the school, two teachers of mixed groups of 4–7-year-olds, given the choice, would opt for the flexibility of a set of hollow blocks, as opposed to specific, purpose-made home corner equipment. This seems an interesting proposition but one that may need working through on an action-research basis. These teachers are in the habit of letting block structures remain *in situ* overnight and for several days, where there is continuity of a particular theme. This would often be necessary if hollow blocks were to replace a permanent home corner. Children might spend all their available time in building their house one day, and would need further time to use it in their dramatic play, after which they might feel the need to modify their design in the light of this experience. At its best, play with hollow blocks is highly complex in its integration of social, imaginative and technical processes.

Some schools reserve hollow blocks for outdoor use; others allow them to be transported in and out of doors and used flexibly in different locations.

A group of children made an office with desks constructed from hollow blocks. They also stripped the graphics area of telephones, paper, pencils, etc., to equip it.

The need to negotiate this kind of alternative use/rearranging of the environment is a theme throughout this chapter and the next. Hollow blocks make useful steps for reaching up when building high and children find it easier to make a solid flight of stairs with them than with smaller blocks. However, the more they are seen as general-purpose blocks, the more scattered they become and less available for large-scale construction.

Storage of hollow blocks can be a problem. Trolleys can be purchased, or made, which means blocks need not be kept in the room where they are to be used. We have seen examples of hollow blocks being turned temporarily into couches when not in use for building, with scatter cushions for comfort.

Oddments

Boxes of oddments are useful to have around the block area, adding a rogue element to blockplay, which sometimes causes the children to stop and think a bit harder than usual. They can create the conflict and contradiction discussed in Chapter 7 as the mechanisms by which learning is advanced. We acquired some small circular offcuts that were used decoratively or to create small details, such as the eye of an elephant (Figure 4.20). A larger circular offcut was highly prized and on one occasion inspired the arrangement shown in Figure 9.1.

Quantities of Blocks

Some children, even at the age of 6, will build until all the blocks have been used. This seems to tell them they have finished. It doesn't seem to matter whether the blocks total 20 or 200. Part of the explanation seems to lie in whether the child is guided by what is out there *in the blocks* or the *block situation* rather than standing back and reflecting on what is required for a particular purpose.[8] Children can be helped to distance themselves with adult help and gradually become more competent at doing this independently.

For some, 'using all of the blocks' seems to be part of the plan. A classic 'stunt' is to create a base area and to erect onto this a volumetric solid using

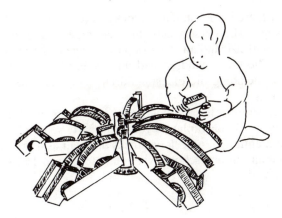

Figure 9.1

every block regardless of shape, form and size, without it falling. Whatever the reasons for the observed phenomenon of 'using all the blocks', it isn't much help in deciding how many, of which blocks, are enough.

The quarter unit is the most useful basic building block.[9] We urge suppliers/ manufacturers to offer supplementary packs of quarters so that groups can build up stocks of these without having to buy complete block sets each time. The project groups would agree that one complete classroom set is adequate for four children, while more than one set is ideal.

After observing children's blockplay with two sets, one group began to see how their pattern-making might be extended by the addition of multiples of the cross, the 'T', the 'L', arch, eliptical and circular curves and quarter circles. With the commitment and support of the headteacher, this group took the plunge and invested heavily in these extra blocks. The exploration and creation of shape and pattern took off in a big way, as can be seen in some of the examples in this book where it is obvious that non-standard sets of blocks are in use (Figures 3.14, 5.3, 5.12, 7.23 and 9.1). This experiment with extra blocks demonstrated to us that children are obviously capable of soaring to greater heights than we ever imagined.

Blocks for All

A sufficient range and quantity of blocks should, ideally, be planned on a whole-school basis. A colleague[10] involved in developing equal opportunities in construction play throughout the primary school in which she taught drew up a whole-school policy based on consultations with colleagues in other schools and her own experience and observations across the 3–11 age-range. Included in her recommendations was the provision of a wide range of construction materials for each age-group. Some materials were to be carried over from one year to the next and eventually dropped to be replaced by something more demanding, or offering more scope for further development. Of all the materials considered, free-standing blocks were retained in the plan across the entire age-range. The nursery class had the largest range of building blocks in terms of type and size and all classes up to the age of 7 were equipped with unit floor blocks. The older children had unit table blocks and Poleidoblocs. The whole school, including the oldest children, had access to a shared reserve of unit floor blocks.

Our own experience has led colleagues in schools involved in the project to extend provision for blockplay beyond the early-years classrooms. As in the example just mentioned, unit floor blocks are held as a shared resource for the older children and in one school every class from 3 to 11 has a set.

CARE

When any of the groups took delivery of new blocks, unpacking them was shared with the children. The smell of the wood is at its most pungent, the feel of the blocks at its smoothest. Children don't easily forget 'the day the blocks came' if a ceremony is made of it.

A colleague recalls the interest in unpacking the new unit blocks. Each block was examined and spontaneously commented on by the children: 'This one's heavy. This one isn't.' 'Smell this.' Someone picked up a wedge and said: 'What's this, what's this mousie?'

If display and storage have not already been organized, this is a good time to involve the children in discussing possibilities. Children who experience blocks in this way are aware of what is at stake when we ask them not to use cars with metal parts on them, because of the damage this can cause.

A set of unit blocks needs to be treated like a jigsaw puzzle in that every block is part of the whole. Missing blocks should be tracked down at the end of the session. The result of not doing so is a basket of oddments in the not-too-distant future and a built-in handicap for the children's blockplay development. It is recommended that oddments be kept in separate containers from sets.

Use of unit blocks outdoors causes very heavy wear if this is on concrete. The corners and edges become scuffed and rounded, making it difficult to stand the blocks upright. Building boards are recommended outdoors.

MIXING MEDIA

The ways in which material is presented are often determined by custom and convenience rather than having any natural or logical basis. In several chapters we have discussed the pros and cons of mixing unit blocks with other media, such as miniature play people, trains, tracks, boats, farm animals, zoo animals. Some children are habitual mixers; others like a place for everything and everything in its place. Adults fall into similar patterns. We need to cater for both, encouraging the mixers to take it plain occasionally, and the tidy-minded to break bounds now and again. Our observations suggest that mixed-media play, at its best, employs both prediction and improvisation, routine and initiative.

We need to observe what happens when children are mixing media, to see whether this adds to the complexity of play, whether it offers evidence of children making interesting associations and whether mixing results in creative transformations. If mixing appears to contribute little to the situation, this may not be an indication to limit the practice. It might mean we need to go on investigating how to improve it.

Greater transformational play occurs when blocks are loaded up as 'shopping' and taken off to the home corner to be 'eaten' as cakes and sandwiches and pieces of cheese. Cylinders have been used as rolling pins. The use of blocks as guns is discussed more fully in the next chapter. The children are making some interesting correspondences and imaginative transformations when they use blocks like this, for which we should give them credit, before helping them organize a substitution.[11]

A colleague summarizes the issue of whether equipment should be allowed to wander by suggesting that the child who is concerned with the general idea of moving things from point to point, i.e. 'transporting', can transport anything, whereas builders *need blocks*.

SAMENESS AND DIFFERENCE

Some colleagues would argue for variety in the provision of blockplay: using different spaces, surfaces, types of block, etc. Changes can call forth a re-appraisal of aspects of blockplay by all concerned. There are different problems to explore and resolve as we saw in the case where children were attempting to build on a slope in the playground in Chapter 6. However, we would place the idea of variety firmly within the context of a stable framework of regularly providing blockplay in the same place and in the same way. Continuity and progression are both taken care of by this means.

SUPPORTING AND ENRICHING ACTIVITIES

Great interest was shown in books on the architecture of different cultures that illuminate both sameness and difference. Often children would look through a book together, discussing various features of buildings. In their subsequent constructions it was sometimes possible to detect the transfer of images and ideas.

Conversely, they were quick to recognize similarities between their own work and images in books and pictures. The headteacher of one of the project schools was sharing her love of classical Greek architecture with the children.

They pointed out to her that they, too, made buildings like those in her photographs.

Pattern is a dominant aspect of blockplay and as awareness of this developed we began to seek out examples of pattern in both the made and natural world to share with the children. Decorative patterns on fabric, wallpaper, floor tiles, and so on, were looked at and displayed. This has fed into both the blockplay and two-dimensional pattern-making.

Field Trips

Children were taken out occasionally to look at and sketch the built environment. This had an impact on both their two- and three-dimensional work.

Some groups researched the children's literature at their local libraries to find books that might link up with blockplay or current interests being worked out in the block area (Appendix IV). It is not always easy to anticipate what they might consider as a suitable target for blockplay. After a visit from the 'animal man', they created snakes, a giraffe and even a fantailed pigeon.

Display

Displays of photographs give pleasure as well as informing children, colleagues, parents and visitors. Life-size as well as scaled-down illustrations of unit blocks, with the block name printed beneath, were wall mounted for decoration and reference. This was translated into Punjabi and Gujurati in one nursery school where most of the children and parents and a member of staff were multilingual.

One school made the illustrated block vocabulary into a small reference book to help the children in planning their structures and another mounted it on loose-leaf card.

RECORD-KEEPING MATERIALS

We found adults and children more likely to engage in routine record-keeping when pads and pencils were kept permanently in the block area. Clip-boards with attached pencils became standard equipment in some groups. A camera is an invaluable aid in record-keeping in the block area. An audio-cassette recorder with external, i.e. directional, microphone is worth keeping to hand.

Children's name cards were extremely useful when a photograph was being taken. The name card was placed near to the structure to be photographed to help with identification after the photographs were processed. If left to memory alone, the relating of photographed structures to their creators can be a strain especially when a film has been in the camera for many weeks, or several films are used in rapid succession.

Name cards were also used by children as token 'messages' to the adult who perhaps wasn't available at the time. A card placed next to a structure was found very useful in allowing adult and child to catch up with each other for a discussion later on. This strategy could be used more generally as an aid to formative record-keeping in overcoming what one colleague calls the 'artist unknown' problem. We are unable to identify a lot of what goes on in our early-years classrooms for want of a simple system like this.

Although name cards were found to be extremely useful in identifying completed structures, knowledge of the processes the child used in creating the structure were irretrievably lost if this was the only record. Our records need to reflect both processes and products. Bennett and Kell (1989, p. 29), in a study of the teaching of 4-year-olds in reception classes, comment on a tendency for teachers to 'limit their assessment to the "products" of children's work. Rarely did they attempt to ascertain the processes or strategies deployed by children in coming to their finished product'. Awareness of the risks of over-reliance on one record-keeping strategy can help to ensure this tendency is reduced.

SUMMARY AND CONCLUSIONS

Children can only fully commit themselves to discovering the creative poss-ibilities of play with blocks if they have the right setting for this. The siting of the area and the regular availability of blocks within a physically defined space require the kind of thinking on the part of educators that leads to a re-examination of the whole environment offered to young children. In other words, by looking at how to offer blockplay it is necessary to look at how we offer each area of material provision and the way each is juxtaposed with others.

Building surfaces can include both floor and table, as well as building boards. Methods of storage and presentation affect the situation in important ways and children need to be aware of the different types and quantity of blocks there are on offer, and have easy access to them. The limitations of the situation in terms of space and/or materials can be experienced positively as problem-solving opportunities, especially where there is active help and support from adults.

Experience suggests that there is ample scope for the development of blockplay across the 3–11 age-range. Some schools plan the resourcing of this on a whole-school basis, with some blocks being held as a shared resource.

The care and concern we show in siting the block area and in the choice and presentation of blocks are all ways of indicating that we adults value this activity. Books, stories, outings, architecture, interest tables and displays are all ways of supporting and enhancing it.

Record-keeping offers a different way of valuing blockplay. Pads of paper and a camera if possible are best kept in the area so that adults can make a record by writing about, photographing or sketching the events that take place there. When children see their blockplay valued, they, too, are encouraged to record their experiences. Record-keeping can also play an important part in our efforts to discover exactly what happens when media are mixed and whether mixing can be accomplished without this resulting in the break-up of sets or the undermining of blockplay as valuable in its own right.

Blockplay can offer children deeply worthwhile experiences. To do so, it needs to be offered with insight based on experience and reflection of how to tailor the setting to allow for support with flexibility in the way it is accommodated, resourced and presented.

NOTES

1. There is a growing body of research pointing to the general finding that the 'ecology' of the educational setting, i.e. the relative balance and distribution of space, time, materials and people, makes an important difference to whether the planned curriculum can be achieved. Nash (1981) suggests spatial organization should reflect awareness of the strengths and weaknesses of young children in organizing themselves. Their distractability can be aggravated by injudicious arrangements, or used to lure them into related areas. Grouping of activities, says Nash, should aim at cutting down unnecessary movement, prolonging play and encouraging continuity between activities so that learning is transferred. Separation of activities gives the opposite message. Kinsman and Berk (1979) report how different age-groups dealt with the removal of the partition separating the home corner and block area in one group and the changes that occurred in play as a result of this 'natural' experiment.

2. This observation confirms the finding of Elkins (1980) that children tended not to cross environmental boundaries in their blockplay.

3. Gramza and Witt (1969) found that the spatial presentation of blocks from which children could select was more influential than colour.

4. Hulson and Reich (1931) reported that a group of 4-year-olds showed a marked preference for the basic unit block, i.e. the block we renamed the quarter unit. Moyer and von Haller (1956) report on the frequencies with which children chose particular unit blocks in an experimental situation. Slats, arches and a block similar to the half unit (our terminology) came out as most frequently chosen.

5. The standard unit blocks used in the study were made and supplied by Community Playthings, Robertsbridge, Surrey. The table blocks were supplied by James Galt, of Altrincham.

6. Poleidoblocs were obtainable in 1987 from E. J. Arnold, Leeds, and were accompanied by a detailed account of their origin, development and use and an appended empirical study by Anderson, Thornhill and Smith (1969).

7. Research into various aspects of play with hollow blocks includes Bender (1978), who progressively increases the number of hollow blocks available and observes the effect on play; Amor (1980), who reports on an action research project involving teachers of 3–7-year-olds; Rogers (1985) contrasts unit and hollow blocks in an observational study; and Haworth (1989) recorded on video-tape, the development of play in each of four different construction materials in the third term at school of a group of 5–6-year-olds. A colleague of Haworth's, Dot Orgill, directed the filming of sequences with hollow blocks, which illuminate the potential of this material for both simple and complex play in a range of social groupings from solitary to collaborative.

8. Elkins (1980), in a small-scale study of blockplay, asked children how they decided whether they had finished. Replies indicated the exhaustion of block supplies as one reason. Others suggested their structure had to look right according to spatial or aesthetic frames of reference or if a plan had been carried through.

9. See note 7 (Bender, 1978). An explanation for the general usefulness of the quarter unit may be in its versatility. According to Smith (1978, p. 21), there are over forty distinctly different ways in which two of these blocks can be combined.

10. Carol Bates, formerly of Elliot Bank Primary School, London Borough of Lewisham.

11. Hutt *et al.* (1988) describe the early-years classroom as a series of micro-environments and observe that the mixing of materials between these tends to be discouraged.

10
SHARING THE RESOURCES AND THE RESPONSIBILITIES: CREATING A FAVOURABLE ENVIRONMENT
Froebel Blockplay Research Group

WHAT BLOCKS AFFORD

Blockplay involves risk-taking; the processes of observation and reflection; the generation, testing and evaluation of theories; and the application of mathematical and scientific understandings in the solving of meaningful practical problems. It requires technical and social competence. The blockplay context offers both the possibility of considering ideas that are different from one's own and of discovering common ground. It also provides opportunities for pooling materials, ideas and skills.

EQUALITY OF ACCESS

When we make available a resource with as much to offer as blocks, we need to ensure that all the children in our groups have equal access to it. Our background reading suggested a greater tendency for boys rather than girls to use the block area[1] and this was borne out by our own early observations. We cannot assume that this is a free choice in the widest sense, particularly for girls. It seems more a case of a self-perpetuating cycle that becomes inextricably bound up with territory and dominance. In a small-scale study of play with hollow blocks, Judd (1988) arranged a 'girls only' session in which she joined. The boys were hostile, as this cut across their customary occupation of the block area. When Judd was called away, they physically attacked the structure, which the girls had made and were playing in, beating it with sticks. The girls fled. Our experience suggests that the question of access cannot be left to work itself out. Young children, in particular, need the personal involvement of adults *long term* to support their emerging understanding and tolerance of the feelings and rights of others. In fact research[2] indicates that the

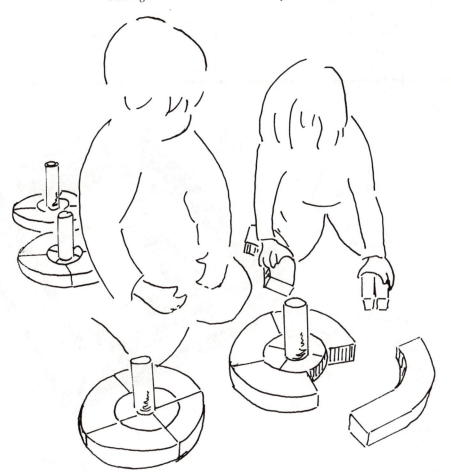

Figure 10.1

block area itself and the home corner can provide the most enabling contexts for the development of these attributes because of the high levels of interaction that occur in these settings and the co-operation that develops during the course of dramatic and constructional/dramatic play. One study (Pellegrini, 1983) found that groups engaging in this type of play used more mature forms of language and a greater range of language than that found in other types of play situation. The effects towards increased co-operation and dramatic play in these areas were found in all the studies to be influenced by age, so mixed-age grouping would appear to offer opportunities for the youngest children to benefit from play with their older peers.

Figure 10.1 shows a four-and-a-half-year-old and a newcomer working in partnership, with the younger child returning from a block hunt with blocks for another repeat of the module the older child has created. Some 'tutoring' was

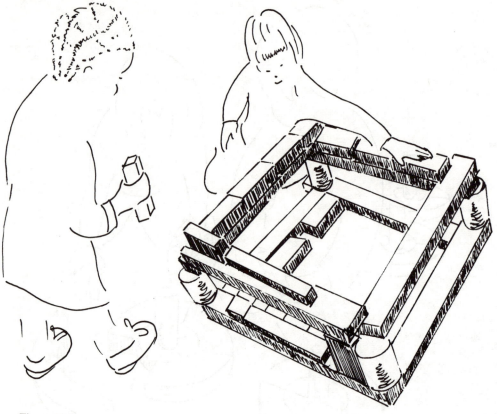

Figure 10.2

offered by the older child when he saw that not all the blocks being offered were suitable for his purpose.[3]

Rubin and Maioni (1975) have demonstrated a relationship between role play and the ability to recognize and represent the feelings of another. We saw that this could also happen in solitary play, with the example of Andrew in Chapter 3, and occasionally two children shared in role play.

Two 4-year-olds, Neil and Paul, have been engaged in dramatic play with cars and a road layout made from blocks. Throughout the game they negotiated and renegotiated roles and dialogue: 'You say . . . then I'll . . .' They explored a number of roles including 'inventors' and some rather disruptive monsters who, in mid-mayhem, were brought to heel by Paul who said: 'I know. Let's be babies. They don't break things.'

The same study found that role play was also related to competence in representing the spatial viewpoint of another, which, as we have seen in other chapters, is an important aspect of collaborative problem-solving relating to constructional aspects of the situation (Figure 10.2).[4]

The implications from these findings make it essential that the block area and blockplay do not become the monopoly of those most able to grab it. When this happens in any area of activity intended for all, patterns of dominance for some and avoidance for others can be set in train. In human terms, the waste is immeasurable both at the individual and species levels. If it is accepted by the children that the block area is the territory of certain individuals, some children may simply get into a non-block-area habit.

GENDER

In our study girls in one group were reported as more likely to play with blocks when these were set out on a table rather than in the block area. This is not offered here as a strategy but to illustrate the point. There should not be any no-go areas for individuals or groups.

Although the idea of 'girls only' sessions may be tempting as a way of trying to break the cycle of domination by boys, early-years staff have generally been unwilling to go along that path (McGill, 1986). If Judd's (1988) experience is any indication, the effect might be to aggravate the situation. In the present study we opted for integration from the start. Our feeling was that there is a risk inherent in officially segregated play, where groups are defined by gender, of perpetuating and appearing to support ideas of gender difference, even where this is organized only on a very occasional basis.

Our experience suggests that children needing guidance include pushy girls and boys as well as timid boys and girls. In addition to questions of access, children may need to have modelled for them how to say firmly and without hostility: 'No thanks, I don't need any help just now.'

Interpersonal Perceptions

Gaining access is sometimes bound up with children's perceptions and those held by adults of the appropriateness of particular activities for one group or another: only for 'big' children/'little' children, older/younger, girls/boys. This in turn can set up self-reinforcing patterns of use/non-use, expertise/lack of expertise.

A new child was watching the adult and several children playing with blocks. 'Would you like to play with the blocks, Anita?' asked the teacher. Anita didn't refuse, but simply said: 'Blocks are boys' toys.'[5] *Over the next few days, however, perhaps as a result of seeing the adult playing with both girls and boys using blocks, she began to join in, sitting beside the teacher.*

The adult was very conscious of the sense of risk and apprehension that must have accompanied this step for Anita and how vital it was that she was enabled to have a very positive experience with the blocks. On one occasion, she made a series of sofa beds to accommodate various members of her family.

Girls often focus on domestic themes. Rather than seeing this as stereotypical and a cue for intervention strategies to be employed, we have taken the more celebratory view that when girls design furniture, create room layouts, build their own stables for My Little Pony and houses for their dolls, instead of asking Father Christmas to fetch them, this represents a great leap forward for humankind.

The influence on development of non-use, or infrequent use, of materials became clearer when we noted the qualitative change that occurred in the constructions of girls once they were using blocks on a regular basis. Observations made at a very early stage in our study show tendencies for girls to build small, enclosing, two-dimensional structures and boys to build vertically and to incorporate more dramatic movement in their blockplay by the use of cars. This seemed to confirm the findings of Erikson (1978), who observed the blockplay of 10–12-year-olds in an experimental situation. Erikson explains these characteristics in terms of differences in the ways in which males and females experience and represent space.[6] In our own study, the differences gradually disappeared until we could no longer differentiate structures on the basis of gender. The children who planned to build 'right up as far as God' were two girls. How much higher can one go?

One possible explanation of our finding is that the boys brought greater initial self-confidence to the material, which enabled them to take the risk of building upwards from the outset. For the girls this might have been too big a first step in an unfamiliar medium. They were perhaps demonstrating greater initial reflectiveness in their approach, which boys picked up on a little later.

Mixed Building

Analysis of our unstructured video-recordings indicates that where there is a free flow of children in and out of the block area and plenty of room to circulate, it is more likely that girl–boy partnerships will occur and sometimes achieve long-term status in relation to this activity. If boys and girls have something different and complementary as well as their samenesses to contribute to the situation, then it is important that cross-gender co-operation be encouraged so that girls and boys can learn from each other. Cross-gender play signals mutual acceptance and respect, not only to the players themselves but also to their classmates and for this reason alone should be supported and encouraged.[7]

NEW CHILDREN

Other children who may need special consideration are those new to the group, especially bilingual children new to English.[8] New children often have difficulty in making reflective choices from the wide range of play materials available and/or in gaining access to particular areas. During this transitional period it is important that children be helped to link their past experience with the present.[9] As part of the early familiarization experience, some schools lend out albums of photographs illustrating various aspects of school life, including the various activities available. Alternatively, collections of photographs are available in school for visiting children, so that their first experience of school can be at one remove. In these early days, in the company of a parent or other caretaker, they are introduced to the different activity areas. In the project groups it is also usual for a member of staff to partner new children either discreetly or more openly if this is needed, as they feel their way into the activities and the group. Colleagues noted how comfortable new children seem to be in the block area, particularly bilingual children, new to English. The block area is a clearly defined, sometimes partly enclosed area. Writing about language and learning in multi-ethnic classrooms, Wiles (1985, p. 86) observes how new children joining nursery or reception classes may spend long periods on one activity, using this as an excuse to observe. We have noticed, with great interest, that new parents when visiting with their children before starting school also often choose the block area to sit in where they, too, observe what is going on both within and beyond the block area.

New children especially need to feel they will not be verbally got at by adults as they play with the blocks. This is one of the things they will learn from observing the behaviour of adults with other children.

Although there are opportunities to observe and listen, there is no absolute need in the block area to interact verbally with other people. As a solitary activity, blocks offer immediate sensory feedback, so the child can use them independently. They also offer an *alternative* to speech in representing experience, and accordingly may be an important tool of thought in helping children make links from one language to another.

Figure 10.3 shows an arrangement made in her first week at school by Marianna (3 y.), who was bilingual and new to English. The block area was her headquarters. From the adjustments she continuously made to her arrangement, it seemed that her concern was to make exactly matching horizontal and vertical rows, using the strategy of 1:1 correspondence. She sang throughout in her first language. On a previous occasion she was heard counting blocks, also in her first language.

An important issue in relation to bilingual children new to English is that of record-keeping. Care needs to be taken that positive perceptions are created, both in terms of the children's own feelings of confidence and independence and in our own professional assessments of their educational needs. The example of Marianna shows that rich records, which are not speech dependent in the way the information is gathered, can be obtained of children's progress in many content areas of the curriculum, e.g. maths, science and problem-solving.

While some bilingual children who are new to the group and new to English may prefer to observe and listen rather than talk, blocks do allow for nonthreatening, nonverbal interaction, which children or sensitive adults can initiate. As already noted, blocks provide immediate sensory feedback from the

Figure 10.3   Figure 10.4

actions performed with them. In a twosome, each partner can cue in to the same observable events. This makes blockplay an ideal context for shared focusing and reciprocity, i.e. turn-taking exchanges in which the participants tailor their responses to each other's successive moves, as in conversational exchanges.[10] Two children demonstrate this process in the next section.

SPECIAL NEEDS

Children who were deaf or had partial hearing and/or speech collaborated with us in our study of blockplay. Semhar (4 y.) had little hearing or speech when the observation relating to Figure 10.4 was made.

She is creating a pattern with the blocks in which she strives for equivalence and visual harmony, in a reflected design. Beside her, trying to help, is a 3-year-old newcomer to the group, whose actions indicate she hasn't worked out how Semhar is organizing the placing of her blocks. Whenever Semhar turns her back to rummage through the blocks, looking for exactly what she needs, her friend places a block on the structure at random, then looks in Semhar's direction for a reaction. Semhar turns, notes the expression on her friend's face, suspects something is going on, then follows her friend's gaze to her construction. With a grin, she removes the odd block. The friend waits until Semhar's back is turned once more, replaces the rejected block and again waits to see what will happen. The earlier sequence of moves is repeated, with much laughter from both children.

The sequence now becomes a turn-taking game between the two. Each time Semhar turns away to search for a block the friend quickly pops on her block. Semhar turns back, they exchange glances, indicating to each other that the game is still 'on'. Semhar follows her friend's gaze, as she knows this will lead her to where the unwanted block has been placed, and removes it. Despite the distraction, Semhar manages to carry on with her pattern-making throughout, until it is completed to her satisfaction.

On finishing, she steps back to look at it, holding out an arm, to indicate 'hold on a minute'. The friend can barely restrain her impatience. When Semhar's achievement has been duly celebrated by herself and others in the group, she allows her friend to topple the structure, joining in the laughter.

It would be difficult to fault Semhar's technique. Indeed, we could take lessons from her and her teachers at home and school, who have enabled her to become a leader. Perhaps the most important strategy, that of shared control between the participants, is worth singling out. In the episode between Semhar and her friend, the game was initiated by the younger child but it was Semhar who enabled it to develop into a mutually enjoyable game, with the moves being worked out between them. This sharing of control has been discussed in several earlier chapters and is an important feature of all effective interaction, verbal and nonverbal. Perhaps we should not be surprised young children are experts at this. They are still very close to the period in their lives when nonverbal interaction was the chief means of communication between them and their caregivers.

Concern for Others

An adult who was counselling a child about the taking of blocks from the buildings of others did so in a way aimed at helping him to decentre: 'Your work is important but so is theirs.' His justification was that he needed the blocks as he hadn't enough to finish his structure. The amount of help children need in decentring and recognizing the needs of others and the effect of their behaviour on others varies from one occasion to another and from child to child.

Feelings of anger may be aroused by what appears to be unthinking, uncaring behaviour on the part of individuals. In particular, young children shouldn't be left without adult support to handle the difficulties some of their peers may be experiencing in moving with due care around the block area. Without help, patterns of intolerance can be set up that become self-fulfilling. One teacher saw this as creating a special need for her group to learn ways of coping with negative feelings as well as for the sharing of positive helping strategies.

BODY AWARENESS

Some names seem to be indivisibly associated with falling masonry. Those who simply enjoy pushing over buildings are relatively easily redeployed. However, individual children differ in the amount of support and guidance they need in becoming aware of their own bodies and body movement in relation to the spaces they occupy and other shapes and forms within it. A child may need help in developing what Papert (1980, p. 7) calls the 'intuitive geometry needed to get around in space'.[11]

Our concepts of space develop out of awareness of our own bodies. This is reflected in the language used in some cultures to denote positions in space: the word 'eye' can mean 'before'; 'back' can mean 'behind'; and 'ground' can mean 'under' (Werner, 1957, pp. 167–81).

The block area may have much to offer children in gaining greater body/spatial awareness, provided they don't become anxious about accidental demolition. Blockplay has all the ingredients of three-dimensional space scaled down and offers a unique opportunity to think about movement, physical balance, spatial relationships, sequence, speed and timing of movement, direction, distance, size, shape, area and volume.

As children construct with unit blocks, they move bodily, in parallel with them: along, up, down and around. They may build from the inside out or the outside in. They can compare their height to that of their structures: as tall as, not as tall as, smaller than. Children connect blocks in lines and then retrace the line by walking along it.

In moving about in the block area and seeing things from different viewpoints, children can learn that appearances may change but shape doesn't. Papert (1980) emphasizes the need for children to be able to identify with what they want to learn, not only in terms of motivation but also in the projecting of body knowledge into the structuring of materials. No one need be at a disadvantage in the block area, if they have a mature partner who can help them to become conscious of their own bodies and to relate this to their blockplay.

In Chapter 3 we asked whether better and more effective use could be made of gesture in helping communicate ideas in the block area. Gesture is certainly well suited to conveying the kinaesthetic, space–time dimensions of blockplay and may be particularly effective in highlighting these.

Gaining control of such material as blocks is intrinsically worthwhile. It may also be important in the longer term in affording access to activities such as the programming of computerized equipment e.g., Papert's drawing 'Turtle'. As guidance for children writing programs for the 'Turtle', Papert urges them to perform the movements they want it to make and then to translate this into a written program.

We have no easy solutions to offer in terms of adequate staffing for the block area to ensure equality of access. We do suggest, however, that children needing extra help in developing a range of competencies should be the concern of the whole school community and not of the individual teacher.

CONFIDENCE AND AUTONOMY

Initially, some children need adult help in approaching the material before they can go on to gain confidence and autonomy in its use. It is sufficient for some children to have a supportive adult presence in the block area. Others may be drawn towards an adult who is using the material and doesn't seem to mind if others join in. The point is reached when the adult can fade into the background, letting the children take over.

Barr *et al.* (1990, pp. 5–6) list six dimensions that make up an interwoven 'continuum of learning': confidence and autonomy, experience, strategies, knowledge and understanding, and reflectiveness. Without confidence and the ability to think and act independently with the material, the remaining dimensions of learning in relation to it will be seriously stunted. Bruner (1968, p. 118) suggests that unless an individual achieves a degree of competence in something, it is difficult to become interested in it, i.e. 'we get interested in what we get good at'. An expectation that adults will spend some time every day in the block area is an assurance that those who feel better with an adult present will not lose out. Where we are aware of this we can let individuals know our intentions at the beginning of a session and help them plan their time accordingly.

COLLABORATION

Where space is restricted, impromptu partnering of any kind occurs less often than when children circulate freely in the block area. Colleagues who are anxious to encourage boys and girls to play together, older children to partner younger ones and children of all levels of competence in the various aspects of blockplay, from technical to social, to help each other, would be wise to bear this in mind when allocating space to different activities.

In more restricted circumstances, children may have to take turns in the block area and be invited to choose a partner to play with. Experience suggests that, in these circumstances, same-sex, 'best friend' choices are invariably made. However, there were times during the study when the adult wanted to know how particular children, who would probably not choose each other, would get on in 'arranged' partnerships. The children never grumbled when this happened but we have to take care not to exploit their relative lack of power in the making of such decisions in school. On several occasions the arranged encounter, judged from the adult viewpoint, called forth more complex play and more mature behaviour in both partners than would have been the case if they had played alone or with a regular partner. This is not a plea for more engineering of partnerships but an indication of a strategy that might be employed where free access to the block area and movement within it is restricted, resulting in reduced opportunity for children to explore a range of partnerships.

Adults and Peers as Partners

Our own observations and those of other researchers indicate that different but complementary roles are played by adults and peers in the development of aspects of the situation. Pellegrini (1984) found that adult presence related to less peer interaction in the case of 3-year-old children and greater concentration on the material, while older children were not significantly influenced by adult presence in either this or the social aspects of the situation. However, in the case of both age-groups, adult absence and peer presence resulted in higher levels of interaction and co-operation. The influence of the adult is complex and it may be that, as we saw in Chapter 7, in the discussion of the apprenticeship model of adult–child partnering, that the child adopts the adult model of interaction in adult-absent situations with peers. This implies that we need to *organize* to be absent (as opposed to doing this by default), as well as for our presence in the block area.

Builders and Consultants

Observing others, studying their work and working methods, offering comments and advice, asking questions, all seem to be important early-years precursors to the full-blown technological processes set out in such documents as *Technology 5–16 in the National Curriculum* (National Curriculum Council, 1989).

We have noted how actively interested children are, as students of blockplay, in each other's work, especially while it is in progress. Some children have a tendency to give what amounts to a 'master class', i.e. an explanatory commentary to building companions, children and adults who express an interest.

If collaboration emerges from such beginnings, then it is important to allow for children to be engaged in discussion with each other in the block area, observing or circulating, as well as actually building. Allowance needs to be calculated in terms of our own reasoned expectations, space, time and noise levels.

Since such interacting is as important as actual construction, there may be no observable 'product' to show for the time a child was in the block area. Someone may have spent their entire time in a consultant or observer capacity.

Cramped conditions have the effect of inhibiting circulation, or, where children persist in attempting to circulate in small spaces, in falling masonry. This is annoying not only for the builder but can also lead to noise escalation and an all-round increase in tension, with the effects reaching beyond the block area.

SPACE AND TIME

Children need sufficient time to mix social aspects of blockplay with construction. This tends to work itself out where there is an open-door policy to blockplay. In one school where space and time were at a premium, the teacher and nursery nurse worked out with their group of 5-year-olds a solution to the problem. The children were aware of the available space and the counterclaims on it. They were also aware of the popularity of blocks and some of the frustrations of having to share space and time. They decided that no more than two children at a time should be in the block area and that they should be able to play until they had finished. They added that people in the block area must be considerate of those not in it and vice versa. Their involvement in this discussion and decision-making was on the basis of genuine consultation between experts. They were therefore highly motivated in subsequently ensuring the agreement was followed.

Drop-In Centre

Sometimes we are asked by colleagues how we distinguish between children who are actively observing and those who are simply 'hanging about'. There are many nonverbal indications, similar to those discussed earlier in the chapter. A few moments spent observing is usually sufficient to establish who is doing what. One strategy is to discover what children are attending to by following their gaze. The fate of those who are bored, between activities, tired or waiting for a friend is a matter for professional decision-making in its own right and beyond the scope of our present discussion.

Organizing for Continuity

In earlier chapters we have highlighted the way in which children repeat and practise various routines until they can produce a form with very little conscious effort. We came to the conclusion that there was a need to acknowledge this in our planning and to allow for the possibility that children might want to return, day in day out, to practise getting something right. We have also noticed how a theme may take several days to develop in all its differentiated detail. Jemima worked out her ideas of a swimming pool over a period of days. Each time some of the features represented on the previous day were carried forward while others were replaced by something else. Sunbeds appeared every day but a huge towel rack was replaced by a diving board and so on. This is the revision and refining of ideas that, according to Eisner (1982), is made possible through our externalized representations.

Where blockplay is freely available throughout the day and from day to day, revising and refining presents few problems. In other circumstances, special dispensation might be granted for someone to continue to work at something where a continuing theme had been observed. One reception-class colleague now occasionally arranges for structures to be left overnight and sometimes for days on end, so that children can carry on from where they left off. At one point, a 'block city' was under construction. The groups involved would vary from day to day on an agreed basis.

'Hit and Run'

Matterson (1990, p. 152) reports on the disappointment expressed by many nursery groups in the quality of blockplay observed by them and suggests that a possible drawback for some is lack of time. In playgroups, for example, everything may have to be cleared away after every half-day session. This, suggests Matterson, may discourage children from embarking on the sort of blockplay that develops slowly over a period of days and may give rise to what is described in Hirsch (1984, p. 192) as a 'hit-and-run' approach to building. Aside from the real, practical difficulties faced by some groups, this description could also apply in any situation where insufficient time is allowed for play to develop, because it is regarded as a time-filler rather than as part of the mainstream curriculum.

For groups with time and space difficulties, Matterson suggests it might be interesting to see what would happen if the adult made a sketch of what had been done and rebuilt it the following morning before the children arrive. This would be worth trying, especially if the children are consulted and can advise and help with the sketching process. It would be even better if the children could also help with the rebuilding, but that may result in them not getting any further forward from day to day! During the present study, many children became very interested in sketching their constructions. At first they did this because they saw adults doing it, then increasingly in their own right. Sometimes they were encouraged and helped to do this, where they had indicated they wanted to continue the following day. Very powerful organizing strategies are being practised here, which contribute to the children's developing sense of autonomy.

Special Dispensations

Sometimes colleagues have supported the need of one child, or a partnership, to use the whole space, the whole block supply and the whole day if necessary, in carrying an idea through to completion. This has never set up a massive chain reaction. Only children who are really committed to something would want to be in this situation for any length of time. Children like being asked to do favours for other people, especially when they are not so concerned for themselves. They appreciate fairness in the negotiation of special privileges, especially if they are consulted.

Shared History

We found the building up of a shared history of blockplay through experience, talk, observation and record-keeping between adults and children on both a group and one-to-one basis significantly diminished any shortfall in the physical circumstances of blockplay.

RULES

Rules negotiated by all the parties concerned can be experienced as enabling rather than repressing. Sometimes *re*negotiation is needed, on a one-to-one basis, where new children are being admitted to ongoing groups. Do we consult young children enough? They certainly respond very positively to having their advice asked. Here, the role of the adult is to chair discussion and be final arbiter.

Rules in the block area may involve safety, e.g. throwing of blocks, knocking down of structures, the height of structures, walking on blocks, building too close to other structures, etc. They may involve the defining of the block area; the prohibition of traffic through it; keeping a clear area around the block supply so that everyone can get to it; sharing of space, time and materials; and respect for other people's efforts and 'ownership' of structures. There is often a need to recycle blocks immediately they are finished with. Where this involves the dismantling of a building, demolition 'rights' and procedures need to be agreed with the 'owner'. The use of other toys and media in the block area needs to be discussed; care of blocks, responsibility for clearing away and methods of storing are other aspects of the situation that become easier to manage if there are *community* understandings and agreements about these. Self-monitoring and helping each other keep to the agreements tend to follow naturally, once these have been reached.

The formulation and reformulation of rules in our different groups took place in the context and at the time when the behaviour of concern arose. For example, we did not pre-empt the kicking down of structures or the taking away and using of blocks as guns with sermons about not doing so. This seemed too theoretical an approach with young children. Far greater impact was achieved when discussion took place where and when cause-and-effect connections could be made on a factual and personal basis.

Non-Accidental Collapsing of Structures

All children at some time (and some more persistently) find the impulse to aim a kick at or push a structure irresistible. The effect is immediate and dramatic and usually sends up the child's level of excitement, leading to more of the same. This may communicate itself to others, affecting concentration and co-operation.

Sometimes, the same act may be a more calculated expression of interest in balance, blocks, separation, trajectory, etc. These might be regarded as legitimate targets for theorizing and experimentation.

There needs to be some leeway for discretion and professional judgement to be used about how structures are dismantled. Occasionally some reflecting, systematic dismantling, could be shared by adult and builder, where the structural and sequential relationships between the blocks become a natural focus for interaction.

Our general view was that safety should be given precedence over every other consideration. Structures collapse frequently without any deliberate action on anyone's part. The more reflective the children are over such incidents, the more they may learn about blocks, balance, separation and trajectory.

A complete ban on kicking or pushing over structures in the block area regardless of motive needs to be matched with alternative opportunities for children to get their kicks or to explore dynamic schema elsewhere.

Anxiety

Structures that collapse unexpectedly cause some children great anxiety. Perhaps they feel the material is in control and does what it wants to. We need to be sensitive to such feelings. There are times for reminders about being careful and times when it is more appropriate to offer reassurance and help in rebuilding. This approach can contribute positively to the child's emerging sense of blocks as material that can be structured, destructured and re-structured through *reflective* action.

Guns

Gun play may not always be what it seems. Often children are expressing concern with the spatial idea of beginning and ending as they represent to themselves the flight path of a missile between gun and target. The 'target' (if this is another child) must mentally represent the distance, direction and speed at which the 'missile' is travelling, in order to fall to the ground in roughly the right spot at the right time, or get out of the way. While acknowledging the formal aspects of the game, some colleagues made a stand on moral grounds about the use of the 'L' block as a gun. Others made their objections on entirely practical grounds: the blocks belong to a set and must remain with the other blocks in the block area. The moral argument, being the more theoretical, may be more difficult for the younger children to come to terms with than the practical one, but this doesn't mean we shouldn't make it.

Guns were not the only cause for blocks to be removed from the block area. Sometimes children would fill up handbags, carts and prams and take them elsewhere. In these circumstances we would try to recognize the underlying need, which was seldom for blocks as such, and provide for that.

SAFETY AND NOISE

Rules differ from one group to the next, according to circumstances, but there are a few situations calling for discussion and agreement between adults and children that seem to crop up universally.

Height

For young children, building upwards on a monumental scale is an experience uniquely afforded by blocks. The control of three-dimensional space involves a gigantic imaginative as well as technical leap forward for the child, akin to that which compelled our stone-age ancestors to begin heaving huge slabs of stone into the upright position, as reminders of important aspects of their lives. Building higher than oneself seems to be of psychological importance.

While bearing in mind the possible affective significance of building high, common sense also has to play a part in how high is high enough, in which circumstances. Perhaps building over a certain height needs to be accompanied by a rule that states 'only when an adult is present'.

We have noticed how experienced builders seem to sense, split seconds before a building is going to fall, that this is going to happen and they will 'steer' the falling structure, with a hand, away from other buildings and people.

One group of nursery children found for themselves that they could increase their own height as builders inch by inch, by adding chairs to a stack, which had started as a single chair (Figure 10.5). This enabled them to stay level with structures, as these rose upwards. The crunch came, almost literally, when one day the stack of chairs teetered and the builder grabbed his block structure to steady himself. Fortunately an adult was standing by and managed to catch him. Since then, the use of chairs has been put on a problem-solving basis in this group. As in other schools, building high goes through phases when it becomes a group 'thing' for a period. In this group, when the spirit is moving in that direction, the children are helped to work out and test how many stacked chairs make a safe building platform. Four chairs tends to be the average – provided the back of the chair is to the front of the builder. A stepstool with a broad platform surrounded by a handrail was also tried, along with other alternatives. The stepstool proved inflexible compared to chairs in terms of adjustable height. It offered only one building position, three feet in the air, which made it more useful as an aerial viewing platform. These examples are offered to show the problem-solving potential rather than as recipes.

In general, before pronouncing on the legitimacy of an activity, we need to assess, in each instance, the possible significance of what is being attempted. It may be necessary to offer alternative channels to satisfy some needs. If the concern is uniquely to do with blocks, as in building high, we should reckon to go as far as is reasonable in helping the children work out and test appropriate procedures.

Noise

A second common concern is the noise and risk-taking that can occur when blocks are being cleared away. Noise can be very disturbing if it is carried on near to other continuing activities. The dropping of blocks and throwing them into boxes and containers are among the chief causes. An outright ban is the

Figure 10.5

only way to deal with throwing. Blocks fall usually because children are tempted to carry too many. Girls often hit on the time-honoured method of turning up the hem of their dresses to use as a sling. Many blocks at a time can be carried in this way. Unloading is usually by the cascade method and is very noisy! Some children discover the chin as a way of securing a stack of blocks to be carried. Other carrying experiments have been observed, such as standing blocks upright in a row, then attempting to pick them all up at once as if they were a concertina. This isn't guaranteed to work with more than three blocks. The effort that goes into devising methods for picking up and carrying blocks is rarely labour saving and sometimes hazardous, so vigilance that doesn't stifle creativity is needed.

As a result of experience, we recommend there should always be at least two people to lift trays or other large receptacles containing blocks, one of whom should be an adult. The 3–4-year-olds were very keen to demonstrate how strong they were by picking these up single-handedly. It is one thing to raise a tray of blocks and yet another to set it down safely. Adult backs have been strained in this way. Pregnant teachers should aim to oversee the lifting and setting down of full trays and boxes rather than doing this themselves.

CHAOS

We discovered very early in our study that once the area has become a sea of rubble the children will abandon it. This can mean there is very little play in the area after the initial wave of activity. Experience suggests regular checks and some modest tidying throughout the session are needed. Chaos has no beginning, middle or end to it and consequently is very worrying to adults as well as children. A group of adults attending a blockplay workshop became so anxious about the prospect of repacking blocks into their respective containers after use that they would have preferred not to use them: 'We'll never get them back in again, the way they were.' This is no different from the child who advised her friend against using too many blocks, in anticipation of tidying up. Another child who had been noticeably reluctant to play with blocks, volunteered the reason: 'You have to put them away.' She was often 'taken ill' at tidying-up time and would assume a prostrate position. The problem for her was not confined to blocks but seemed to be connected to a more general pattern of anxiety about tidying up rather than laziness which, from our observations and knowledge of individual children, seemed an inadequate explanation of their reluctance to become involved in clearing away.

As the adults in the study group, we can identify with anxieties about clearing up. However, we went on to discover with the children some of the satisfactions, even joys, of clearing away.

ORDER

It is very liberating to be able to create order out of apparent chaos. Sorting things out is no more than seeking and finding patterns and using these as the basis on which to organize our behaviour. In Chapter 7 we looked at problem-solving as a process. Here, in the clearing-up situation, we have a real-world problem to solve. We could do a great deal worse than make the solving of it the basis of some of our mathematics teaching and learning – our own as well as the children's.

After much experience of helping the children to clear away, we now consider this a very important, cognitively stretching activity as well as one that offers the opportunity to experience feelings of being in control as well as the benefits and pleasures of teamwork.

When clearing away is shared by adults and children, the onerous aspects of the task tend to disappear. It is important to get the time and timing right. Warnings for those still building prior to clearing away are best given personally, to ensure that the most absorbed are aware of the time. The least helpful warning is that given over the public address system! This is a signal for the less committed to disappear from the scene fast, their work abandoned, and for others to start clearing immediately while some are still working.

Depending on the quantity of blocks to be cleared and the method of storing, time allowed for this will differ from one group to another. It is worth doing several timed runs, not to see how fast it can be done but how long it takes to clear the area when account is taken of the teaching–learning aspects of the situation.

Colleagues who have a block area that also doubles as the group gathering point for stories, registration, discussion, etc., will appreciate the wisdom of having the timing worked out so that there is orderly transition from one kind of use to another. The worst possible scenario occurs when children are coming in from outdoor play, or other areas, before tidying is complete. Where outdoor play starts later than that indoors, care needs to be taken if the continuity of indoor play is not to be disturbed when the doors are opened. The inclination to abandon work can be hard to resist, even where there are community understandings that the activity in hand must be finished before another is begun. Relative to other activities, there is often a lot of tidying to do in the block area, especially where some complex building was taking place. The frustration of seeing others who perhaps had less to put away disappearing outdoors is too much for some children and they take the soft option of slipping away, leaving any rubble behind them. We can anticipate this and be on hand to encourage children to finish, even if this means helping to build to the child's instructions and putting the majority of blocks away afterwards, so long as this is done by negotiation and not simply done for them.

The study group was united in stressing the need for equal weight to be given to outdoor as well as indoor play, provided staffing is adequate, and would not subscribe to the practice of a compulsory indoor period for all for anything other than security reasons. Observation indicates that the fragmentation of play, which can result from staggered timetabling, encourages the 'hit-and-run' approach described earlier.

Teamwork between adults is essential where there is more than one adult involved with a group. Observation is the best way of finding out how children actually behave at transition times and what happens if our timing slips out of synchronization. The wisdom of adults checking with each other a little before something is to happen has been found a wise policy as it enables everyone to behave more thoughtfully than when things seem to 'just happen'.

SUMMARY AND CONCLUSIONS

Although we have given several instances of practice in this chapter and the previous one, these are not intended as prescriptions. As we suggested at the beginning of Chapter 9, our own ideas are still being formed about what constitutes a favourable environment and will continue, so long as we go on reflecting through our record-keeping and in our discussions with each other and the children.

Sharing the resources and responsibilities is as much a part of blockplay as exploring, patterning and building. They are all intimately and dynamically bound up with each other.

Signs that blockplay is going well can be judged in terms of the amount of positive interaction and the social and technical complexity of play. These are facilitated by good, systematic record-keeping and partnership between adults and between adults and children, especially in the negotiation of conditions and procedures for blockplay.

Equality of access to blockplay has been fully explored. What is at stake when we consider access strategies is not simply a bit of carpet but the early-years curriculum. There is a prior need to establish feelings of confidence and autonomy before other dimensions of learning can benefit from blockplay.

The business of creating and *maintaining* a favourable environment for blockplay provides a rich context for problem-solving. The wider classroom may be regarded as a system of relationships and inter-relationships. What happens in the block area affects other activities and what happens elsewhere affects the block area. In terms of the block area, as distinct from the rest of the environment, many practical problems to do with safety, storage and transport have to be considered. This can be done using a process model such as that described in Chapter 7.

Problem-solving in blockplay is not confined to how to make roads and such like. It is also to do with making roads, in this space, with the co-operation of this group of people.

NOTES

1. Parry (1978); Amor (1980); Smith (1983); Halliday, McNaughton and Glynn (1985); and Judd (1988). Although Elkins (1980) makes no direct reference to this, her small-scale study of blockplay involved a self-selected group of eighteen boys and two girls.

2. Pellegrini (1983, 1984, 1985); Rogers (1985); and Rubin and Seibel (1979, 1985).

3. See note 12, Chapter 4.

4. This research also found a relationship between role play and understandings of classification: part–whole, some–all and class-inclusion relationships. The common bond between role play, the ability to represent the feelings and viewpoint of another and understandings of classification is that they are all concerned with reciprocal relations (Rubin and Seibel, 1979, p. 172).

5. For a review of research methodology and research into sex-typed toy choices, see Eisenberg (1983). An interesting fact to emerge is that children use 'significantly more sex-role reasoning to justify others' choices (likes and dislikes) than to explain their own choices' (*ibid*. p. 60).

6. Budd, Clance and Simerly (1985) review research that has replicated Erikson's study with the same results. They question the use of gender-biased toys in the original and replication studies. In their own study, which corrects for this bias, they could find no evidence to support the theory of innate differences.

7. Sprafkin *et al.* (1983) offer a review of research on cross-gender play.

8. For guidance on the stages of English learning for bilingual children, see Barr *et al.* (1990, p. 41).

9. Cleave, Jowett and Bate (1982); Barrett (1986); Watt (1987); and Ghaye and Pascal (1988).

10. See Wood, McMahon and Cranstoun (1980), Chapter 4. The descriptions Trevarthen (1975) and Bruner and Watson (1983) give of shared focusing between infants and their caretakers are very similar to that described here.

11. See Gerhardt (1973) and Sutcliffe, Billett and Duncan (1987) for further elaboration of these ideas.

REFLECTIONS
Tina Bruce

Most of the important learning we achieve throughout our lives happens without our being aware of it. We adjust an idea here, rearrange a thought, come to terms with a feeling, add a bit there, put something into words. We do this in a constantly changing world in constantly changing ways. Those who work with very young children, and with children with severe physical impairments, are particularly aware of the slow, gradual learning we hardly notice day by day. It is only when we look back at a photograph of baby Jo or Joan six months ago that we realize the progress, changes and development.

The blockplay project has not been about the 'whoopee, eureka' kind of learning, although there have been exciting moments when this has been experienced. It has really been about the steady, quiet and deep learning that is not easy to see at a glance. The children have learnt, as this book demonstrates.

The interactions, transactions, partnerships between children and also between adults and children in their own classrooms have been of central importance. Children and adults have learnt with and through each other, functioning as research communities (Macauley, 1990; Pascal, 1990).

Deep learning does not happen overnight. That is the value of collaborative research. We have been learning together for about four years now, and the network established has remained despite adults or children moving to new schools and settings. There have been moments when, because we are human, the inter-relationships between feelings, thinking and what we know and understand cause pain or struggle. This is part of learning. Perhaps most important, though, is the way a web of social relationships has led to the basic trust and will to learn together which has empowered us to learn in ways that have developed the curriculum. Blockplay has only been the mechanism for a wider exploration of the curriculum, as it was for Froebel more than two hundred years ago in his community school.

The blockplay project has taken the pioneering approach of the educator, using research and literature from the past and present in the practical setting of today. We have, in a modern-day context, used a traditional and time-honoured piece of equipment, Froebel's Gifts, as a starting-point through which to explore the curriculum needs of the young and not so young in five schools and more. We needed a focus, which the blocks gave us. They provided a reason for adults and children to get together and interact, to learn and develop, to share common thoughts and feelings and to find that each of us is also unique.

We salute the past, for the past leads us to the future if it is carefully reflected upon. Froebel helped us to explore the disadvantages of didactic teaching. Harriet Johnson led us to look at the limitations of an unwittingly *laissez-faire* approach. We have been confronted by historic and continuing debates and arguments, which are important for each generation of educators to explore. We hope that in this book we have shown in the children's learning, through an interactionist approach to the curriculum, new insights, understandings, feelings, ideas and relationships that now take the curriculum forward.

Early childhood education still needs its pioneering workforce of educators. Pioneering on behalf of children to ensure a quality curriculum takes energy that is informed and supported by the fusion of theory, research and practice. Research alone cannot do this. Nor can practice in isolation from theory. Educators combine the two as they work with children in their own classrooms. This book has celebrated and shared the learning of a group of children working with educators in the Froebel Blockplay Project.

APPENDIX I
THE RESEARCH PROPOSAL
Tina Bruce

Three approaches that have influenced the character of the early-years curriculum (*laissez-faire*, didactic and interactionist) had interested me before becoming the research director (Bruce, 1985, 1987, 1989). An area of provision in which to observe the effect of these different curriculum approaches was needed. I chose blockplay as it was part of the Froebelian tradition in the early childhood curriculum. Froebel developed one of the earliest sets of blocks in his Gifts.

LAISSEZ-FAIRE

This approach is typified by adults carefully setting up a block area and leaving the children to use it freely without adult intervention; that is unless safety or bullying becomes an issue. Its slogan might be 'If you set things up right, the children will learn.'

DIDACTIC

This approach encourages adults to work with children in very direct ways. It might involve encouraging a child to carry out an adult-initiated task, such as building a tower, house, etc., in a particular way. Its slogan might be 'Children are like blotting paper. They absorb the experiences you decide to give them.'

INTERACTIONIST

The third approach is interactionist, and leads to transactional behaviour between adults and children. It involves adults in play-partnering with children. Its slogan might be: 'At times the adult leads, and at times the child leads.' The adult's initiatives develop through knowing the educational possibilities of blockplay appropriate at that time.

The interactionist approach offers a sensitive approach to children, which respects both deep intuitive and articulated knowledge.

REDEFINING THE RESEARCH PROPOSAL

The research proposal aimed to explore these three approaches, and gave what Wynne Harlen (1982) would call a 'possible line of direction' for the research project. Because the other participants began to act on and contribute their own concerns, developing from this starting-point, the potential domination of the research proposal quickly receded. It is explored in Chapter 2, and it is important to note that without it there would have been no starting-point and therefore no research project.

WHERE THE RESEARCH PROPOSAL LED US

Ruth Jonathan (1981, p. 166) suggests that 'The most exemplary empirical research in the field of education would simply be work in which prior assumptions were made explicit, uncontrolled variables were allowed for in alternative explanations, and the predictive limitations of the findings were clearly indicated'.

The situation for those participating in the Froebel Blockplay Project was, as Elden (1981, p. 262) suggests that it may well lessen 'one's belief not only in a particular pre-packaged framework, but also in the whole idea of pre-packaging.' Elden differentiates between pre-packaging inquiry and structuring inquiry.

THE RESEARCH PROPOSAL AS A CATALYST

The research proposal was really a catalyst in observing ourselves and the children. It led us to look at the context in which blockplay takes place, the timing, use of space, type of block, management and organization of blockplay, including race and gender issues, and consideration of children with special educational needs. It led us to look at symbolic behaviour. It impinged on the content of the child's learning. It addressed the question whether children really do learn maths, science, technology, language, arts, music, movement, geography and history while playing with blocks. Early childhood educators have operated on the assumption that children do. They see this occurring in an integrated way rather than such learning taking place as separated subjects.

The blockplay project proposal set us on the path to explore the curriculum as a whole, but not in a prestructured way. Those involved are convinced that it was all the richer for developing from its starting-point in an organic way, and that it covered what it set out to do with more breadth, more deeply and with more sense of ownership by participants because of this.

OUR UNARTICULATED BIASES

We are all biased, but we are not always aware of how and why. Researchers sometimes believe they can be objective. This is unlikely to be possible in educational research. As Margaret Clark (1989, p. 7) says, 'Even researchers are not value-free in their choice of topics, approach and in the findings they emphasise'.

If educators are to use research findings in their work with young children, it is important to know the influences and biases upon researchers.

THE RESEARCH DIRECTOR

The research director is a Froebel-trained, qualified teacher of hearing-impaired children, and a teacher educator in the primary-age phase. During the 1970s she was the teacher in the Froebel Project research school, working with the research fellow, Chris Athey (1990). This project (1972–7) explored children's learning, 3–5 years, through parental partnership.

THE PAST INFLUENCES THE PRESENT AND THE FUTURE

Chris Athey's nursery project at the Froebel Institute College went against the current conventions, which emphasized experimental design and statistics. Although Chris Athey's nursery project took these seriously, her approach was very different because of the way it was steeped in educational principles and philosophy first and foremost, using current research and theory to support it. It was in the line of a strong Froebelian tradition, greatly developed through the work of Susan Isaacs in the 1930s (Margaret Roberts, opening speech, Redford House Nursery, November 1989).

The focus of Chris Athey's work was on particular aspects of how to observe children in school, using the Piagetian schema in particular as an observation tool. A schema is an observable pattern of behaviour that can be generalized by the child. This research project aimed to share with parents insights into how children learn. Parents were encouraged to be partners in finding out more. They helped with observations, data collection and discussion.

There were three strands in Chris Athey's project that had a deep and lasting influence on the way I, as the research director, designed and initiated the blockplay project with guidance from Marten Shipman, then Dean of the School of Education at the Roehampton Institute:

1. Chris Athey had encouraged teachers working with her to see themselves as educators in the pioneer tradition, combining theory with practice.
2. A traditional Froebelian concern that educational research needs to be based on educational principles and philosophy that is translated, explored and extended through the use of current theory and research into good classroom practice.
3. Everything was articulated, discussed and reflected upon with the research fellow, colleagues and parents.

It became apparent that in both Chris Athey's nursery project, and the blockplay project we were working in the framework Elden (1981, p. 262) suggests and 'sharing control over the research process'.

In both projects the research directors expected to write up the experience. Chris Athey did so in her book, *Extending Thought in Young Children* (1990). In the Froebel Blockplay Project, because five schools were involved together with the research assistant, the research director felt, as Elden (1981, p. 261) says, 'caught between the old roles I knew and a new one I didn't know'.

It gradually became clear that everyone wanted to and should be involved in writing up the Froebel Blockplay Project. Once the idea took form, it was taken up with enthusiasm by everyone.

THE PARTICIPANTS IN THE FIVE SCHOOLS

Everyone involved in the project had some form of link with the Froebel Institute College, either through initial or inservice training or both. Everyone in the Froebel Blockplay Project was aware of the philosophy of the Froebel Institute, which was a shared backcloth to the project.

The participating schools were Danebury Primary School, London; Eastwood Nursery School, London; Grove House Nursery School, Ealing; Holman Hunt Primary

School and Partial Hearing Unit, London; and Our Lady of Victories RC Primary School, Putney, London. The children were between 3 and 6 years of age.

THE RESEARCH ASSISTANT

The research assistant had trained both as a nursery nurse and teacher and had studied educational research. She was actively involved in the playgroup movement at local level as a participating parent, and also as a playgroup course tutor.

A particular concern for many years has been the deskilling of parents, nursery nurses and teachers by experts and a growing interest in the methodology of participative classroom research. The research assistant's original role was to make a literature search, and to set up and carry out the work to be done in the schools, working with them and reporting developments to the research director and the group. In this way she became an important bridge between schools and college. She signalled common issues in ways that expressed and held meanings for the group. Many, including the research assistant, have commented on the similarity between this role and that of deputy head.

During the second year of the project, her role developed and extended considerably. Because she developed an overview of both theory and research literature, and the classroom practice being explored, she had a view unavailable to the rest of us. Just as the role of the teachers, nursery nurses and project director moved forward in sharing the control of the research process, so her role extended. Indeed, it became obvious that she would be the most appropriate person to edit this book.

APPENDIX II
HOW WE WORKED TOGETHER
Tina Bruce

The Froebel Blockplay Research Group (1987–90) has been a collaborative study, funded by the Froebel governing body, who generously gave a further two years' funding from 1988. Participants met regularly in the Centre for Early Childhood Studies at the Froebel Institute, and were involved at an early stage in the planning and carrying out of the study.

Throughout the project, blockplay was seen as a vehicle through which to encourage the development of insights into the whole curriculum. In developing from the research proposal in an organic way, through discussion and planning, the group has made classroom observations, interventions and reflected on the place of blockplay in the early childhood curriculum as a whole.

A continuation of this spirit is reflected in the way participants wanted to contribute in the writing of this book. The book has developed as a natural extension of our work together. Although we reflect each other's views and have undoubtedly been influenced by each other, sensing we have a shared framework, we still remain as unique individuals who have experienced and been touched by the project each in our own way.

Different chapters reflect perspectives of different participants in the project.

THE APPROACH TAKEN IN THE BLOCKPLAY PROJECT

From the beginning, those participating developed their own thinking in an organic way, through reading, meetings in college, in school and in the classroom.

Schools were initially invited to join the project on the basis that they were near the college, and that overall there would be diversity of provision, socioeconomic background, ethnic mix, and include children with special educational needs. One non-local school was invited in order that these conditions were satisfied.

THE POWER OF GROUP SUPPORT

At the early meetings of the collaborative group, it became apparent that the participants had an expectation that the research director would explain what they needed to do, and that the research assistant would visit them in schools and help them to put this into action.

They were clearly puzzled and a little unnerved when, at the first meeting, they were asked to help formulate what would be studied. They were polite but, if the truth be told, probably shared the experiences of those participating in the Ford Teaching Project: 'We grumbled about the apparent lack of guidance from the central team, although with hindsight we can see that this was deliberate, presumably aimed at ensuring our personal involvement in the actual classroom research' (Bowen, Green and Pols, 1975, p. 33).

In the case of the blockplay project, it was not deliberate but an inevitable outcome of a determination to find the kind of balance 'which endeavours to create quality criteria for research without becoming a fore-structure that pre-determines content' (Letiche, 1988, p. 37).

The framework of the study group inevitably emerged from the general principles of early childhood education expressed in *Early Childhood Education* (Bruce, 1987). The project has developed in the way Elden (1981, p. 265) suggests: 'If the people in a particular organisational setting are to learn from and use the research, then it should be in their language and deal with concrete issues they see as important. This is more likely if they participate in planning and carrying out the research work.'

In contrast to the Ford project, perhaps because of everyone's awareness of the principles of early childhood philosophy, there did not seem to be difficulty in establishing shared principles. However, as might be predicted, we did need to explore the diverse ways these principles might be translated into practice (Bruce, 1987).

The teachers in the Ford project (Bowen, Green and Pols, 1975, p. 37) noted that 'the help and encouragement of the central team was very important'. The meetings with the research assistant in school, and with the research director, research assistant and whole group in college were part of this. 'The support of others experiencing the same problems seemed to us to be of tremendous importance' (*ibid.* p. 36).

Sharing problems was certainly important in the blockplay project, but even more so was sharing the learning. The enjoyment and celebration of the children's learning were central aspects.

HOW WE EXPLORED

Meetings in College

Three meetings per term took place in the Centre for Early Childhood Education of the Froebel Institute. Each school tried to send at least one representative, although typically there would be more than one. Only occasionally was this not possible, and the research assistant would always make sure the school was updated in this instance. The schools reflected the chronic shortage and difficulties in staffing, and it has been a real achievement to keep up this level of attendance and participation for more than three years.

Initially, six schools participated, but early on a crisis-level staffing situation made it impractical for one school to attend meetings. With regret on all sides, the school withdrew after the first term. Of the remaining five, the one with the most difficulty in attending was, predictably, the only school that was not local.

Visits to Schools

The research assistant made regular visits to the schools. In the first term, she visited each school once. One school made an outing to the college primary base. The video taken was used in subsequent discussion. During visits, either slides or video film was taken, and subsequently used in the group discussions.

Data-Gathering and Interpreting

The research assistant gathered data (video, photographs and written records) during these visits. These were shared with the host school. In turn, participating schools made written records (see Chapter 8), which they have shared with parents and the group.

WHAT WE EXPLORED: ESTABLISHING A BASELINE

The research director set a baseline condition, which was that initially participants should note how they were currently working with blocks. This helped the group to consider constraints, resources and presentation. A survey of existing provision formed a part of this, and resulted in a request for help from toy manufacturers (see the Acknowledgements). Headteachers of the participating schools have also made blocks a priority when ordering equipment both in the nursery and other classes.

WHAT WE READ

The theory and research literature under review was chosen to help us focus on particular aspects in the depth we wanted. Literature was selected through discussion of the concerns of the group as part of the organic development from the research proposal, and the original search of the literature.

FINDING APPROPRIATE WAYS TO DESCRIBE CHILDREN'S BLOCKPLAY

During the second year, the group requested that we should look at the terminology used to describe Piagetian schemas (Nicoll *et al.*, 1986; Sharp, 1986; Matthews, 1988; Boyd and Bauers, 1989; Nutbrown, 1989; Athey, 1990; Northampton Schema Booklet, 1990; Bruce, 1987, 1991). It was interesting to compare this with the terminology used by Guanella (1934) and Johnson (1933) in describing children's block structures. The research assistant combined these in a revised simpler version of our earlier identification chart.

A recurring problem was the way architectural terms (e.g. floor) were not useful in describing blockplay. This is because they tend to set an image in the mind, unlike the Piagetian terminology, which is content free. The group wanted terminology that dealt with processes and yet described children's products and behaviour patterns adequately, and in ways which did not prestructure the manner in which they were perceived by the adult or child. This is also explored in the set of slides and the video-tape arising from the work of the project that was produced during 1990 and 1991.

RESIDENCIES

During the autumn and spring terms of the second year, it was decided through discussion that the best way forward would be for the research assistant to take a residency in each school. She would become attached to each school for a month (one and a half days a week). She would use the other half day to keep in touch with the other four schools. Heads of the schools agreed to this, and were invited with the College Principal and Chair of the Funding Body to a semi-social meeting. Slides and video-tapes were shown of the children's blockplay.

During the residencies in school, the research assistant showed children slides and video-tapes of themselves. She also showed these at staff meetings and parents evenings. A feature of the residencies was that blockplay of particular children could be examined in more depth, but always in the context of the whole curriculum.

Schools would use the research assistant's residency in the school as they thought best. For example, one nursery nurse asked to write up and analyse her observations of blockplay while the research assistant took her place in the classroom. In another school, the research assistant worked in the classroom in a general way so that staff could focus specifically on blockplay.

THE LAST FORMAL STAGE OF THE BLOCKPLAY PROJECT

This has involved the collaborative writing up of the project so that the work can be shared. It has meant both small groups meeting and the whole group continuing to meet regularly. In this way the chapters that were written collaboratively emerged over the year. It demonstrates the commitment of those who work with young children. It is important to note that this stage has taken nearly three years. Writing up collaborative research is a lengthy process and, in reality, requires at least as much time as the research itself, for reflection is an important part of the process.

SEEING OURSELVES AS EDUCATORS

It is important to take up the educator issue raised in the Introduction to the book. At the last stage of the blockplay project, in the five schools, of the teachers involved, they are all either taking further qualifications, have been promoted or both. Of the nursery nurses involved, there have been more staff changes during the life of the project but it is interesting that of those who have been participating throughout, three have taken steps towards training as teachers. All feel confident in discussion, lead sessions in inservice work and with parents and take a major part in the development of good record-keeping.

Another important development in the way nursery nurses and teachers now see themselves as educators is demonstrated by their desire to share in the writing of this book. Participants in the project also seem to have become catalysts for continuity with progression in two of the three primary schools. Blockplay is becoming valued beyond the nursery years. The reception class in one school has worked with the research assistant and demonstrated some of the work at the local teachers centre. The mathematics post-holder has also drawn on the work of the project.

In the second primary school, there has been general inservice work for the infant and junior staff arising from discussion with the nursery staff and research assistant. As a result, there is now a set of unit blocks in every classroom from nursery to top-junior level.

In the third primary school, staff changes have made such work impractical. Rich blockplay is also being developed in new schools as teachers and nursery nurses move, through promotion, and as different participants give talks and workshops.

It may be that all of this would have happened anyway, but it seems likely that the blockplay project has empowered people by raising the confidence of participants in their academic and intellectual selves and in the sense that they want to take more responsibility in their professional lives.

APPENDIX III
USE OF BLOCKS
Pat Gura

The analysis that follows is based on observational records kept in the first eighteen months of the study and represents an overview of the five groups involved.

Of the total amount of blockplay recorded in the course of the present study, children between the ages of 3 and 4-plus years spent *more* time exploring (1) the properties of blocks and learning to combine them at increasing levels of integration and complexity; and (2) a range of general cognitive concerns, particularly those relating to space and movement, than they did in creating figurative representations with them.

Children from 4-plus to 5-plus spent at least as much time on these aspects of blockplay as on figurative representations. On this evidence, there seems to be considerable scope for children to continue to develop their competence in the medium well beyond the fifth year.

A further category of play that was way ahead of figurative use for children across the age-range 3–5-plus was (3) the creation of two- and three-dimensional patterns. Finally, after the age of 6, the lead was taken by (4) figurative representations.

FIGURATIVE REPRESENTATIONS

The following list is of types of construction where there was, in the observer's view, some visual correspondence between the structure and its given name. They are presented in order of frequency:

3–5 years and above

1. Houses (Figures 4.13 and III.1), monumental or public buildings and places including towers, shops (Figure 3.8); castles, palaces, churches, schools, bridges (Figure III.2); and swimming bath/pools, hospital, hotel, blocks of flats, parks, football stadium, farms, zoos, car park, garage. Often the children named actual buildings/places, e.g. London Bridge.
2. Well below this group of subjects came human or humanoid figures (Figures III.3 and III.4); furniture, including beds, chairs, tables, settees; forms of transport,

Figure III.1

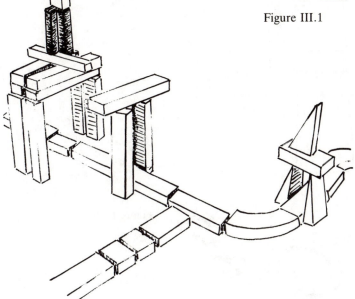

Figure III.2

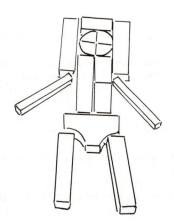

Figure III.3   Figure III.4

Figure III.5

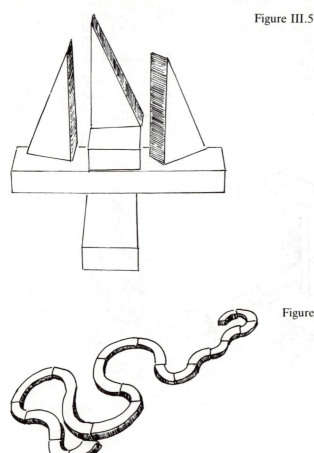

Figure III.6

including boats (Figure III.5); trains, aeroplanes, spaceships, cars, rocket, see-saws; and roads and paths.
3.   The last group consists of subjects each recorded between one and three times: caterpillar, elephant, fairwheel, snail, snake (Figure III.6), giraffe, fantailed pigeon, tree, star, flower, letters of the alphabet, computer, car-wash, decoration (Figure 9.1), clocks, wheel-clamp, fish, birds and birds' nests.

5-plus to 6-plus years

Analysis of the records of the blockplay of 6-year-old children after eighteen months' regular access to blocks indicates a greater likelihood that use of blocks will be for the purpose of figurative representation and is often undertaken collaboratively. The range and frequency of topics is similar to that of the younger children: castles and palaces, school, house, church. Newcomers to the list were a dance-hall, a dinosaur and a guillotine.

There is a greater tendency for the 6-year-old to make a group of structures relating to one superordinate idea: water with a bridge and road; aeroplane with hangar;

spaceship and spacecraft; supermarket with trolleys and a car park; house with car, aunts, uncles and naughty babies.

In general, there is greater differentiation of the subject-matter, i.e. more detail and greater structural integration as well as increased use of blocks three-dimensionally. One house and a school had upper storeys connected with stairs and walls with integral windows; castle walls have battlements. *This level of structural integration was only just becoming apparent in the work of a few children.* Integral windows and stairs still present problems for many and so far we have not recorded a bridge over a road that is going anywhere. Bridges were still being represented as simple, three-block vertical enclosures (Figure III.2), a function perhaps of the way in which a child experiences bridges? When you are on a bridge, you can't see the arch and when you can see the arch, you can't see the way it connects with everything else! The ways in which children have tried to tackle some of these technical problems are discussed and illustrated in Chapter 7.

IMAGINATIVE PLAY

Children with a good working knowledge of blocks sometimes create block structures to use in play with model cars, play people, etc. This is the *stage design* discussed in Chapter 3, where reference was made to the three characteristics, noted by Cuffaro (1984, p. 125), which dramatic play with blocks requires of the child. The second of these was the need to deal with reality and scale in translating ideas to the medium. As in creating figurative representations, the function the structure is to serve is adapted to the materials and the materials to it.

Of the total amount of blockplay recorded in the study, only a small proportion of structures were planned and constructed with imaginative play in mind. This was due in part to the bias of the study, in which equipment such as Mobilo, farm animals, play people, cars, etc., was removed from the immediate blockplay area. Tina Bruce explains the reasoning behind this in Chapter 2. There are indications from our study that once a good pattern of block construction is established in a group, mixed-media imaginative play will follow for some children. The physical separation of the two kinds of play material seems to encourage reflection in choosing and using them. For further discussion on combining blocks with accessories, see Chapters 9 and 10.

APPENDIX IV
LIST OF BOOKS USED IN RELATION TO BLOCKPLAY
Compiled by Danebury Nursery Class

STORIES AND POEMS

Hadithi, M. and Kennawau, A. (1990) *Lazy Lion*, Hodder & Stoughton, Sevenoaks.
Hutchins, P. (1971) *Changes, Changes*, The Bodley Head, London.
Peppe, R. (1981) *The Mice who Lived in a Shoe*, Viking Kestrel, London.
Pfanner, L. (1987) *Louise Builds a House*, Collins, London.
Stevenson, R. L. (1988) *Block City*, Anderson Press, London.
(Various folk tales, such as 'The Three Little Pigs', 'Little Red Riding Hood', etc., and fairy tales, such as 'Sleeping Beauty', 'Beauty and the Beast', etc.).

INFORMATION

Hernandez, X., Comes, P. and Watson, L. (1990) *A Town through History*, Wayland, Hove.
Karavasil, J. (1983) *Houses and Homes Around the World* (International Picture Library), Macmillan, Basingstoke.
Macaulay, D. (1977) *Castle*, Collins, London.
Macaulay, D. (1975) *Pyramid*, Collins, London.
Macaulay, D. (1974) *City*, Collins, London.
Macaulay, D. (1976) *Underground*, Collins, London.
Pluckrose, H. (1990) *Ways to . . . Build it*, Franklin Watts, London.
Sorrell, A. and Birley, A. (1970) *Imperial Rome*, Lutterworth Press, London.
Taylor, A. C. (1986) *Buildings of Delight*, Victor Gollancz, London.
Turner, D. (1983) *The Man-Made Wonders of the World* (International Picture Library), Macmillan, Basingstoke.
Unstead, R. J. (1986) *See Inside a Roman Town*, Kingfisher Books, London.
Young, C. and King, C. (1989) *Castles, Pyramids and Palaces*, Usborne, London.

ADULT REFERENCE

Breckon, A. and Prest, D. (1983) *Craft, Design and Technology*, Thames/Hutchinson, London.

REFERENCES

Abbott, J. S. C. (1833) *The Mother at Home*, American Tract Society, New York, NY.

Amor, C. (1980) *Very Large Blocks* (unpublished report), ILEA Television and Publications, London.

Anderson, V., Thornhill, R. G. and Smith, M. (1969) *Poleidoblocs*, ESA, Arnold & Son, Leeds.

Anon (1693) *Arche Noah*, Dillinger, Germany.

Arnheim, R. (1970) *Visual Thinking*, Faber & Faber, London.

Association of Teachers of Mathematics (1980) *Language and Mathematics*, Association of Mathematics, Derby.

Athey, C. (1980) Parental involvement in nursery education, *Early Childhood*, Vol. 1, no. 3, pp. 4–9.

Athey, C. (1981) Parental involvement in nursery education, *Early Child Development and Care*, Vol. 7, no. 4, pp. 253–67.

Athey, C. (1990) *Extending Thought in Young Children: A Parent–Teacher Partnership*, Paul Chapman Publishing, London.

Ausubel, D. K. (1978) *Educational Psychology: A Cognitive View*, Holt, Rinehart & Winston, New York, NY.

Azmitia, M. (1988) Peer interactions and problem solving: when are two heads better than one? *Child Development*, Vol. 59, no. 1, pp. 87–96.

Bailey, M. W. (1933) A scale of block construction for young children, *Child Development*, Vol. 4, no. 2, pp. 121–39.

Banta, M. A. (1980) *Unit Blocks: A Curriculum for Early Learning*, The Early Childhood Learning Center, Department of Early Childhood Education, University of the District of Columbia, New York, NY, ERIC Document 206401.

Barnes, R. (1987) *Teaching Art to Young Children*, Allen & Unwin, London.

Barr, M., Ellis, S., Hester, H. and Thomas, A. (1990) *Primary Language Record*, Inner London Education Authority, London.

Barrett, G. (1986) *Starting School: An Evaluation of the Experience*, Final Report to AMMA.

Barthes, R. (1973) *Mythologies*, Paladin, St Albans.

Bender, J. (1978) Large hollow blocks: relationship of quantity to blockbuilding behaviour, *Young Children*, Vol. 33, no. 6, pp. 17–33.

Bennett, N. and Kell, J. (1989) *A Good Start? Four Year Olds in Infant Schools*, Blackwell, Oxford.

Bergamini, D. (1972) *Mathematics*, Time Life International, The Netherlands.

Berk, L. E. (1985) Why children talk to themselves, *Young Children*, Vol. 40, no. 5, pp. 46–52.

Billett, S. and Matusiak, C. (1988) Nursery children as map makers, *Education 3–13*, Vol. 16, no. 1, pp. 41–5.

Blenkin, G. M. and Kelly, A. V. (eds.) (1987) *Early Childhood Education: A Developmental Curriculum*, Paul Chapman Publishing, London.

Blenkin, G. M. and Whitehead, M. R. (1988) Creating a context for development, in Blenkin and Kelly (eds.) op. cit.

Block, J. (1984) *Sex Role Identity and Ego Development*, Jossey Bass, San Francisco, Calif.

Board of Education (1908) *Report of the Consultative Committee upon the School Attendance of Children below the Age of Five*, HMSO, London.

Bowen, R. B., Green, L. L. J. and Pols, R. (1975) The Ford Project: the teacher as researcher, *British Journal of In-Service Education*, Vol. 2, no. 1, pp. 35–41.

Bruce, T. (1976) *A Comparative Study of the Montessori Method and a Piaget-Based Conceptualisation of the Pre-School Curriculum*, unpublished MA dissertation, University of London.

Bruce, T. (1985) It's all very well in practice, but what about in theory? *Early Child Development and Care*, Vol. 19, no. 3, pp. 151–73.

Bruce, T. (1987) *Early Childhood Education*, Hodder & Stoughton, Sevenoaks.

Bruce, T. (1989) Constructive play, *Child Education*, May, pp. 25–8.

Bruce, T. (1991) *Time to Play in Early Childhood Education*, Hodder & Stoughton, Sevenoaks.

Bruner, J. S. (1968) *Towards a Theory of Instruction*, Norton, New York, NY.

Bruner, J. S. (1973) Organisation of early skilled action, *Child Development*, Vol. 44, pp. 1–11.

Bruner, J. S. (1974) The nature and uses of immaturity, in K. Connolly and J. S. Bruner (eds.) *The Growth of Competence*, Academic Press, London.

Bruner, J., Wood, D. and Ross, G. (1976) The role of tutoring in problem-solving, *Journal of Child Psychology and Psychiatry*, Vol. 17, pp. 89–100.

Bruner, J. S. and Watson, R. (1983) *Child's Talk: Learning to Use Language*, Oxford University Press.

Budd, B. E., Clance, P. R. and Simerly, E. D. (1985) Spatial configurations: Erikson re-examined, *Sex Roles*, Vol. 12, nos. 5–6, pp. 571–7.

Buhler, C. (1945) *From Birth to Maturity: An Outline of the Psychological Development of the Child*, Kegan Paul, Trench, Trubner & Co., London.

Choat, E. (1978) *Children's Acquisition of Mathematics*, NFER, Windsor.

Clark, M. M. (1988) *Children Under Five: Educational Research and Evidence* (Final Report to DES), Gordon & Breach, London.

Clark, M. M. (1989) *Understanding Educational Research*, Gordon & Breach, London.

Cleave, S. and Brown, S. (1989) *Four Year Olds in School: Meeting their Needs*, NFER, Slough.

Cleave, S., Jowett, S. and Bate, M. (1982) *And So to School: A Study of Continuity from Pre-School to Infant School*, NFER, Nelson.

Cleveland Teachers in Early Education (1987) *How Your Child Learns*, The Avenue Primary School (Nursery), Cleveland.

Cockroft, W. H. (1982) *Mathematics Counts: Report of the Committee of Inquiry into the Teaching of Mathematics in Schools*, HMSO, London.

Comenius, J. A. (1832) *Neuer Orbis Pictus*, Loflund & Sohn, Stuttgart.

Comenius, J. A. (1896) *School of Infancy*, Heath, Boston, Mass.

Conolly, K. (1975) The growth of skill, in R. Lewin (ed.) *Child Alive*, Temple Smith, London.

Corsaro, W. (1979) 'We're friends, right?' Children's use of access rituals in a nursery school, *Language in Society*, no. 8, pp. 315–36.

Cuffaro, H. K. (1984) Dramatic play: the experience of blockbuilding, in E. S. Hirsch (ed.) op. cit., pp. 121–51.

De Loach, J. S. and Brown, A. L. (1987) The early emergence of planning skills in children, in J. S. Bruner and H. Haste (eds.) *Making Sense: The Child's Construction of the World*, Methuen, London.

DES (1987) *Report of the Task Group on Assessment and Testing*, HMSO, London.

DES (1989a) *English in the National Curriculum*, HMSO, London.

DES (1989b) *Report by HM Inspectors on a Survey of the Quality of Education for Four-Year-Olds in Primary Classes*, DES Publications Despatch Centre, London.

DES (1989c) *Aspects of Primary Education: The Teaching of Mathematics*, Report by HM Inspectors, HMSO, London.

DeVries, R. with Kohlberg, L. (1987) *Programs of Early Education: The Constructivist View*, Longman, London, and New York, NY.

Dewey, J. (1916) *Democracy and Education*, Macmillan, New York, NY.

Dillon-Goodson, B. (1982) The development of hierarchical organization: the reproduction, planning and perception of multiarch block structures, in Forman (ed.) op. cit.

Donaldson, M. (1978) *Children's Minds*, Fontana/Collins, Glasgow.

Duckworth, E. (1972) The having of wonderful ideas, *Harvard Educational Review*, Vol. 42, no. 2, pp. 217–31.

Duckworth, E. (1979) Either we're too early and they can't learn it, or we're too late and they know it already: the dilemma of applying Piaget, *Harvard Educational Review*, Vol. 49, no. 3, pp. 297–311.

Dyson, A. H. (1988) Appreciate the drawings and dictating of young children, *Young Children*, Vol. 43, no. 3, pp. 25–32.

Dweck, C. S. and Legett, E. L. (1988) A social-cognitive approach to motivation and personality, *Psychological Review*, Vol. 95, no. 2, pp. 256–73.

Early Years Curriculum Group (1989) *Early Childhood Education: The Early Years Curriculum and the National Curriculum*, Trentam Books, Stoke-on-Trent.

Easen, P. R. and Green, D. A. (1987) Developing real problem-solving in the primary classroom, in R. Fisher (ed.) *Problem-Solving in Primary Schools*, Blackwell, Oxford.

Ebbeck, M. (1984) Equity for boys and girls: some important issues, *Early Child Development and Care*, Vol. 18, nos. 1–2, pp. 119–31.

Edgeworth, M. and Lovell Edgeworth, R. (1798) *Essays on Practical Education*, London, and 2nd edn, 1801, London.

Edwards, V. and Redfern, A. (1988) *At Home in School: Parent Participation in Primary Education*, Routledge, London.

Eisenberg, N. (1983) Sex-typed toy choices: what do they signify? in M. B. Liss (ed.) *Social and Cognitive Skills: Sex Roles and Children's Play*, Academic Press, New York, NY.

Eisner, E. W. (1982) *Cognition and Curriculum*, Longman, New York, NY.

Elden, M. (1981) Sharing the research work, in P. Reason and J. Rowan (eds.) *Human Enquiry*, Wiley, Chichester.

Elkins, C. (1980) Blockplay (unpublished dissertation, Diploma in Education), University of Nottingham Faculty and School of Education.

Erikson, E. H. (1978) *Toys and Reasons: Stages in the Ritualisation of Experience*, Marion Boyars, London.

Evans, G. W. (1980) Environmental cognition, *Psychological Bulletin*, Vol. 88, pp. 259–87.

Ferguson, E. S. (1977) The mind's eye: nonverbal thought in technology, *Science*, Vol. 197, pp. 827–36.

Feynman, R. P. (1990) *What Do You Care What Other People Think? Further Adventures of a Curious Character*, Unwin Hyman, London.

Fletcher, C. (1988) A framework for practitioner research (paper delivered at the conference, Practitioner Research: Who, What and How?), New Hall College, Cambridge.

Forman, G. (1982) A search for the origins of equivalence concepts: through a microanalysis of blockplay, in G. Forman (ed.) op. cit.

Forman, G. (ed.) (1982) *Action and Thought*, Academic Press, New York, NY.

Franklin, M. B. (1973) Non-verbal representation in young children: a cognitive perspective, *Young Children*, Vol. 29, no. 1, pp. 33–52.

Fritzsch, K. E. and Bachmann, M. (1966) *An Illustrated History of Toys*, Abbey Library, London.

Froebel, F. (1887) *The Education of Man* (W. N. Hailmann (trans.)), Appleton, New York, NY.

Froebel, F. (1895) *Pedagogics of the Kindergarten* (J. Jarvis (trans.)), Appleton, New York, NY.

Garvey, C. (1977) *Play*, Collins/Fontana Open Books, London.

Gelfer, J. I. and Perkins, P. G. (1987) Young children's acquisitions of selected art concepts using the medium of blocks with teacher guidance, *Early Child Development and Care*, Vol. 27, pp. 19–30.

Gelfer, J. I. and Perkins, P. G. (1988) A new look at an old friend, *Early Child Development and Care*, Vol. 30, pp. 59–69.

Gelman, R. and Gallistel, C. R. (1983) The understanding of number, in M. Donaldson, R. Grieve and S. Pratt (eds.) *Early Childhood Development and Education*, Blackwell, Oxford.

Gerhardt, L. A. (1973) *Moving and Knowing: The Young Child Orients Himself in Space*, Prentice-Hall, Englewood Cliffs, NJ.

Gesell, A. (1940) *The First Years of Life*, Harper, New York, NY.

Gesell, A. (1952) *Infant Development*, Hamish Hamilton, London.

Ghaye, A. and Pascal, C. (1988) *Four Year Old Children in Reception Classrooms: Participant Perceptions and Practice*, Worcester College of Higher Education.

Gibson, J. J. (1979) *The Ecological Approach to Visual Perception*, Houghton Mifflin, Boston, Mass.

Goetz, E. M. (1981) The effects of minimal praise on the creative block building of three year olds, *Child Study Journal*, Vol. 11, no. 2, pp. 55–67.

Goetz, E. M. and Baer, D. M. (1973) Social control of form diversity and the emergence of new forms in children's block building, *Journal of Behaviour Analysis*, Vol. 6, pp. 209–17.

Goldammer, H. (1882) *The Gifts of the Kindergarten* (W. Wright (trans.)), Williams & Norgate, London.

Golomb, C. (1972) Evolution of the human figure in a three dimensional medium, *Developmental Psychology*, Vol. 6, pp. 385–91.

Goodnow, J. (1977) *Children's Drawings*, Fontana/Open Books, London.

Gramza, A. F. and Witt, P. A. (1969) Choices of coloured blocks in the play of preschool children, *Perceptual and Motor Skills*, Vol. 29, pp. 783–7.

Guanella, F. M. (1934) Blockbuilding activities of young children, *Archives of Psychology*, no. 174, pp. 1–92.

Halliday, J., McNaughton, S. and Glynn, T. (1985) Influencing children's choice of play activities at kindergarten through teacher participation, *New Zealand Journal of Educational Studies*, Vol. 20, no. 1, pp. 48–58.

Halpern, E., Corrigan, R. and Alvierez, O. (1981) Two types of under? Implications for the relationship between cognition and language, *International Journal of Psycholinguistics*, Vol. 8, no. 4, 24, pp. 34–56.

Halpern, E., Corrigan, R. and Alvierez, O. (1983) In, on and under: Examining the relationship between cognitive and language skills, *International Journal of Behavioural Development*, Vol. 6, pp. 153–166.

Harlen, W. (1982) Evaluation and Assessment, in C. Richards (ed.) *New Directions in Primary Education*, Falmer, Lewes.

Harlen, W. (1983) *Guides to Assessment in Education: Science*, Macmillan Education, London.

Harlen, W. and Black, P. (1989) Space probe, *The Times Educational Supplement*, 29 December.

Harnet, P. (1988) Personal symbols, *The Times Educational Supplement*, 4 March.

Hatcher, B. A. (1983) Putting young cartographers on the map, *Childhood Education*, Vol. 59, pp. 311–15.

Haworth, J. (1989) *Construction Play* (video), Edgehill College of Higher Education, Chorley.

Hazen, N. L. (1982) Spatial exploration and spatial knowledge: individual and developmental differences in very young children, *Child Development*, Vol. 53, pp. 826–33.

Higginson, W. (1982) Symbols, icons and mathematical understanding, *Visible Language*, Vol. XVI, no. 3, pp. 239–48.

Hirsch, S. (ed.) (1984) *The Block Book*, National Association for the Education of Young Children, Washington, DC.

Hirsch, E. S. (1984) Practical considerations for the classroom teacher, in E. S. Hirsch (ed.) op. cit.

Hitz, R. and Driscoll, A. (1988) Praise or encouragement? *Young Children*, Vol. 43, no. 5, pp. 6–13.

Hohmann, M., Banet, B. and Weikart, D. P. (1979) *Young Children in Action*, High Scope Press, Ypsilanti, Mich.

Holton, G. (1973) *Thematic Origins of Scientific Thought*, Harvard University Press, Cambridge, Mass.

Honig, A. (1990) Working with young children (lecture in the Third Series organized by the Centre for Early Childhood Studies, Froebel Institute College, jointly with the Under Fives Unit, National Children's Bureau), London.

Hughes, E. R. and Rogers, J. (1979) *Conceptual Powers of Children: An Appraisal through Mathematics and Science*, Schools Council Publications, Macmillan Education, London.

Hughes, M. (1981) Play and problem solving, reported in C. Hutt *et al.* (1988) op. cit.

Hughes, M. (1986) *Children and Number: Difficulties in Learning Mathematics*, Blackwell, Oxford.

Hulson, E. and Reich, H. (1931) Blocks and the four year old, *Childhood Education*, Vol. 8, pp. 66–8.

Hutt, J. S., Tyler, S., Hutt, C. and Christopherson, H. (1988) *Play, Exploration and Learning: A Natural History of the Pre-School*, Routledge, London.

Isaacs, N. (1930) Children's 'why?' questions, in S. Isaacs (1930) *Intellectual Growth in Children*, Routledge & Kegan Paul, London.

Isaacs, S. (1930) *Intellectual Growth in Children*, Routledge & Kegan Paul, London.

Isaacs, S. (1933) *Social Development in Young Children* (student's abridged edition, abridged and extended by D. May (1951)), Routledge & Kegan Paul, London.

Isaacson, Z. (1989) Taking sides: the tensions between creativity and utilitarian skills, *The Times Educational Supplement*, 27 October.

Johnson, H. M. (1929) *Children in the Nursery School*, John Day, New York, NY.

Johnson, H. M. (1933) The art of blockbuilding, reprinted in Provenzo and Brett (1983) op. cit.

Jonathan, R. (1981) Empirical research and educational theory, in B. Simon and J. Willcocks (eds.) (1981) *Research and Practice in the Primary Classroom*, Routledge & Kegan Paul, London.

Jones, D. (1980) *Toy with Idea*, Norfolk Museums Service, Norwich.

Jonson, B. (1960) *Bartholomew Fair*, Methuen, London. First published 1614.

Jowett, B. (ed.) (1953) *Plato: Dialogues, Vol. IV, Laws*, Oxford University Press.

Judd, R. (1988) A study into how gender is reinforced and reproduced in the nursery in relation to large blockplay (unpublished essay, Certificate in Early Childhood Education), Froebel Institute College, London.

Kamii, C. and De Vries, R. (1977) Piaget for early education, in M. D. Day and R. K. Parker (eds.) *The Pre-School in Action: Exploring Early Childhood Programs*, Allyn & Bacon, Newton, Mass.

Katz, L. (1990) Early childhood education (lecture), Centre for Early Childhood Studies, Froebel Institute College, London.

Katz, L. G. and Chard, S. C. (1989) *Engaging Children's Minds: The Project Approach*, Ablex, Norwood, NJ.

Kellogg, R. (1979) *Children's Drawings, Children's Minds*, Avon, New York, NY.

Kepes, G. (ed.) (1965) *Structure in Art and in Science*, Studio Vista, London.

Kinsman, C. and Berk, L. (1979) Joining the block and housekeeping areas, *Young Children*, Vol. 35, no. 1, pp. 66–75.

Krashen, S. (1981) *First Language Acquisition and Second Language Learning*, Pergamon Press, Oxford.

Krotzsch, W. (1917) *Rhymus und Form in der frein Kinderzeichnung*, Schulwissenschaftlicher Verlag, U. Haase, Leipzig (cited in Guanella, op. cit.).

Kuschner, D. (1989) Put your name on your painting, but the blocks go back on the shelves, *Young Children*, Vol. 45, no. 1, pp. 49–58.

Letiche, H. (1988) Facilitating self-evaluation (paper delivered at the conference, Practitioner Research, Who, What and How?), New Hall College, Cambridge.

Liss, M. B. (ed.) (1983) *Social and Cognitive Skills: Sex Roles in Children's Play*, Academic Press, New York.

Locke, J. (1884) *Some Thoughts Concerning Education* (R. H. Quick (ed.)), Cambridge University Press.

Longman (1988) *Dictionary of the English Language* (5th impression), Longman, Harlow.

Lunzer, E. A. (1959) Intellectual development in the play of young children, *Educational Review*, Vol. 11, pp. 205–17.

Macauley, H. (1990) Learning structures for the young child: a review of the literature, *Early Child Development and Care*, Vol. 59, pp. 87–124.

Malkus, U. C., Feldman, D. H. and Gardner, H. W. (1988) Dimensions of mind in early childhood, in A. D. Pellegrini (ed.) (1988) *Psychological Bases for Early Education*, Wiley, Chichester.

Manson, G. (1954) Wright in the nursery class, *National Froebel Foundation Bulletin*, no. 86, pp. 10–17.

Matterson, E. (1990) *Play with a Purpose for Under Sevens* (3rd edn), Penguin Books, Harmondsworth.

Matthews, J. (1984) Children's drawings: are young children really scribbling? *Early Child Development and Care*, Vol. 18, pp. 1–39.

Matthews, J. (1987) The young child's early representation and drawing, in G. M. Blenkin and A. V. Kelly (eds.) op. cit.

McGill, L. (1986) *First Reflections: Equal Opportunities in the Early Years*, Inner London Education Authority, London.

Meek, M. (1985) Play and paradoxes: some considerations of imagination and language, in G. Wells and J. Nicholls (eds.) (1985) *Language and Learning: An Interactional Perspective*, Falmer Press, Lewes.

Metz, M. (1988) The development of mathematical understanding, in Blenkin and Kelly (eds.) op. cit.

Milloy, I. (1987) Craft, design and technology in the primary school: let's keep it primary, *Education 3–13*, Vol. 18, no. 1, pp. 11–19.

Montessori, M. (1912) *The Montessori Method*, Heinemann, London.

Mortimore, P., Sammons, P., Stoll, L., Lewis, D. and Ecob, R. (1988) *School Matters: The Junior Years*, Open Books, Wells.

Mounts, N. S. and Roopnarine, J. (1987) Social cognitive play patterns in same age and mixed age pre-school classrooms, *American Educational Research Journal*, Vol. 24, no. 3, pp. 463–76.

Moyer, K. E. and von Haller, G. B. (1956) Experimental study of children's block preferences and use of blocks in play, *Journal of Genetic Development*, Vol. 89, pp. 3–10.

Moyles, J. (1989) *Just Playing?* Open University Press, Milton Keynes.

Nash, B. C. (1981) The effects of classroom spatial organisation on 4–5 year old children learning, *British Journal of Educational Psychology*, Vol. 51, pp. 144–55.

National Curriculum Council (1989) *Technology 5–16 in the National Curriculum*, NCC, York.

Nesbit, E. (1913) *Wings and the Child, or, The Building of Magic Cities*, Hodder & Stoughton, London.

Newson, J. and Newson, E. (1979) *Toys and Playthings in Development and Remediation*, Allen & Unwin, London.

Nias, J. (1987) *Seeing Anew: Teachers' Theories in Action*, Deakin University, Victoria.

Nicolls, R. (ed.) with Sedgwick, J., Duncan, J., Clarke, J., Curwen, L. and McDougall, B. (1986) *Rumpus Schema Extra*, Cleveland Teachers in Early Education, Cleveland.

Noss, R. (1983) Doing mathematics while learning logo, *Mathematics Teaching*, Vol. 104, pp. 5–10.

Nutbrown, C. (1988) Patterns in paintings, patterns in play: young children learning, *Topic 7*, Issue 1, Spring, NFER, Windsor.

Nutbrown, C. (1989) Up, down and round, *Child Education*, Vol. 66, no. 5, pp. 14–15.

Osborn, A. and Milbank, D. (1987) *The Effects of Early Education*, Clarendon Press, Oxford.

Papert, S. (1980) *Mindstorms: Children, Computers and Powerful Ideas*, Harvester, Brighton.

Parry, M. (1978) *Play with Bricks*, Arnold & Son, Leeds.

Pascal, C. (1990) *Under Fives in Infant Classrooms*, Trentam Books, Stoke-on-Trent.

Payne, M. (1990) Teaching art appreciation in the nursery school: its relevance for 3–4 year olds, *Early Child Development and Care*, Vol. 61, pp. 93–106.

Pellegrini, A. D. (1983) Sociolinguistic contexts of the pre-school, *Journal of Applied Developmental Psychology*, Vol. 4, no. 4, pp. 397–405.

Pellegrini, A. D. (1984) The social cognitive ecology of preschool classrooms: contextual relations revisited, *International Journal of Behavioural Development*, Vol. 17, pp. 321–32.

Pellegrini, A. D. (1985) Social cognitive aspects of children's play: the effects of age, gender and activity centres, *Journal of Applied Psychology*, Vol. 6, pp. 129–40.

Piaget, J. (1926) *The Language and Thought of the Young Child*, Kegan Paul, Trench & Trubner, London.

Piaget, J. (1953) *The Origin of Intelligence in the Child*, Routledge & Kegan Paul, London.

Piaget, J. (1962) *Play, Dreams, and Imitation in Childhood*, Routledge & Kegan Paul, London.

Piaget, J. (1969) *The Mechanisms of Perception*, Routledge & Kegan Paul, London.

Piaget, J. and Garcia, R. (1971) Physio-geometric explanation and analysis, in J. Piaget (1971) *Understanding Causality*, Norton, New York, NY.

Pick, H. L. (jnr) (1976) Transactional constructivist approach to environmental knowing: a commentary, in G. Moore and R. Golledge (eds.) (1976) *Environmental Knowing*, Dowden, Hutchinson & Ross, Stroudsberg, Pa.

Pimm, D. (1981) Mathematics? I speak it fluently, in A. Floyd (ed.) (1981) *Developing Mathematical Thinking*, Addison-Wesley with the Open University, Wokingham.

Pratt, C. (1924) *Experimental Practice in the City and Country School*, Dutton, New York, NY.

Provenzo, E. F. (jnr) and Brett, A. (1983) *The Complete Block Book*, Syracuse University Press, Syracuse, NY.

Pugh, G. and De'Ath, E. (1989) *Working towards Partnership in the Early Years*, National Children's Bureau, London.

Raven, J. (1980) *Parents, Teachers and Children*, Hodder & Stoughton for the Scottish Council for Educational Research, Sevenoaks.

Reifel, S. (1984) Block construction: children's developmental landmarks in the representation of space, *Young Children*, Vol. 40, no. 1, pp. 61–7.

Reifel, S. and Greenfield, P. M. (1982) Structural development in a symbolic medium: the representational use of block constructions, in G. Forman (ed.) op. cit.

Roberts, M. and Tamburrini, J. (eds.) (1981) *Child Development 0–5*, Holmes McDougall, Edinburgh.

Rogers, D. W. (1985) Relationship between blockplay and the social development of young children, *Early Child Development and Care*, Vol. 20, pp. 245–61.

Rousseau, J. J. (1892) *Emile, or, Concerning Education* (J. Steeg (trans.)), Heath, Lexington, Mass.

Rubin, K. H. and Maioni, T. L. (1975) Play preference and its relation to egocentrism, popularity and classification skills, *Merril Palmer Quarterly*, Vol. 21, no. 3, pp. 171–9.

Rubin, K. H. and Seibel, C. G. (1979) The effects of ecological setting on the cognitive and social behaviors of the schoolers (paper presented at the Annual Meeting of the American Research Association), San Francisco, Calif.

Ruddock, J. (1985) A study in the dissemination of action research, in M. Shipman (ed.) *Educational Research*, Falmer, London.

Sacks, O. (1989) *Seeing Voices: A Journey into the World of the Deaf*, Picador, London.

Sauvy, J. and Sauvy, S. (1974) *The Child's Discovery of Space*, Penguin Books, Harmondsworth.

Schirrmacher, R. (1986) Talking with young children about their art, *Young Children*, Vol. 41, no. 5, pp. 3–7.

Shapiro, E. (1978) Copying and inventing: similarities and contrasts in process and performance, in N. R. Smith and M. B. Franklin (eds.) op. cit.

Sharp, A. (1986) *The Learning and Development of 3–5 Year Olds: Schema*, City of Sheffield Education Department.

Sheridan, M. A. (1975) *The Developmental Progress of Young Children* (3rd edn), HMSO, London.

Shotwell, J. (1979) Counting steps, in H. Gardner and D. Wolf (eds.) (1979) *Early Symbolizations. New Directions for Child Development (no. 3)*, Jossey-Bass, San Francisco, Calif.

Sigel, I. E. (1986) Early social experience and the development of representational competence, in W. Fowler (ed.) (1986) *Early Experience and the Development of Competence*, Jossey-Bass, London.

Silin, J. (1987) The early childhood educator's knowledge: a reconsideration, in L. Katz (ed.) *Current Topics in Early Childhood Education*, Vol. 7, ERIC, pp. 17–31.

Smith, A. B. (1983) Sex differences in activities in early childhood centres, *New Zealand Journal of Psychology*, Vol. 12, pp. 74–81.

Smith, N. R. (1978) Developmental origins of structural variation and symbol form, in N. R. Smith and M. B. Franklin (eds.) op. cit.

Smith, N. R. and Franklin, M. B. (eds.) (1978) *Symbolic Functioning in Early Childhood*, Lawrence Erlbaum Associates, Hillsdale, NJ.

Smith, P. K. and Simon, T. (1984) Object play, problem-solving and creativity in children, in P. K. Smith (ed.) (1984) *Play in Animals and Humans*, Blackwell, Oxford.

Smith, T. (1980) *Parents and Pre-School*, Grant McIntyre, Oxford.

Spencer, C. and Darvizeh, Z. (1983) Young children's place description maps and route finding: a comparison of nursery school children in Iran and Great Britain, *International Journal of Early Education*, Vol. 15, no. 1, pp. 26–31.

Spencer, C., Harrison, N. and Darvizeh, Z. (1980) The development of iconic mapping ability in young children, *International Journal of Early Childhood*, Vol. 12, pp. 57–63.

Sprafkin, C., Sebin, L. A., Dervier, C. and Connor, J. M. (1983) Sex differentiated play: cognitive consequences and early interventions, in M. B. Liss (ed.) *Social and Cognitive Skills: Sex Roles and Children's Play*, Academic Press, New York, NY.

Stevenson, R. L. (1985) *A Child's Garden of Verses*, Victor Gollancz, London.

Sutcliffe, M., Billett, S. and Duncan, J. (1987) Learning to move and moving to learn in the nursery years, *British Journal of Physical Education*, Vol. 18, no. 4, pp. 157–9.

Sutton-Smith, B. (1975) The useless made useful: play as variability training, *School Review*, Vol. 83, pp. 197–214.

Sylva, K., Roy, C. and Painter, M. (1980) *Childwatching at Playgroup and Nursery School*, Grant McIntyre, London.

Taylor, H. and Hartley, B. (eds.) (1986) *Design it, Build it, Use it*, Curriculum Development Unit, Brent Education Department, London.

Thomas, N. (1985) *Improving Primary Schools*, Inner London Education Authority Committee on Primary Education, London.

Tizard, B., Phelps, J. P. and Plewis, I. (1976) Play in pre-school centres, part 1, *Journal of Child Psychology and Psychiatry*, Vol. 17, pp. 251–64.

Trachtenberg, M. and Hymen, I. (1986) *Architecture from Prehistory to Post Modernism: The Western Tradition*, Academy Editions, London.

Trevarthen, C. (1975) Early attempts at speech, in R. Lewin (ed.) (1975) *Child Alive*, Temple Smith, London.

Vereecken, P. (1961) *Spatial Development: Constructive Praxia from Birth to the Age of Seven*, Walters, Groningen, Holland.

Vygotsky, L. S. (1962) *Thought and Language*. MIT Press, Cambridge, Mass.

Vygotsky, L. S. (1978) *Mind and Society: The Development of Higher Psychological Processes*, Harvard University Press, Cambridge, Mass.

Walkerdine, V. (1982) From content to text: a psychosemiotic approach to abstract thought, in M. Beveridge (ed.) (1982) *Children Thinking through Language*, Edward Arnold, London.

Waterland, L. (1985) *Read with Me: An Apprenticeship Approach to Reading*, Thimble Press, Stroud.

Watt, J. (1987) Continuity in early education, in M. M. Clark (ed.) (1987) *Roles, Responsibilities and Relationships in the Education of the Young Child (Educational Review Occasional Publication no. 13)*, Faculty of Education, University of Birmingham.

Wells, H. G. (1911) *Floor Games*, Palmer, London.

Wells, H. G. (1931) *Little Wars*, Dent, London.

Wells, G. (1987) *The Meaning Makers: Children Learning Language and Using Language to Learn*, Hodder & Stoughton, Sevenoaks.

Werner, H. (1957) *Comparative Psychology of Mental Development*, Incorporated University Press, New York, NY.

Whitehead, M. (1990) *Language and Literacy in the Early Years: An Approach for Education Students*, Paul Chapman Publishing, London.

Wilderspin, S. (1823) *On the Importance of Educating the Infant Poor*, Goyder, London.

Wilderspin, S. (1834) *The Infant System* (6th edn), Hodson, London.

Wilderspin, S. (1840) *A System for the Education of the Young*, Hodson, London.

Wiles, S. (1985) Language and learning in multi-ethnic classrooms: strategies for supporting bilingual students, in G. Wells and J. Nicholls (eds.) (1985) *Language and Learning: An Interactional Perspective*, Falmer Press, Lewes.

Williams, C. K. and Kamii, C. (1986) How do children learn by handling objects? *Young Children*, Vol. 42, no. 1, pp. 23–6.

Wolf, D. and Gardner, H. (1978) Style and sequence in early symbolic play, in N. R. Smith and M. B. Franklin (eds.) op. cit.

Wolf, D. and Gardner, H. (1980) Beyond playing and polishing: a developmental view of art history, in J. Hausman (ed.) (1980) *Arts and the Schools*, McGraw-Hill, New York, NY.

Wood, D. (1988) *How Children Think and Learn*, Blackwell, Oxford.

Wood, D., Bruner, J. S. and Ross, G. (1976) The role of play tutoring in problem solving, *Journal of Child Psychology and Psychiatry*, Vol. 17, pp. 89–100.

Wood, D., McMahon, L. and Cranstoun, Y. (1980) *Working with Under Fives*, Grant McIntyre, London.

Wood, D. and Wood, H. (1986) *Teaching and Talking with Deaf Children*, Wiley, Chichester.

Wood, H. and Wood, D. (1983) Questioning the pre-school child, *Educational Review*, Vol. 35, no. 2, pp. 149–62.

Wright, Frank Lloyd (1932) *An Autobiography*, Longman, London.

Zervigon-Hakes, A. (1984) Materials mastery and symbolic development in construction play: stages of development, *Early Child Development and Care*, Vol. 17, pp. 37–48.

Zimiles, H. (1977) A radical progressive solution to the problem of evaluation, in L. G. Katz (ed.) (1977) *Current Topics in Early Childhood Education, Vol. 1*, Ablex, Norwood, NJ.

INDEX